PRAEGER LIBRARY OF AFRICAN AFFAIRS

LESOTHO, BOTSWANA, AND SWAZILAND

The Praeger Library of African Affairs is intended to provide clear, authoritative, and objective information about the historical, political, cultural, and economic background of modern Africa. Individual countries and groupings of countries will be dealt with as will general themes affecting the whole continent and its relations with the rest of the world. The library appears under the general editorship of Colin Legum, and each volume is written by an acknowledged expert on its subject.

ALREADY PUBLISHED

ETHIOPIA: A New Political History *Richard Greenfield*
ZAMBIA *Richard Hall*
SOUTH AFRICA: A Political and Economic History *Alex Hepple*
THE LITERATURE AND THOUGHT OF MODERN AFRICA:
A Survey *Claude Wauthier*

Richard P. Stevens

LESOTHO,
BOTSWANA, &
SWAZILAND

THE FORMER HIGH COMMISSION TERRITORIES
IN SOUTHERN AFRICA

FREDERICK A. PRAEGER, *Publishers*
New York · Washington · London

FREDERICK A. PRAEGER, INC., *Publishers*
111 Fourth Avenue, New York, N.Y. 10003, U.S.A.
77-79 Charlotte Street, London, W.1, England

PUBLISHED IN THE UNITED STATES OF AMERICA IN 1967
by Frederick A. Praeger, Inc., Publishers

Library of Congress Catalog Card Number: 66-18923

PRINTED IN GREAT BRITAIN

CONTENTS

CONTENTS

ACKNOWLEDGEMENTS

The author is especially indebted to Dr H. George Henry, whose contributions on the economics of the three Territories places the political and constitutional developments in proper context. Welcome suggestions were made by Dr John Marcum, Director of the Lincoln University African Area and Language Program. Dr Edward Muth of the University of Basutoland, Bechuanaland and Swaziland also supplied the author with valuable materials. Lincoln University assisted the author with a research grant through the Babcock Fund and the Acting Librarian, Mr Emery Wimbish, made every effort to facilitate the author's efforts.

INTRODUCTION

BASUTOLAND (newly named Lesotho), Bechuanaland (Botswana) and Swaziland were formerly jointly referred to as the Protectorates, the High Commission Territories or the British Southern African Territories. For historical, political and economic reasons their development began later than that of the other British dependencies in Africa. None of the Territories had a Legislative Council before 1960. Embedded in the apartheid complex of South Africa, they have presented Britain with one of the most intractable and politically explosive of its remaining colonial problems. Even now, the immediate political issues are by no means clear cut and the ultimate consequences of recent elections or independence cannot be predicted with certainty.

In general, the three countries may be described as isolated, land-locked, rather poor, underdeveloped areas where nature has not been over generous towards those who would wrest a living from the land. Although the inhabitants are mainly Africans of the Bantu language group, they have markedly different physical environments and economies. Lesotho, with an area of 11,716 square miles (roughly the size of Belgium), is for the most part hilly or mountainous, with elevations up to 11,000 feet. The country is traversed by a multitude of perennial streams, including the headwaters of the Orange river and a considerable part of its tributary, the Caledon. The population has been estimated at 975,000, of whom approximately 2,000 are Europeans, and about 117,000 are employed in South Africa. Most of the population lives in the heavily-populated western lowlands; this includes about 10,000 in Maseru, the capital. Of the three countries, Lesotho is the poorest. Apart from some diamonds, there is slight evidence of other exploitable minerals. Water resources have not as yet been utilised.

Larger than the British Isles, Botswana is bounded by South Africa, South-West Africa, Zambia (at a point on the map) and

Rhodesia. The country is a tableland at a mean altitude of 3,300 feet and with elevations up to 5,000 feet, and is estimated to cover some 220,000 square miles. The regional differences of climate, soil and vegetation are considerable. Most of the west and south-west consists of Kalahari sand-veld and is largely uninhabited, although it is not desert in the strict sense since it includes many large tracts of savannah. Everywhere, water is in short supply. The 1965 census places the population at 542,104, of whom 3,900 are Europeans. The population is concentrated in the sub-tropical to temperate eastern region, which is better watered and straddles the railroad to the north. Essentially it is the livestock industry which has raised the economy above the bare subsistence level.

Very rich in minerals, Swaziland stands in marked contrast to the other two states. Together with one of the world's largest asbestos mines, mountains of high-grade iron ore provide attractive incentives for outside investment. Highly developed forest enterprises, commercial crops, livestock and a host of exploitable minerals make this small country of 6,705 square miles a potentially viable state. The very attractiveness of the country resulted in the alienation of most of the land to Europeans. Even today, after government action and Swazi land-purchases, some 43 per cent of the land is owned by approximately 10,000 Europeans out of the country's total population of 280,000. The bulk of the population has scarcely benefited from the country's resources and is engaged in subsistence agriculture. Swaziland has a pleasant elevation in the west, with mountainous veld averaging about 3,500 to over 5,000 feet. The middle veld averages about 2,000 feet and rainfall is plentiful. On the east, the low veld provides good grazing and is highly fertile, though the rainfall is low.

Past administration and history still justify consideration of the three countries collectively. They all came under British protection during the latter part of the nineteenth century and the beginning of the twentieth during the course of the struggle between the Boers and the British for dominance in southern Africa—Basutoland in 1884, Bechuanaland in 1885 and Swaziland in 1906. In each of the Territories the High Commissioner, acting through a Resident Commissioner, was proclaimed sole legislative authority in a system known as indirect rule. The administrative responsibility for internal affairs was left on the whole to the chiefs, who continued to exercise their traditional political and judicial authority and in addition regulated the economic life of their people. If the inhabitants were not entirely satisfied with this arrangement, fear of their South African neighbour deflected the force of their protests. As British Protectorates they were afforded security with stagnation. But traditional leaders, unaware of the economic forces which were transforming their lives, and without real decision-making power, could not respond to this new challenge without major institutional changes. However, any fundamental change in the traditional structure of society—a condition for political advancement or constitutional evolution—seemed to invite the loosening of British protection and, conversely, the encroachment of the historic enemy. Even today, with only Swaziland to gain independence, some would doubt whether this assumption can yet be discarded.

In any event, the abolition in late 1964 of the office of High Commissioner—combined since 1961 with that of British Ambassador to South Africa—reflected the changed political status of the Territories as each advanced towards independence under its respective constitution. Already, in October 1963, the post of Resident Commissioner was upgraded to Queen's Commissioner in Bechuanaland and Swaziland. A similar step was taken for Basutoland in August 1964 and thus each Territory received the equivalent of a Governor responsible directly to the Secretary of State for the Colonies. Henceforth, the British Ambassador to South Africa would be informed about aspects of the three Territories' affairs affecting foreign relations or defence, but he would have no further responsibility for purely territorial matters. This change, long demanded by nationalist leaders as a condition for proper political and economic advancement, was more than a symbolic act demanded by the times. Hopefully, it marked the end of an era of contradiction and uncertainty as Britain debated the relative merits of its various commitments and involvements in southern Africa.

The office of High Commissioner was originally attached to that of the Governor of Cape Colony in recognition of the fact that negotiations had to be carried on with various tribes living beyond the Cape Colony boundaries. With the creation of the Union of South Africa in 1910, the office was attached to that of Governor-General. However, the Statute of Westminster of 1931, which defined a new relationship between the various Commonwealth or Dominion governments on the one hand and the British government on the other, necessitated the separation of the office of High Commissioner from that of Governor-General, the latter office now representing merely the Crown and not the British government. Only in this way could the Protectorates remain as Britain's responsibility. This move also emphasised the differences of policy between the two governments and left the inhabitants, as they preferred, outside the Union of South Africa. It did not, however, give them the advantages of the regular British colonial service. For now, in addition to his usual functions, His Majesty's High Commissioner to South Africa remained responsible for the administration of Basutoland, Bechuanaland and Swaziland. Since the office of High Commissioner fell not under the Colonial Office but under the Commonwealth Relations Office, the Territories were placed in the anomalous position of being worse off than other British colonies and protectorates inasmuch as these could theoretically evolve towards independence. The High Commission Territories remained in a political limbo without prospect of change except in the direction of incorporation into South Africa. Even the development of local government was therefore twenty to forty years behind the times as compared with other British African territories.

When the self-governing colonies of Natal, Cape, Orange Free State and Transvaal were united in 1910 in the Union of South Africa, the three High Commission Territories were maintained as separate units as a result of African apprehension about the new government. The British government therefore showed itself from the start more responsive to political than to geographic or economic factors. In response to a petition from a deputation of chiefs who went to England in 1909 requesting that Basutoland be excluded from the projected Union, the British government declared that 'it was the purpose of His Majesty and His Majesty's Government, who are his advisers, that they should continue in the enjoyment of the privileges which they hitherto possessed'.

Although not included in the Union, the South African government, taking over the collection of customs from the Cape Colony, agreed to pay a fixed percentage to each of the Territories. In Basutoland and Swaziland, the Union government also ran the postal services, and in all three Territories the general law of the Union prevailed. South African rail services, omnibuses and currency were used, while South African citizens were employed in most administrative positions. The net effect was to make the Territories total captives of the South African economy and lent credence to the assumption that, eventually, they would be incorporated.

The 1909 draft Act of Union did indeed envisage a time when the government of the Territories would be handed over to the Union. The preamble to the Act declared that 'it is expedient to provide for the eventual . . . transfer to the Union of such parts of South Africa as are not originally included therein'. In a Schedule to the Act, it was provided in detail how such a transfer might take place. Upon receiving addresses from both Houses of the Union Parliament, the King-in-Council was empowered to grant a transfer of government upon the terms and conditions set forth in the same Schedule, conditions which forbade the alienation of land, the sale of liquor and the imposition of differential tariffs. In the event of transfer, responsibility for the administration was to be vested in the Prime Minister, advised by a commission of not more than three members appointed by the Governor-General-in-Council. Amendments to the Schedule would require Crown assent. The obvious intention was to ensure that the inhabitants of the Territories, in the event of transfer, would at least not be in any worse position, and, during debate on the Act, the responsible Ministers gave assurances that Parliament would have the fullest opportunity of discussing and, if so inclined, of disapproving any proposal of transfer. It was also promised, although not spelled out in precise form, that the inhabitants of the Territories would be first 'consulted' and their wishes taken into account. These assurances were repeated and emphasised over the next forty years. Although a request for transfer was never made by the Union government in the official form provided, the matter was raised privately and publicly over the years. That the request was not made formally was indicative of South Africa's growing fears that it would suffer a public rebuke from the peoples of the Territories as well as from the British government.

Hertzog was the first South African Prime Minister to raise the question of transfer with the British government. He expressed as his personal view that the time was then ripe. But in a statement in the Union Parliament in 1925, Hertzog said he would not press for incorporation unless 'the people—natives as well as Europeans—are prepared and desire to come in'.[1] In 1934, the Prime Minister again called for transfer and went on to suggest that, if it were delayed, difficulties might arise for the inhabitants of the Territories, especially with regard to their rights and privileges in the Union.[2] At a meeting in 1935 with the Secretary of State for the Dominions, J. H. Thomas, the Prime Minister pressed his point. By way of reply, Thomas repeated his suggestions, already made by way of instructions to the High Commissioner, that methods of co-operation between the Union government and the administration of the Territories be worked out. It was suggested that the Territories be given representation on various South African control boards and that South Africa associate itself financially with territorial development schemes then getting under way, largely as the outcome of Sir Alan Pim's critical reports. If at any time a change were to take place, said the Secretary, it could only be with the good will and co-operation of all parties.[3]

But this suggestion that South Africa contribute to schemes of bene-faction was viewed as a dangerous inroad by the inhabitants of the Territories. Hertzog's clumsy announcement in Parliament of a £35,000 contribution 'to help to secure the good will of the Natives for the hand-over' seemed adequate justification for this distrust. Consequently, when the offer was communicated to the African authorities in the Territories by their Resident Commissioners, 'accompanied by assurances that they would incur no liability by accepting Union money, it became clear that these assurances were not enough to dispel their fear of what might happen if their areas should eventually be incorporated in the Union. So strong a feeling against acceptance of the contribution was in fact expressed by the African authorities, that the High Commissioner eventually found himself compelled to inform the Union government that he could not hope for some time to ask that the contribution be actually paid. The offer was in consequence withdrawn by the Union government.'[4] The fact that South Africa, as a self-governing Dominion, was probably not bound by any conditions contained in the Schedule to the Act of Union, further contributed to the unwillingness of the Territories to risk closer ties with South Africa.

After much misunderstanding as to whether the Secretary of State had actually promised to use such influence 'as would advance the establishment of a disposition towards the Union',[5] Hertzog agreed in 1937 that, if transfer occurred, it would take place along lines laid down in the Schedule, and a memorandum, though unpublished, was prepared to this effect. By letter of December 29, 1937, Hertzog stated that the administration of the Transkei Territories by the Union would provide a model to be followed in the High Commission Territories, if they were transferred to the Union.[6] More important, in 1938 a Joint Advisory Council, consisting of officers of the Union government and the Resident Commissioners, was set up to study the possibilities of co-operation in the development of the Territories. These co-operative moves were facilitated by the Union government's announcement that 'the paramountcy of native interests in native areas' would be maintained. To many influential and 'liberal' people, there no longer seemed any adequate reason for further postponement of transfer, since such a policy coincided with British policy for the Protectorates.[7] The likelihood of independence for the Territories was not even considered. Fortunately for the Protectorates, the second world war put an end to these discussions and the question of transfer was left in abeyance until 1949.

The Nationalist victory of 1948 which brought Dr D. F. Malan to power as Prime Minister of South Africa again revived discussion on the question of transfer. At the Commonwealth Conference of 1949, Malan criticised the attitude of the British government and warned that his government was considering a petition to the British Parliament for the transfer of the Territories. Returning from the Conference, Malan told the House of Assembly: 'It is one of the greatest anomalies existing that within the borders of a sovereign independent nation there should be areas which are administered by another power from outside its borders. It is an absurdity which few nations would tolerate.'[8] In 1950, the Prime Minister stressed to the visiting Secretary of State for Commonwealth Relations, Patrick Gordon Walker, that delay in effecting transfer implied a 'position of inferiority' for the Union as a member of the Commonwealth, on the grounds that no other member of that association would tolerate being 'compelled to harbour territories, entirely dependent upon her economically and largely also for defence, but belonging to and governed by another country'.[9] South Africa's resentment was underscored in 1952 when Malan threatened to regard the Protectorates as 'foreign territory' and thus deprive the administering authority of basic facilities. This, he added, was not so much a threat as a plain statement of fact. He urged a policy of gradually preparing the way for eventual transfer.[10] The Union Parliament resolved in 1954 that the transfer of the Territories 'should take place as soon as possible' and that negotiations should be resumed.[11] Prime Minister Strijdom's assurance in 1955, that 'if the Territories are transferred to us we shall treat them in the same sympathetic way in which we have always treated the native territories within the Union', was hardly comforting to the peoples of the Protectorates. These 'assurances' were combined with a more moderate approach by the Prime Minister, who told his party conference that the problem of the Territories would be settled by 'agreement' and 'between friends', a possible reflection of certain Nationalist opinion

that 'while sovereignty could remain with Britain, the administration
of the three Territories should be progressively transferred to South
African hands'.[12]

British response to these overtures was a repeated adherence to the
principle of consultation with the inhabitants of the Territories, and
no sign was given of any desire to enter into negotiations on the subject. If, as Tshekedi Khama observed, this was but a further example
of British procrastination, it implicitly served warning that the policies
of the Nationalist government would have to be changed to secure
agreement. Tshekedi's advice, on the other hand, that no time should
be lost in preparing the people of the Territories 'for the responsible
task of stating their own case to the British government' through the
establishment of a more representative form of government 'by concurrently creating Local, Legislative and Executive Councils',[13] was
no longer falling on deaf ears. The advent of the Nationalist government, with its declared policy of total apartheid, at least had the merit
of clearing the air of misconceptions, since incorporation of the
Territories fitted all too logically into its total schemes.

Publication in 1956 of the Tomlinson Commission Report on
'separate development' revealed that all three Territories were theoretically incorporated in the proposed Bantustan system. Although Dr
H. F. Verwoerd, then South African Minister for Native Affairs,
denied that their inclusion was a basic requirement for the success of
his policy, some of the maps in the Report clearly indicated that
transfer of the Territories would permit the carrying out of the
Bantustan project. Without the Territories, the Bantustan system
would remain a painfully unconvincing project and, with the exception
of the Transkei, could hardly advance beyond the drawing board. The
Commission pointed out that, even if all the land promised in 1936
were added to the reserves, only thirteen per cent of the country would
be set aside for the African population. However, if the High Commission Territories were included in the term South Africa, and if they
were added to existing reserves, the percentage would amount to
nearly forty-five.

Although the incorporation of the Protectorates appeared essential
for the realisation of the Bantustan system as well as a condition for its
acceptance abroad, the Nationalist victory of 1948 and that party's
continued success in parliamentary elections effectively removed the
possibility of negotiated transfer. The failure of South Africa to develop
along liberal British lines made it impossible for Whitehall to accept any

assurances that the paramount interests of the Protectorates would be maintained. As an opposition member of the South African Parliament has recently observed, 'if it had not been for the tragedy of 1948 . . . and if the United Party had remained in power, the three territories would have become part of South Africa'.[14] The vigorous pursuit of apartheid by Malan and his successors, Strijdom and Verwoerd, as well as the departure of South Africa from the Commonwealth as a Republic in 1961, put the final seal on this development. Reluctantly at first, the British government pushed on after 1959 towards the goal of internal self-government for the Protectorates. From there it was only logical that independence would follow.

The replacement of Her Majesty's High Commissioner by Her Majesty's Ambassador, responsible to the Foreign Office, and the transfer of the Territories to the Colonial Office on December 1, 1961, still under the Ambassador in his capacity as High Commissioner for the Territories, provided a more proper framework for the development of the Protectorates. It also provided concrete evidence of Britain's decision not to carry through the transfer. By abolishing the office of High Commissioner in 1964, the process of setting the Territories on their own paths was complete.

Faced with Britain's determination to advance the Territories to independence, Verwoerd was induced to dismiss the possibility of incorporation as incompatible with that policy. 'This candid admission of reality had never been matched by any of Dr Verwoerd's predecessors as Prime Minister, and it clearly revealed his inability to conceive of full independence for the Bantustans and by implication for the High Commission Territories as part of that scheme.'[15] On September 3, 1963, Verwoerd went on to recast South Africa's attitude towards the High Commission Territories. 'If South Africa were to be, or to become, the guardian, the protector or helper of these adjacent Territories, instead of the United Kingdom', he proclaimed, 'South Africa could lead them far better and much more quickly to independence and economic prosperity than Great Britain can do.' Britain, he said, 'might guide them to political freedom, but she is almost powerless to regulate the ultimate economic situation or to achieve the economic viability of these areas for their peoples'. Two days later, in reply to world criticism that he was attempting to 'take over' or 'incorporate' the Territories, the Prime Minister denied that incorporation was sought. He insisted that this would be contrary to his government's policy of separate development 'which has as its objective the political independence of the Bantu nations'.[16]

By offering to 'guide' the Territories to political independence and economic prosperity, Verwoerd was making a variation on the theme of a half century of efforts to bring the Territories under South African control. Although incorporation was clearly out of the question, the Nationalist government saw new opportunities to effect the same end. The fact that the Protectorates were becoming places of asylum for South African refugees, together with the possibility that these countries might become hostile states on and within South Africa's borders, could not go unnoticed. Border posts, barbed-wire fences, passport control, curtailment of railway passenger service, air flight restrictions and some return of workers: all demonstrated South Africa's ability to adversely affect life in the Territories. But alternating with these displays of force, Verwoerd showed that he could co-operate with any government in the Territories which sought South African friendship. Friendly relations, he said, were in accord with South Africa's policy of separate development. Moreover, he expressed confidence that independent governments would be better guarantors of their own interests than the British government.

On the election of Seretse Khama as first Prime Minister of Bechuanaland in early 1965, Verwoerd sent his own personal congratulations. It was also announced that the ban against Seretse Khama's entering South Africa had been lifted the previous October. There was also abundant evidence that the South African government, directly or indirectly, was providing financial and other assistance for the parties of Chief Jonathan in Basutoland and King Sobhuza in Swaziland. These moves could be interpreted as being entirely consistent with Verwoerd's earlier comments that he would make the Territories 'democratic states in which the masses would not be dominated by a small group of authoritarians'. In other words, the tribal system would be resuscitated, as was being attempted in South Africa, and an alliance would be formed with the chiefs, at the expense of the young political parties and nationalist movements.

The danger of acquiescence on the part of the indigenous population to South Africa's blandishments is perhaps greatest in Swaziland, one of the more backward traditional societies in southern Africa. Thanks to the entrenched position of the King and his inner circle of aristocrats, together with a powerful white community of supporters, South Africa is able to find natural allies fearful of the 'subversive' ideas of modern African nationalism. This group totally dominates the country's first Legislative Council and seeks British permission for an early vote on independence.

In Lesotho there is less possibility that either the supporters of chieftainship or any other substantial group would be party to a direct 'deal' with South Africa. Nevertheless, the fact that approximately one half of the adult male population finds employment in South Africa strengthens the hand of those who stress the importance of maintaining good relations with the Republic. Intimations that South Africa might even transfer certain adjacent lands to a friendly Lesotho and Swaziland also bolster the position of conservative chiefly elements.

Botswana is less precariously situated vis-à-vis South Africa and it alone of the three countries has a geographical link with an independent black African state, Zambia. Although the party of Seretse Khama, supported by the chiefs of the country, may wield control for some time it is not inclined to accept dictation from South Africa. Nor is the new government prepared to provoke or unnecessarily offend its mighty neighbour. At the same time, as an escape route to the north, Botswana must of necessity prove troublesome to South Africa. The very success of a non-racial government here or in the other countries presents a fundamental threat to the apartheid system.

Each of the three states is particularly vulnerable to economic pressures from South Africa. These pressures need not take the form of overtly hostile actions. Rather, the potential danger is that they might be strangled through slow, undramatic administrative and economic measures, all of which might be entirely 'legitimate'. The inhabitants could thus be unnerved into accepting steady capitulation in order to avoid open confrontation. At the very least, a Bantustan psychology might be effected with a minimum of effort. On the other hand, South Africa can be prevented from using these Territories as hostages in her conflict with the rest of Africa if a great infusion of capital, as recommended in the Morse Report of 1959, is immediately forthcoming. Economic development of the Territories, with a corresponding reduction of dependence on South Africa, can weight the balance more favourably on the side of these countries. A United Nations presence, both economically and politically, together with firm insistence upon international right of access, will also strengthen the determination of the former Territories not to abandon their desire to develop independently.

PART I

FROM BASUTOLAND
TO LESOTHO

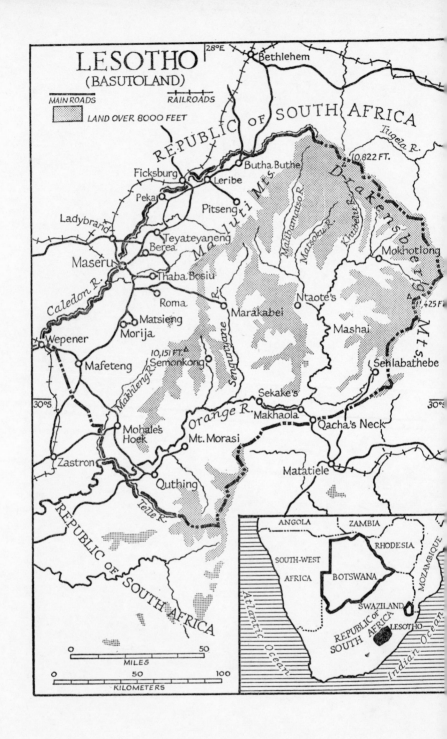

I

THE BASUTO NATION, FROM BIRTH TO
COLONIAL STATUS, 1823–1884

THE BASUTO,* one of the youngest tribal groupings in Africa,
trace their national origin back to 1823, when the young Chief
Moshoeshoe had become the acknowledged leader of most
Basuto clans. These clans, together with the Nguni† speaking peoples,
constituted the two main linguistic divisions of the Southern Bantu,
who had begun migrating into southern Africa during the thirteenth
and fourteenth centuries. By 1620, the Suto and Nguni had crossed the
Limpopo river and begun scattering the weakly organised Khoisan‡
people, who had been the country's only inhabitants since prehistoric
times. Many of the Bushmen were killed or fled to the Kalahari Desert,
west of the grassy highland veld, while the Hottentots moved towards
the Cape of Good Hope. The Nguni, in turn, took the semitropical
coastlands of modern Natal whereas the Suto remained in the interior,
between the Drakensberg Mountains and the Kalahari. The southern
branch of the Suto arrived during the seventeenth century in the
modern Orange Free State; the northern Suto remained in the Trans-
vaal.¹ Over the centuries, the Suto frequently intermarried with the
Bushmen and, by the end of the eighteenth century, a number of
individualistic Suto groupings were thickly settled in the valley of the
Caledon river, the north-western boundary of present-day Lesotho.
But until the appearance of Moshoeshoe no single chief had succeeded
in securing a dominant position among them.

In 1820, the 'Wars of Calamity', part of the chain reaction flowing
from the activities of Shaka, the Chief of the Zulu clan of the Nguni to
the east, were affecting the Suto clans along the Caledon. Many Basuto
were driven from their homes, which in most cases were completely

---

* Basuto (pl.); Masuto (sing.); Suto or Sesotho—the language; Lesotho—the country.
† The generic term Nguni included the Zulu.
‡ Khoisan included Hottentot and Bushmen.

broken up, and were so reduced that cannibalism became not uncommon.[2] It was during this period of upheaval that Moshoeshoe, a minor Chief known only for his reputation as a raider, consolidated his position in the region. Moshoeshoe secured himself in the impregnable fortress of Thaba Bosiu—the 'mountain that grows taller by night'— a flat-topped crag wide enough even to graze large herds. From this vantage point he could easily check any contenders for power as leaders of tribal fragments joined him to form the Basuto nation. Despite this strength, Moshoeshoe respected the greater striking power of the Zulu and decided to avoid conflict. As a real political alternative, Moshoeshoe resorted to diplomacy, an art in which he was to become highly skilled, and undertook to provide Shaka with an annual tribute.

The Coming of the Europeans

The threat from the Zulu soon gave way to that of the Boers from the south. Shortly after the founding and settlement of Cape Town in 1652 by Jan van Riebeeck, the Dutch began fighting their Bushmen and Hottentot neighbours. Increasingly restive under the government of their sponsors, the Netherlands East India Company, the settlers took to 'trekking' and slavery so as to avoid expensive duties and taxes demanded by the Company. As these free farmers, known in Dutch as 'Boers', moved inland seeking better agricultural and grazing lands, their peculiar Calvinistic background combined with the necessities of Trekboer life to mould them into a distinct people. Inasmuch as their 'national' life required them to migrate into the interior, it was only a matter of time until they would come into conflict with those Bantu tribes moving south and westward into the Cape. In 1775 the two great waves met in a momentous encounter on the banks of the Fish river. In this clash between Boer and Xosa, two powerful advancing frontiers struggled for the right to occupy the interior. Subsequent history would be dominated by the manner in which they reacted to, and ultimately overlapped, each other.[3] Of all the Bantu groupings, only the Basuto, Swazi and Ngwato survived the Boer onslaught, due both to their ability to maintain political cohesion and to British protection.

Basuto history entered a new phase as British and Boer interests collided following the British occupation of the Cape Colony in 1806. Occasional parties of Boers began to make their appearance along the Caledon as early as 1831. Moshoeshoe regarded their presence as a serious problem. Impressed by the obvious superiority of their arms, Moshoeshoe was eager to avail himself of other contacts with the outside world. He gratefully accepted such valuable presents as a pistol, a mare and foal and two horses from a German traveller who visited Thaba Bosiu in 1833. Contact with the Korana, a mixed body of Hottentot, Griqua, Bastards and desperadoes, further introduced Moshoeshoe and his people to the use of firearms and horses and they used the horse to an extent unmatched by any other Africa tribe.

Determined to assert their independence of British rule the Boers made the Great Trek across the Orange river in 1837. Their first winter encampment was at Thaba Nchu, about a day's journey from Moshoeshoe's settlement at Thaba Bosiu, where, for the first time, a Bantu tribe fell directly under the control of the Boers. Meanwhile, the British were already preparing to extend their jurisdiction beyond the Orange river, and this decision would inextricably involve the Basuto in the struggle between Boer and British until the resolution of the contest in 1904.

Another important influence was introduced to the Basuto by Adam Krotz, a coloured Christian. Krotz informed Moshoeshoe of a group known as missionaries and his account so impressed the Chief that he was commissioned as an ambassador to persuade a missionary to visit the fortress.[4] Already, however, three French missionaries from the Paris Evangelical Society were on their way and reached Thaba Bosiu in June 1833. Moshoeshoe quickly saw in this group a suitable European balance, which, together with horses and firearms, would enable him to withstand the encroaching Boers. Two of the missionaries were accordingly settled at Morija, twenty-five miles to the south-west, near an outpost in the charge of Moshoeshoe's son, Letsie. The third missionary, Casalis, was permitted to found a mission at Thaba Bosiu. Within a short time Casalis had become a close friend and confidant of the Chief and acted almost as a foreign secretary. In 1850, Moshoeshoe invited Bishop Gray to Basutoland and offered him ground on which to start a Church of England mission. Although the Church of England was not in a position to take up the offer until 1876, Moshoeshoe's desire to encourage various denominations was now clear.

In 1862, Moshoeshoe welcomed another Christian force when two members of the Oblates of Mary Immaculate, a French Roman Catholic missionary order, unexpectedly appeared. They were cordially received by Moshoeshoe, particularly since he had not yet attracted the Church of England. Two of the Chief's sons were commissioned to assist the priests in selecting a suitable site in a fertile valley some fifteen miles south-east of Thaba Bosiu. The new settlement, known to the Basuto as Roma, was to play a significant role some years later, after the ascendancy of the Evangelical 'political' missionaries had been reduced. The establishment by the Catholics of schools, and eventually a printing press, which competed with Morija, also stimulated a rivalry which at times bore the hallmarks of all the traditional religious animosities inherent in the French situation. But if religious rivalry had its undesirable aspects, it also served to lay the foundations of a broad elementary educational system and made the Basuto the most literate people in Africa.

Early missionaries were not always circumspect in political matters and their attempts to influence the Paramount Chief brought considerable criticism, not only from the Boers, but from British administrators. But whatever their shortcomings, the Evangelical missionaries advised and helped the Basuto in their struggle with the Boers, who coveted Basuto wheat-growing country. To the missionaries, the Basuto owe in no small measure their written language, their literature, the preservation of their oral traditions and their recorded history. Of especial importance to the Basuto was the power of the pen which these men of world-wide contacts could utilise on their behalf. At a time when the anti-slavery movement was enjoying popular support in Europe, these missionaries commanded an influence far out of proportion to their numbers and resources. Soon they came to be regarded as indispensable intermediaries between Moshoeshoe and the British authorities.

At this point, Moshoeshoe had little idea of British power, since its expansion northward had been slow and unspectacular. Not until 1835 did British rule reach the south bank of the Orange river. In any event, Moshoeshoe quickly perceived the enmity existing between the two European groups. After a visit in 1837 from the Boer leader, Piet Retief, who reportedly had imprisoned Chief Sikonyela, Moshoeshoe began to weigh the advantages of British protection. When it was learned that Commandant Andries Pretorius, reputedly the best of the Boer leaders, had committed the unheard-of offence of executing an envoy from the Zulu chief, Dingane, Moshoeshoe was prompted to seek British protection.

In 1842, Moshoeshoe officially inquired on what terms Britain would be willing to 'recognise' the tribe of the Basuto. The result was an agreement, signed in October 1843 by Sir George Napier, admitting

Moshoeshoe as 'a friend and ally of Cape Colony' and roughly describing the boundaries of his territory. This document would henceforth be cited as proof that Basutoland had acquired the status of a Protected State and could not be treated as either a colony or a protectorate. Moshoeshoe was obliged by the treaty to preserve order in his own area and to prevent violence in adjacent regions of the Cape Colony. By this time, Moshoeshoe probably had some 51,000 people under his control and the number continued to grow as scattered clans and individuals placed themselves under his protection.

Despite British recognition, failure to agree on the demarcation of the western boundary proved a source of constant conflict. British attempts to mediate the dispute between the Boer settlers and the Basuto were unsuccessful, and, in order to secure peace in these regions beyond the Cape Colony borders, Britain found it necessary, in February 1848, to declare her sovereignty over the territory north of the Orange river. Before this step was taken, however, the British High Commissioner assured Moshoeshoe that he would remain independent and would be allowed to govern his tribe according to custom. It was only on this assurance, given in January 1848, that Moshoeshoe agreed to come under British jurisdiction.

Moshoeshoe realised, however, that British control and influence north of the Orange was little more than nominal and that the Boers were continuing their preparations for a contest of power. He began arming his people against Boer encroachment and took the lead in forming a confederation of tribes in the upper Cape Colony. Indeed, so tenuous was British control amid growing tension and unrest that the British government decided to abandon its jurisdiction in the 'Orange River Sovereignty'. Not only was there conflict between the Boers and Moshoeshoe, but, increasingly, Moshoeshoe opposed British authorities who, it seemed, sought to maintain peace at the expense of the Basuto. It has even been suggested that Moshoeshoe's anger with the British induced him to request an alliance with the Boer leader, Andries Pretorius. Although there is little likelihood that either party would have seriously entertained such an idea, Moshoeshoe apparently did request that Pretorius intervene to prevent further bloodshed in the Sovereignty.

Disagreement between Moshoeshoe and the British High Commissioner, Sir George Cathcart, induced the latter to hold Moshoeshoe responsible for the past activities of his subordinates. He felt a show of force against Moshoeshoe would make it possible to abandon the

Orange river jurisdiction with less likelihood of a Basuto attack against the four Transvaal republics (recognised by Britain in the Sand River Convention of 1852 and united in 1860 to form the South African Republic). As Britain drew closer to the Boers and thus 'undermined the whole humanitarian assumption that one of the main functions of British power in South Africa was to supervise and manage the relations between whites and natives',[5] Moshoeshoe was given no alternative but to fight or be ruined.

In the ensuing conflict, the British forces could gain no immediate victory and British power seemed thoroughly discredited in the area. Moshoeshoe correctly assessed that he now had an opportunity to sue for peace on favourable terms. Realising that British power would certainly increase and that British friendship was necessary for survival, Moshoeshoe despatched a letter to Cathcart on December 20, 1852. Often described as the most politic document ever penned in South Africa, Moshoeshoe informed the High Commissioner: 'You have chastised, let it be enough, I pray you; and let me be no longer considered an enemy of the Queen.'[6] Moshoeshoe's tactics were successful and he was everywhere hailed as a victor in the wake of British withdrawal. Moshoeshoe was left supreme from the northern waters of the Caledon and Orange down the Caledon valley to the Cape Colony frontier along the Orange. Thus, at the age of about sixty-seven, Moshoeshoe was at the height of his power and, except for the Zulu King, he was the most powerful chief in southern Africa.

The abandonment of British jurisdiction in the Orange River Sovereignty in favour of the Boers was formally announced in August 1854, and Moshoeshoe thereby ceased to be even a titular subject of the British Crown. He still maintained, however, that he was in alliance with the British. But he refused to recognise the so-called Warden Line as his western boundary, a demarcation drawn up under British direction. Although adamant on this vital matter, Moshoeshoe was keenly aware of the limitations imposed upon him by reason of the new Anglo-Boer accord. Consequently, when Josias P. Hoffman, first President of the Orange Free State, made friendly overtures, Moshoeshoe responded quickly. Hoffman, who owed his election to his reputation for being able to 'manage' Moshoeshoe, had, as Acting President, invited the Chief to Bloemfontein for the formal departure of the British. There he met with the members of the new government, who were aware of their dependence on Moshoeshoe's forbearance and respect for a boundary which he was known to detest. Hoffman subsequently commissioned Joseph M. Orpen to visit Thaba Bosiu to ascertain the minimal terms acceptable to Moshoeshoe and this was followed by a state visit in August 1854. Resplendent in a French military uniform, Moshoeshoe acknowledged the President's arrival with prolonged salutes. Despite the expressions of friendship, Hoffman was unable to secure the Chief's assent to a border definition. The President was driven out of office a few months later for making a present to Moshoeshoe of a keg of powder to replace what had been blown away in salutes. Whatever hope there had been that Hoffman's friendship with Moshoeshoe might have led to better relations between the two governments was now removed.

Border clashes became more frequent after 1855, and in 1858 the Orange Free State declared war on the Basuto in order to secure the Warden Line as their eastern boundary. The fighting was inconclusive and peace was brought about through British mediation. In the first Award of Aliwal North, all the northern portion of the Warden Line was reaffirmed as the boundary between the Orange Free State and the country of Moshoeshoe. On the southern part some concessions were made to the claims of the Basuto. Moshoeshoe let it be known, however, that he would regard the Award as binding only so long as he considered it expedient.

Seven years of tenuous peace followed, marred by frequent minor breaches of order. British responsibility for these disturbances was underlined by Sir George Grey, the new Governor and High Commissioner who replaced Cathcart in late 1854. The British government, he said, had abandoned sovereignty in the Orange river without having demarcated the boundary between the Basuto and the Free State Boers. The latter's government had to face the pressure of farmers holding grants which extended over the lands actually occupied by the Basuto. Even two private meetings between Moshoeshoe and Martinus W. Pretorius, who succeeded to the presidency of the South African Republic in 1859, failed to bring agreement. Apart from the exchange of platitudes on the desirability of peace, no progress was made towards a solution of basic issues.

Renewed Appeals for British Protection

In 1860, Moshoeshoe again requested that he be restored as one of the Queen's subjects. He was growing old and was less able than ever to control the rival chiefs, who wanted more land in order to increase their pretensions and their followers. Within their own recognised territories there was a greater congestion of horses and cattle than the country could carry, since the tribes had been deprived of free movement over the wide pastures of their western frontier lands.[7] But Moshoeshoe realised that in any future conflict the Boers would predominate. He therefore sought British protection as a matter of urgency and took advantage of the appointment of a new Cape Colony Governor and High Commissioner, Sir Philip Wodehouse, to renew his petition. Moshoeshoe wrote to Wodehouse, saying that while he was not altogether unable to defend his country, he could not keep it from the constant threat of attack. Security could be had, he told the High Commissioner, only if the Basuto were recognised as the Queen's subjects. Should the Queen be willing to appoint an Agent to live with him and be 'her eyes and ears', he would gladly receive him.

Wodehouse was anxious to know exactly what Moshoeshoe intended in this offer, and sent two commissioners to Basutoland in 1862 to secure clarification. Their report seems to have been a most accurate rendering of Moshoeshoe's ideas. The Basuto, according to Moshoeshoe, did not actually want the British to send magistrates, for, he said: 'If the Government sends magistrates, the Basuto will not understand; it will be like a stone that is too heavy for them to carry.' On the other hand, said Moshoeshoe, the Agent whom he had requested could 'practise the Basutos, and gradually teach them to hear magistrates while he is helping me in political matters'. As for the rest, said the Chief, 'I will be under the Queen as her subject, and my people will be her subjects also, but under me . . . so that the Queen rules my people only through me. I wish to govern my own people by Native Law, by our own laws; but if the Queen wishes after this to introduce other laws into my country, I will be willing; but I should wish such laws to be submitted to the Council of the Basuto; and when they are accepted by my Council I will send the Queen and inform her that they have become law.'[8]

While in favour of sending an Agent as requested, Wodehouse doubted, perhaps with good reason, that the Basuto would have accepted even such qualified jurisdiction as Moshoeshoe proposed. Moreover, the High Commissioner was forbidden by London to make any commitments likely to prove embarrassing or expensive. Although constrained in this matter, Wodehouse did act in 1863 to mediate between the Basuto and the Free State on the basis of the Award of Aliwal North. He was eager to keep Basutoland intact 'lest its dispersed fragments spread confusion throughout the Native world'.[9] But the Basuto subsequently refused to acknowledge the mediation as binding, while the Boers demanded that the Basuto withdraw from the lands assigned to them under the Award. Moshoeshoe made only a pretence of complying and the Boers retaliated with a declaration of war in May 1865. After a year of desultory fighting, the Great Basuto War, as it was known, was brought to an end by the Treaty of Thaba Bosiu. With his people close to starvation, Moshoeshoe was forced to cede his western border territory that contained half the total arable area in all Basutoland. It was by far the most disastrous 'treaty' forced on the Basuto. Within two years, however, the Basuto decided to renew the struggle and were once again faced with the prospect of imminent starvation.

At this crucial juncture Moshoeshoe made a last desperate appeal for British protection. He therefore conferred on his personal emissary 'all authority which may be required to deliver up into the hands of the representatives of Her Majesty's Government at Natal the whole Government of the Basuto Nation, that is to say, all our claims and personal rights, with those of our country, so that we may in all concerns, duties and privileges become the faithful and true subjects of Her Majesty's Government'.[10]

In Natal, Theophilus Shepstone, the power behind the Lieutenant Governor, favoured the request on the twofold ground that in Basuto-land the British government 'would hold the key to South African native politics, and that the annexation of Basutoland to Natal was an essential step towards the fulfilment of his ambition of a Greater Natal'.[11] It was on these same grounds that the Transvaal Republic subsequently sought the incorporation of Basutoland and which through the years has undoubtedly influenced South African policy.

Annexation, 1868

Meanwhile, there had been a change of opinion in Britain towards the Basuto and the Boer republics. The closing down of the French Protestant and the Wesleyan mission stations in the area ceded by the Basuto to the Free State aroused much ill-feeling against the Boers, both in England and in France. This resentment coincided with growing fears that the Free State might push its borders forward in order to secure a seaport on the eastern coast. Dissatisfied with the Conventions and the independence they had conferred on the republics, the imperial

government reversed itself and determined to accept in principle
Moshoeshoe's offer. Wodehouse was thereupon authorised to annex
Basutoland on the explicit and significant condition that not the
British government but Natal should be responsible for the organisation and expenses of its future administration—a decision strongly
criticised by Wodehouse who 'distrusted Shepstone's Native policy, and
was perturbed at the talk in the Natal legislature of taxing the Basuto
in order to swell the exiguous Natal revenues, and of setting aside parts
of Basutoland for white settlement'.[12]

Lest they now be cheated of victory, the Boers hurriedly launched a
large-scale attack on the Kheme plateau, the last remaining Basuto
stronghold. This action forced the British to act with despatch and, on
March 12, 1866, Wodehouse proclaimed that 'the tribe of the Basutos
shall be taken to be for all intents and purposes British subjects, and the
territory of the said tribe shall be taken to be British territory'. It was
subsequently decided that the territory would be administered for the
time being by the High Commissioner rather than be incorporated in
the colony of Natal as originally planned. The attitude of the imperial
government, an attitude which would long characterise the British
approach towards the territory, was summed up by the Secretary of
State who wrote to the High Commissioner: 'The object [of protecting
the Basuto] was to attain such an arrangement as, without involving
the imperial government in any pecuniary liability, should secure
peace around the frontiers of the South African colonies. . . .' Members
of the Cape colonial legislature severely criticised the imperial government for this policy of frugality at the expense of their own vital
interests.

Although the Proclamation of March 12, 1868, clearly extended
British protection to the Basuto, it did not settle the frontier question
between the Free State and the Basuto. The High Commissioner therefore set out to recover through negotiation a part of the surrendered
arable lands and to establish the border through treaty. Realising that
the British annexation of Basutoland was irrevocable, the Free State at
last signed the Convention of Aliwal North on February 12, 1869, by
which the land east of the Caledon reverted to the Basuto. But the
Basuto, who had confidently anticipated the restoration of *all* their
lands, were given barely enough to preserve them from the worst
effects of congestion. That they had lost much of their best grazing
and ploughing land was seen not only in the fact that they began to
develop an economy more pronouncedly agricultural than pastoral,

but above all in the fact that they began to supplement their production with wages earned in the service of whites.[31] The frontiers then laid down and ratified were substantially the same as those recognised today.

The British government soon proved to be less than enthusiastic about its new commitment in Basutoland and seemed to have neither time nor money for its administration. Moreover, the Colonial Office had not yet really considered placing large areas of black Africa under its direct administration, and such administration as existed was generally confined to coastal towns and adjacent areas. Since the annexation of Basutoland was clearly induced by the need for securing peace on the frontiers of the Cape Colony and Natal, it seemed logical that one of these colonies should assume responsibility for administration. Initial arrangements making Basutoland a Crown Protectorate therefore appeared to have been only of a tentative or exploratory character and subject to change on the death of Moshoeshoe.

The Death of Moshoeshoe and Accession of Letsie

Moshoeshoe died on March 1, 1870, and the succession passed to his fifty-nine year old son, Letsie. Whatever conflicting estimates Europeans might have entertained of Moshoeshoe, there can be little doubt that he was held in high esteem, not only by the Basuto as the founder of their nation, but by Africans generally. Indeed, it was Moshoeshoe who had succeeded in creating an original nation-state, one of the few in Africa, possessing established frontiers, a single language, a unified army, a new religion and a central institution of government with its court, chieftaincy and *pitso* system.

Moshoeshoe's policy had been to leave the chiefs in local control while he established his authority throughout the country. Later, he had sought to secure the position of his family and to provide for the devolution of his authority by creating a number of territorial charges under his sons and brothers. Thus, Letsie was placed in the centre of the country as his father's deputy. So long as this practice of creating charges or princedoms was confined to major chiefs, administration was not unduly complicated. Under subsequent Paramount Chiefs, however, the placing of the offspring of lesser houses created a new and embarrassing feature in organisation. Although Moshoeshoe attempted to consolidate control in the hands of his family, his rule was never absolute. Important decisions were made in consultation with his family and other chiefs at a *pitso* or general meeting attended by the tribesmen. Each of his subchiefs did in fact expect to be consulted on matters of importance. The more important 'Laws of Moshoeshoe'— those prohibiting the sale of spirits (1854), punishing witchcraft (1855) and forbidding permanent European settlement (1859)—were all promulgated as laws 'with the advice and concurrence of the great men of the tribe'.

Letsie was formally recognised as Paramount Chief in 1870, shortly after his father's death. During his twenty-one year reign he would show himself to be a man of vastly different character from his father, and some critics would call him irresolute and suspicious. In any event, while Moshoeshoe was still clinging to life, the new High Commissioner, Sir Henry Barkly, visited Letsie in early 1869 and warned him of the impending decision to incorporate Basutoland into Cape Colony.

Annexation to Cape Colony, 1871–1883

The formal Act of Annexation was passed by the Cape legislature in 1871. It was not even considered necessary to consult the Basuto chiefs before this change in government was effected. Annexation, however, did not automatically extend to Basutoland the system of law prevailing in the Cape. The power of making laws and regulations was vested in the Governor, and Cape laws applied only if specifically extended by the Governor or if specifically provided for. Likewise, the Governor decided what class of cases originating in Basutoland would be cognisable by Cape courts. The country was then divided into four administrative districts under the charge of Resident Magistrates— Leribe, Berea, Thaba Bosiu and Cornet Spruit, roughly corresponding to the four areas held by Letsie, his brother Molapo, and the important chiefs Masupha and Morosi. Wide administrative powers were entrusted to a Governor's Agent who was to act as Chief Magistrate in judicial matters. A comprehensive set of regulations for the future government of the area were immediately put in force and these were supplemented by proclamations in 1877 and 1880.

Contrary to the draft regulations proposed in 1868 under Wodehouse, which contemplated the use of the chiefs as the agency of local rule, the new regulations, influenced in their conception by the views of Cape officials, pointed to the progressive substitution of the jurisdiction of magistrates for that of chiefs. The effect of the regulations of 1871 and 1877 was to treat Basutoland as a Native Reserve. Land was to be protected from alienation to Europeans, but in other respects the country was to be brought, for administrative purposes, under the magisterial system as practised in Cape Colony.

The economic life of Basutoland quickly responded to the introduction of orderly government. In 1878, grain was exported to the value of £400,000 and wool to the value of £75,000. Ominously, however, the opening of the Kimberley diamond mines introduced a more profitable employment than traditional pursuits and large numbers of Basuto began migrating in order to secure ready cash.

But whatever the economic benefits of the new regime, the Basuto chiefs were vigorously opposed to the system. An unexpected result of annexation was the request made in 1872 by Letsie and some leading chiefs that Basutoland be given representation in the Cape Parliament. This was refused and their taxes were doubled. The Basuto were not, however, seeking closer integration with the Cape government. Rather, by participating in Parliament, they hoped to share in the discussion of measures which the government intended to apply to Basutoland.[14] Such participation, as time would show, was vitally necessary to national survival and development. In its absence, as the next ninety years would prove, the preservation of tribal law and custom without reference to the complexity of modern society, could only leave the country to the mercy of external economic and political forces which nullified the substance of British protection. In the event, the Cape Parliament refused the request on the unconvincing grounds that if the proposal were granted, the Territory would have to come in all respects under colonial rule.

The climax of the Cape government's policy of direct rule came in 1880 when an attempt was made to disarm the Basuto in accordance with the Cape Peace Preservation Act of 1876. But the Basuto still feared the Boers in the Orange Free State and were rightly distrustful of Britain's unstable colonial policy. Refusing to stake their survival on a tenuous British support, the Basuto resisted the Cape's disarmament demands and the Gun War, costing the Cape government £5,000,000, ensued. In this eight-month war, which also had something of the character of a Basuto civil war during which several chiefs sought to maintain independent control, the forces of the Cape Colony were successfully resisted. An armistice signed in 1881 eventually led to a compromise whereby the Basuto were granted permission to retain their guns if they paid an annual licence fee. But the Cape Colony government, as the Basuto well knew, was in no position to secure the payment of the prescribed fees. Meanwhile, a state of unrest continued and border raids increased.

Crown Colony, 1884

The prestige of the Cape Colony's administration was thus destroyed in Basutoland and the imperial government was requested to relieve the Cape of its charge. Britain at last agreed to take over the administration of the Territory on condition that the Cape Colony guarantee an annual subsidy of £20,000 as a contribution towards any deficiency in revenues. At the same time, recent events had brought the imperial government to appreciate the need for treating the views of the Basuto with greater respect. Accordingly, the Basuto were presented with the option of returning to the independent status enjoyed prior to coming under British protection. The obvious intention, however, was to force recalcitrant chiefs either to accept imperial terms of rule or face the chance of Free State aggression.

The Cape Colony Parliament passed the Basutoland Disannexation Act in September 1883 and in November the chiefs assembled in *pitso* to decide whether or not they wished to become British subjects under the direct rule of the Queen. Letsie and his son Lerotholi accepted at once. Although several important chiefs did not attend the *pitso*, the majority of chiefs put forward a strongly worded plea for British control. The imperial government assented to this request and a Proclamation was issued on March 18, 1884, which embodied an order-in-council of February 21 to that effect. This decision practically coincided with that which resulted in the establishment of the Bechuanaland Protectorate, a move calculated to guard British approaches to the north. The order-in-council of February 1884, the fundamental document in Basutoland's constitutional structure, inaugurated a period of administration under the British government destined to last roughly three-quarters of a century.

2

INDIRECT RULE AND THE DEVELOPMENT OF
ADVISORY INSTITUTIONS, 1884–1910

FROM THE BEGINNING of direct British responsibility, the High Commissioner, Sir Hercules Robinson, made it clear that the system of local rule adopted by the Cape Colony government was to be abandoned in favour of recognising the chiefs as agencies of the administration. Proclamations were issued in March and May of 1884 repealing the Cape Colony regulations and promulgating new ones. A Resident Commissioner was put in charge of the Territory and Assistant Commissioners were appointed. The new regulations dealt, as had the earlier ones, with courts, marriages, taxes, passes, pounds, trading and the sale of spirits. Although many clauses were modelled on the earlier ones, several important changes were made. For example, one of the earlier regulations which had caused particular resentment gave the Governor authority to allocate tribal land. This was not repeated in the 1884 regulations.

The Establishment of Indirect Rule

There has been some disagreement on the type of administration which the British government introduced into Basutoland when it assumed responsibility in 1884. Lord Hailey has said that the British authorities decided to abandon the policy of direct or magisterial rule introduced by the Cape Colony government and chose to maintain the authority of the chiefs. G. I. Jones has described the policy as 'a form of indirect rule in which the British government ruled the nation through its Paramount Chief in a parallel system'.[1] Sir Alan Pim, on the other hand, was of the opinion that 'there was then [1884] and there is now [1935] no rule either direct or indirect by the British government'.[2] This confusion in nomenclature is not unrelated to the dilemma of Basutoland, as will later be shown. In any event, it is worth considering the actual characteristics of the administration as it was laid down in 1884 and the philosophy behind it.

The first instructions to Colonel (Sir) Marshall Clarke, as Resident Commissioner, were exceedingly brief. The British government was of the opinion 'that nothing more could be attempted at first than the protection of life and property, and the maintenance of order on the border . . . [while] the Basuto were to be encouraged to establish internal self-government sufficient to suppress crime and settle inter-tribal disputes'.[3] Little, if any, attention was to be paid to developing the economic and political potentiality of the country. The British government, which was concerned with keeping the costs of empire to a minimum, decided to limit the energies of the local officials to maintaining law and order. Even this charge, however, could sometimes be a formidable and time-consuming task and was sometimes regarded as beyond the competence of the British authorities. On the whole, administrative responsibility was therefore left to the chiefs, a procedure supported by British philanthropists, who were against any sudden dislocation of African cultures. The principle that expenditure should not exceed revenue, which was also laid down in these instructions to the first Resident Commissioner, was to become the touchstone of administrative competence in all the High Commission Territories. 'This neat coincidence of interest between private altruism and government parsimony set a pattern of administration which was to last, in varying degree and despite attempts at improvement, into the fourth and fifth decades of the next century.'[4]

The position of the Resident Commissioner, in these circumstances, was neither easy nor enviable. Law-making power was reserved to the High Commissioner, while the bulk of administration fell to the Paramount Chief. The Resident Commissioner thus filled an anomalous, in-between position, something of an adviser to both. According to the Colonial Office, his primary function was to come to the assistance of the Paramount Chief should the latter find himself in difficulties. If he should venture to take any step on his own initiative, however constructive, he thereby invited accusations of interference. But since he was given control over revenue and made responsible for public works, it could be erroneously assumed that the Resident Commissioner had sufficient power to shape the destiny of the country.

The Consolidation of the Paramountcy

Three main problems concerned the administration during the early days of British rule: (1) the consolidation of the Paramount Chieftainship;

(2) the implications of British sovereignty for non-Basuto residents of the country; (3) the development of representative government. The necessity of consolidating the power of the Paramount Chief seemed self-evident in view of the unending inter-tribal disputes which plagued the country. Action against rebellious chiefs was made the charge of Lerotholi, who had succeeded his father as Paramount Chief in 1891. Lerotholi's victory in 1897 over Chief Masupha was a vindication of the Resident Commissioner's decision not to employ imperial forces in this situation. The Paramount Chief was thus maintained as the supreme head of the indigenous Basuto organisation and became the undisputed symbol of national unity. When Lerotholi died in 1907, to be followed by his son, Letsienyane (Letsie II), the supremacy of the Paramountcy was ensured. Although the consolidation of the Paramountcy, along lines envisaged by Moshoeshoe, was considered essential by the administration for the establishment of order, this development also served to promote national unity. Unlike kingship in Swaziland, however, the paramountcy was entirely of a political character, there being no mystical quality involved which would link the personality of the Paramount Chief in magico-religious rites with either soil or subjects. It was obvious, therefore, that the predominant position held by the Paramount Chief was to a considerable extent the creation of the British administration itself. At a later date, this predominance of the Paramount Chief would create its own problems.

British Sovereignty and Land Rights

During the period of annexation to Cape Colony, some discussion had taken place in Parliament on the question of possible alienation of certain areas of Basutoland. It was the opinion of the Attorney-General that the 1868 Proclamation which made the country British territory in effect made the entire area of Basutoland Crown land. Even then, however, the contrary view was advanced that a cession of sovereign rights did not necessarily involve a surrender of ownership. Although the British government never addressed itself to the question in any definitive manner, in practice it acted as if all land in Basutoland was the property of the Basuto nation. The Paramount Chief was recognised as the hereditary trustee on behalf of the nation.

Linked to this somewhat theoretical problem on the nature of sovereignty, was the more practical one of colonisation. On this point, however, there was never any real dispute. During the negotiations for annexation, it was Moshoeshoe's express wish that Basutoland should be an African territory exclusively reserved for the Basuto—a wish consistently honoured as the cornerstone of government policy. Consequently, Moshoeshoe's Law of Trade (1859) has had a permanent effect in determining the future of settlement in Basutoland by non-Basutos. While welcoming the advent of traders, subject to their obtaining permission of a chief to open shop, the law went on to emphasise that a trader would in no case be given a title to the land he was permitted to occupy. It was under this condition imposed by Moshoeshoe that European and Indian traders began to make their mark in the country during the second half of the nineteenth century. Replies by the High Commissioner in 1906 and 1909 to petitions from the Basutoland Chamber of Commerce requesting land titles were unequivocally in the negative. The High Commissioner stressed that 'he could not but regard any leasing of land to Europeans as an infringement of the cardinal principle of the inalienability from the Basuto of the land of Basutoland'.[5]

The Pitso System

The instructions to the first Resident Commissioner, commanding him to preserve and encourage institutions of self-government, although narrowly conceived in scope, proved most significant for the political evolution of the country. The task was made easier by the Basuto tradition of representative government, as embodied in the tribal council or *pitso*. Moshoeshoe himself had made frequent reference to his sons and other chiefs although he had no formally constituted body of councillors. The Basuto Paramount Chief was bound by the will of the people over whom he ruled and it is in this connection that the Basuto maxim is frequently quoted: '*Morena ke morena ka Batho*' (A chief is a chief by the people).

Until 1864, national *pitsos* were held irregularly as the need arose to discuss particular problems. In 1874, however, at the instigation of the Governor's Agent from Cape Colony, the idea was accepted that national *pitsos* should be held annually. This assembly 'enabled the government to acquaint the people of the laws and regulations in vogue, to correct wrong impressions and to mould public thought; it made the people feel they were governed not as slaves but as men; it was a safety-valve of the best description allowing men to unburden their minds and seek for information and guidance; by such a rough form of parliament could their voices be heard'.[6] An attempt on the part of the Cape Colony government in 1883 to further institutionalise Basuto government was rejected because of opposition to Cape colonial rule.

Between 1879 and 1886 there was an interruption in the annual series of national *pitsos*. Although they were held several times after 1888, they tended to become mere ceremonial occasions for making important announcements and receiving distinguished visitors. Moreover, as the range of matters with which the Paramount Chief had to deal progressively widened, the counsel given him by his immediate advisers became more important than the support of a general *pitso*. It thus seemed that the idea of the national *pitso* was fast passing away.

The Establishment of the National Council, 1903

In these circumstances, the need to organise an effective body representative of public opinion impressed itself upon the Resident Commissioner, Sir Marshall Clarke. In 1886, he therefore took the first steps which eventually led to the establishment in 1903 of the National Council. In a letter to the Paramount Chief, Letsie I, Clarke wrote:

> I send a proposal for the making and the work of a council; this is my own suggestion and is not from the Government. As I wish you to look well into it and tell me openly your opinion after consulting your brothers, sons and councillors, you can tell me what you think, but the matter is of importance and should be carefully considered. I propose keeping 8 nominations for Government so as to be able to give representation in case people are left out or forgotten.
>
> I think while the council is assembled the members should be fed and lodged at Government expense. The Resident Commissioner and the Paramount Chief would be members of the Council.
>
> The Council would meet at least once a year at Maseru at such time as would be fixed by the Resident Commissioner.
>
> The Council would consider any fresh laws which are submitted to it, so far as such laws purely affected the Basuto; it would consider all questions connected with local affairs; it would also receive an account of the manner in which hut tax was spent.
>
> Where serious national cases are referred by the Paramount Chief to the Resident Commissioner they can where advisable be heard by the latter with the Council. The Council cannot make laws, this can

alone be done by the Queen's Government, but it is to give advice and make suggestions as to what it thinks best for the nation.[7]

Letsie pondered the idea for a few years, while the Resident Commissioner was content to let the thought take root. At last, on December 25, 1889, the Paramount Chief wrote the Resident Commissioner as follows:

By this letter I say now it is my duty to reply to your letter, which is a proclamation; I told you I was unable to answer your letter, my being alone, that I will have to meet with my sons and my brothers and the men belonging to the country, those whose names you will find in this letter.

Now Chief I say, Oh, I am speaking to you respectfully, so that the words I am bringing to your notice, you will patiently listen to them.

The matter which I speak about is that I say it is some time that I have been considering about a Council for the Basuto Nation and I have not yet found a nicer way in which it will be conducted, and also a nicer way in which it can be preserved.

Today I say that I consent to this Council being in this country; and that the members of this Council be elected by myself and the nation; this is my request.

Now Chief, I say that in this matter of the Council, I find that this will be a work that will show well; that the hut tax of Basutoland will be of use to the country, because this Council will be for the whole nation; it will be for the representation of the whole of Basutoland.

Chief, I shall be glad and will thank you very much if I be granted these two requests: That I be told the amount of taxes collected each year, and what amount remains at the end of each year. The members of the Council to be elected by me together with the nation.

As for you, Chief, you have a right in this Council, because we will found it on you; so that you may advise us in all things; and you too, can choose whom you wish to be in council. But they are to be people with whom we will understand, and those with whom we will be able to work with for the good of this country.

Again that I be allowed, that if any member of the Council should be found fault with or cause the nation a grievance, that his service be dispensed with and another be appointed in his stead.

Oh Chief, I shall be waiting with great hopes with regard to my requests; and I will thank you very much should my requests be granted.[8]

The Resident Commissioner welcomed Letsie's letter and put his proposals to the High Commissioner, Sir Henry Loch, who received them sympathetically. In April 1890, the High Commissioner approved a set of regulations, subsequently sanctioned by the Secretary of State, for the conduct of a National Council along the lines suggested. Still, there was opposition to be overcome from some of the chiefs, who feared the loss of their powers. The following year, Lerotholi wrote on behalf of his aged father, again requesting that the Council be established. Later that year Letsie himself wrote sending in the names of the members he had nominated to the Council. Letsie, whose strength was rapidly failing, was anxious that the Council should be formed as soon as possible, so that a permanent body capable of dealing with dangerous tribal disputes would be on hand when he died. Until his death in late 1893 he continued to press the Resident Commissioner to summon the Council; but his death, together with the strong opposition of several influential chiefs, delayed the formation of the Council for a decade.

Towards the end of the century, Sir Godfrey Lagden, Resident Commissioner since 1894, and the High Commissioner, Sir Alfred (later Lord) Milner, strongly urged the advisability of considering the proposals for the Council anew. Milner believed the national *pitso* too unwieldy an assembly for serious discussions. Thereafter, the chiefs present at a national *pitso* in May 1899 agreed to the formation of a council of fifty members. But it was not until 1903 that Lerotholi, in failing health and anxious to strengthen the position of his successor, agreed to a meeting of a National Council. The High Commissioner gave his formal approval in May 1903 and thus consummated an object patiently awaited—namely, unanimous agreement by the chiefs upon the subject of a National Council to deal with tribal affairs in consultation with the government.

The Council met for the first time in July 1903. The meeting was held more or less on an experimental basis since its existence was not formally established by proclamation. The regulations approved by the High Commissioner stipulated that the Council was to consist of not more than a hundred members, five being nominated by the Resident Commissioner and the rest by the Paramount Chief. The term of office of members was to be one year, and the Resident Commissioner was recognised as President of the Council. A primary concern of the Council was to maintain itself as the sole custodian of the Basuto national tradition, hoping thereby to gain recognition as the only source of legislation in all matters falling within the field of native affairs. In accord with this plan, the Council adopted a code of rules (subsequently known as the Laws of Lerotholi), based on what was held to be the custom of the Basuto, designed to entrench the position of the chiefs. General procedure in a number of matters was laid down; the recognition of the hereditary character of the chieftainship, an affirmation of the authority to be accorded to the chiefs, a declaration of their right to summon the people for personal service and to make use of certain tribal lands for the support of their household and retainers. At the same time, however, the Laws of Lerotholi recognised the right of the people to hold lands for cultivation, subject to allotment by the chiefs. They also laid down that there should be no punishment or confiscation of property without fair trial. The second session of the Council was held in 1905 and the third in 1908, at which the Resident Commissioner agreed that the Council should meet annually, a practice thereafter observed.

The Establishment of the Basutoland Council, 1910

Fearing the dangerous consequences of the approaching unification of South Africa, a deputation was sent to England by the Paramount Chief in 1908, asking that Basutoland should not be included in any future union. At the same time, the fourth session of the National Council, meeting in 1909, stressed the importance of securing formal confirmation of the Council's position. It was felt that in the event of the colony's transfer to the Union, a Council confirmed in law would serve to protect Basuto interests. The High Commissioner, Lord Selborne, sympathised with these views and gave them his support. The outcome was authorisation by the Secretary of State for the drafting of a proclamation to put the National Council 'on a more regular footing and to regularise existing practice'.[9]

Proclamation 7 of March 3, 1910, provided for the establishment of a Council, to be called the Basutoland Council, 'for discussing the domestic affairs of the territory'. It was to consist of a President (Resident Commissioner) and not more than a hundred members. The Paramount Chief was to be a member under the title of Chief Councillor, and was to have the right to nominate ninety-four persons 'belonging to the Basuto tribe' who were to include 'the principal persons exercising authority as chiefs of the Basuto tribe'. The Paramount Chief's nominees were to be appointed by the Resident Commissioner, if confirmed by him. In addition, the Resident Commissioner was empowered to appoint not more than five persons to be members of the Council.[10] After some exchange of opinion between the Resident Commissioner, the Basutoland Chamber of Commerce, the High Commissioner and the Secretary of State, it was decided that, in the selection of his nominees, the Resident Commissioner would not be prevented from appointing non-Basuto, but in fact no Resident Commissioner ever took advantage of this power.

The powers of the Council, as established under the 1910 Proclamation, were those of advice and criticism. The President was empowered to lay before the Council the draft of any proposed law affecting Basutoland and to invite opinion. Members of Council were also free to discuss the provisions of any proclamation affecting Basutoland and to suggest amendments. A duty was placed on the Resident Commissioner to submit to the Council annually an account both of the revenue collected in the Territory and of its expenditure. The Resident Commissioner was also authorised, in consultation and co-operation with the Paramount Chief, to bring any questions or disputes 'of a purely tribal character' before the Council. And finally, wide powers were given to the Resident Commissioner to determine what matters fell within the competence of the Council. The Council was strictly prohibited from discussing any resolutions upon any matter which, in the opinion of the Resident Commissioner, was not one relating to the domestic affairs of the Territory—a restriction which prevented the Council from dealing with the country's most fundamental problems, all of which originated outside Basutoland.

From the first, however, Moshoeshoe's family (the 'Sons of Moshoeshoe') or their representatives constituted the majority of the Council members, and to that extent it did not take the place of the national *pitso*, where everyone had the right to attend and to express his views. To the government, the value of the Council lay in its providing an influential body with which the administration could discuss measures affecting the general interest. The Council, on the other hand, took a somewhat different view of its own position. Representing mainly the interests of the chiefs, it saw itself as the natural custodian of the traditions from which the chiefs derived their authority over the people. Its concern, therefore, was to keep this field intact against innovations from the administration, subject to one important exception. It was generally prepared to co-operate with the administration in measures likely to promote the general welfare.

This basic difference of opinion on the function of the Basutoland Council did not come to the surface during the first years of its existence, primarily because of the cordial relations the Council enjoyed with the Resident Commissioner, Sir Herbert Sloley. Sloley seemed convinced of the Council's genuine desire to abolish defects in the system of native administration and to control the arbitrary and rapacious decisions of the chiefs' courts.[11] In reality, however, the consolidation of the authority of the Paramount Chief inevitably strengthened the resistance of traditional elements to any suggestion of reform. The Council was an advance, no doubt, but it in no way took the place of the earlier *pitso*, where all were more or less free to ventilate opinions and voice grievances.[12]

3

THE FAILURE OF INDIRECT RULE AND
ADMINISTRATIVE REFORM, 1910–1959

THE GENERAL CONDITION of the Territory appeared promising after the introduction of a more defined system of government in 1910. The population, which had been estimated at 218,900 in 1891, increased to 349,500 in 1904, and between 1911 and 1921 a twenty-three per cent increase not only attested to the favourable effects of peace, but also reflected a great expansion of medical services. Although the Territory ceased to receive the usual contribution of £18,000 from the Cape government, this was replaced by a fixed percentage in 1910 of 0·88575 per cent of the total customs receipts of the Union government, an arrangement which provided a considerably larger sum. The price of wool continued to rise, and, by 1925, the annual average revenue reached £242,053, a substantial increase over the 1904 figure of £96,806. The budget continued to be favourably balanced, with income in excess of expenditure. The ever-increasing number of passes for labour in South Africa, reported as 86,155 in 1904, was also viewed as a favourable development and British authorities co-operated closely with mine recruiters. The opening, in 1906, of both a branch railway line to Maseru and an industrial school; a general expansion of education under a Director of Education; extended mission activity (especially Roman Catholic—fostered by the conversion in 1913 of the heir-presumptive, Letsie II, to that faith); all seemed to confirm that Basutoland was moving into the twentieth century. The two problems of overstocking and erosion had not become so acute as to attract close attention, and there had been no serious drought since 1903 to challenge the resourcefulness of the administration. If there was any apparent drawback in this generally satisfactory picture of progress, it lay in the growing evidence that increasing pressure on the land was leading to soil deterioration and that economic and social services were not keeping up with needs.

Dislocation of Traditional Life

The initial advantages of British administration, adapted as it was to the existing social and economic organisation of Basuto society, were lost, however, with the emergence of a new range of social, political and economic problems. Although the normal routine of Basuto life seemed to survive intact, forces at work were subtly altering its content within the traditional framework. The great increase in population became a serious factor in this undifferentiated agricultural society. The availability of land decreased and soil erosion reached staggering proportions. Traditional Basuto society was unequal to the new burden of monetary taxation and was forced to sacrifice the cream of its manpower to meet the need. The presence of a European civil service and a few thousand other Europeans inevitably introduced new ideas and new needs, to draw off the country's very limited savings and further attract its youth. In addition to these more obvious forces transforming the substance of Basuto life, certain related factors associated with chieftainship and land tenure were operating to retard the development which otherwise might have been expected.

As Basutoland's problems increased in complexity, indirect rule proved incapable of dealing with the situation. Having decided to permit the country 'to develop along its own lines', no effort was made to discover what direction those lines should take. The British government felt that it had played its part and made policy to the extent requested when it decided to support and maintain the authority of the chiefs. Such an interpretation of indirect rule hardly corresponded to its definition as understood in other parts of Africa, where it implied 'not only the acceptance and the preservation of the recognised tribal institutions but making the native authorities a living part of the machinery of the government, and directing the political energies and ability of the people to the development of their own institutions'.[1]

In Basutoland, indirect rule placed the actual burden of policy-making on the shoulders of the chiefs within their very limited sphere of operations. The success of such a system demanded that certain conditions be met. The first of these was that chiefs should be men sufficiently educated to formulate a policy based on an appreciation of the new forces affecting the lives of their people. The second condition was that they be men of sufficient vision to realise that the old chieftainship was a doomed institution, a form of government destined to pass with the development of the people.[2] On both scores, the chiefs were tragically unequal to the task. Moreover, the chiefs, like their people, were increasingly affected by the change from a subsistence to a money economy; inevitably they were involved in the effort to improve their own incomes and found it difficult to discharge their traditional responsibilities.

The existence of the Basutoland Council also operated to dislocate traditional relationships between chiefs and people. Gradually, it ceased to be the custom for chiefs to submit important matters to the opinion of the tribe in local *pitsos*. No longer could it be said of the chiefs that 'their authority was built on the foundation of popular support and maintained by a two way stream of consultation and advice'.[3] In part, this estrangement of chiefs and people could be attributed to the tendency of the British government to encourage the chiefs to look 'upwards towards government for authority and support rather than, as before, to the people'.[4]

The prestige of the chiefs was further impaired by the widespread practice of placing their relatives in positions of authority; this increased the number of chiefs in the Territory and the number of courts which, it was often alleged, were being exploited for financial gain. Moreover, appeals from these courts were difficult and few records were kept of their proceedings. This particular grievance was debated in the Basutoland Council at intervals between 1918 and 1927, largely because of pressure from the Progressive Association, an organisation established by commoners in 1907. The majority on the Council, however, successfully resisted these attacks, arguing that the Laws of Lerotholi were quite sufficient for this purpose. But even this code was ignored when it suited the chiefs' interests.

The defects in the Basuto courts were, however, only a symptom of the general malaise afflicting the country and even the Progressive Association had no real comprehension of all the factors involved. Their elementary education fitted them to be moderately good civil servants but they knew little of societies and development.[5] Significantly, however, the Progressive Association did demand that a proportion of the members of the Council should be elected, a demand which the chiefs successfully parried. The chiefs were also successful in 1929 in obtaining the withdrawal of a draft proclamation, defining relations between the administration and the chiefs on the one hand, and the chiefs and their people on the other. Any measure considered as likely to affect their hereditary rights and prerogatives or any legislation under the Proclamation of 1884 suggesting a legal right to control any of their internal affairs was strenuously opposed.[6]

Crisis and Investigation: The Pim Report

Despite growing complaints and the obvious seriousness of soil erosion, nothing occurred to convince the administration of the need for radical reform until the great drought of 1932-3, coupled with the disastrous effects of expanding worldwide depression, revealed the true magnitude of Basutoland's problems. As early as 1929, the first effects of the general decline in world prices were felt in the country. With the depression in prices, the export value of mohair and wool fell from the 1928 peak of £750,234 to a mere £115,671 in 1932. In the old days, the Basuto stored grain against a bad season, but the growing need for cash forced the Basuto to sell their crops, usually at a very low price, only to buy them back later at a greatly increased price. But in 1932 the traders' stores were virtually empty, and many families were on the verge of starvation. Even grass was eagerly sought as food and whole districts were without any supply of milk. Livestock died by the thousands and the old-type Basuto pony almost disappeared. Government distribution of maize served only to relieve the most extreme suffering. At last, when the rains did come in late 1933, they were torrential, and rapidly increased the process of erosion. Throughout this difficult period, with a few notable exceptions including the Paramount Chief, 'the chiefs behaved badly, doing little or nothing for their starving people'.[7]

In response to this desperate situation, the Secretary of State for Dominion Affairs sent out a commission in September 1934 to report on the financial and economic position of Basutoland and the other Territories. Under the direction of Sir Alan Pim, the commission toured practically the whole country. The commission's report, published in 1935 and generally known as the Pim Report, dealt with most aspects of the situation and made many recommendations. Additional criticism of British administration in the High Commission Territories was stirred by M. L. Hodgson and W. G. Ballinger.

The Pim Report noted that tribal institutions were a means and not an end, and that they were incapable of meeting modern needs without guidance. In this respect, Basutoland was said to have little in common with Britain's usual policy of indirect rule elsewhere in Africa. In Basutoland, it was 'a policy of non-interference, of proffering alliance, of leaving two parallel governments to work in a state of detachment unknown in tropical Africa'.[8] Hodgson and Ballinger argued that by imposing taxation and defining the limits of native and European settlement in the Territories, Britain was doing more than was usually involved in the traditional role of a protecting power, and thus 'the whole basis of her relationship to the protected states [had] altered'.[9] Whatever the exact causes of the Territory's problems, it was estimated that roughly £151,000 spread over ten years was required to deal only with the more urgent problems of soil conservation. These grants were forthcoming under the colonial development and welfare funds and the government was also prompted to undertake serious discussions on the prevailing system of administration.

The Reform of Native Administration

Largely as a result of the Pim Report, the British government accepted the need for immediate administrative reform. After prolonged negotiation, the Resident Commissioner persuaded the Paramount Chief to recognise that reform was both essential and inevitable, and that it was in the interests of the chieftaincy itself. Chief Griffith, who had held the paramountcy for thirty years, thereafter associated himself with reform. The government's proposals were modified to meet his views and to avoid the rigidity of the Bechuanaland proclamations which were stirring considerable legal strife.[10] Eventually, the reform measures were promulgated as the Native Administration Proclamation No 61 and the Native Courts Proclamation No 62, both of 1938. To some extent these proclamations followed the classic ordinances of Nigeria and Tanganyika in attempting to fit indigenous institutions into a new pattern of colonial administration. There was no exact duplication, however, inasmuch as account had to be taken of the fact that British rule in East and West Africa had acquired distinctive characteristics over the previous half century.

Very definite reforms of the native administration were effected in terms of Proclamation 61. Instead of providing for the recognition of a Paramount Chief who might in turn be vested with defined powers by the administration, these powers were specifically vested in 'the person who is recognised by the High Commissioner as holding the office or rank of Paramount Chief'. With firm control over the paramountcy assured, the High Commissioner was recognised as having the right, in consultation with the Paramount Chief, to list the chiefs, sub-chiefs and headmen entitled to recognition as sharers in the native authority. This step was regarded as essential if 'placing' and its attendant evils were to be halted and eradicated. By 1939, an estimated 1,340 chiefs and headmen were so recognised by the administration. Just as the High Commissioner was empowered to recognise any chief, sub-chief or headman, all such offices could be revoked at his discretion.

On their part, the Paramount Chief and subordinate native authorities accepted a statutory obligation to maintain good order and good government. They also received restricted powers of arrest. The Paramount Chief was given power to make 'orders' concerning such matters as noxious weeds, soil erosion and grazing, subject to reservation by the Resident Commissioner. In addition, he was empowered, with the approval of the High Commissioner, to make 'rules' for the peace, order and welfare of the Basuto.

In terms of the Native Courts Proclamation, the right to hold court was restricted to persons given a warrant by the Resident Commissioner. By 1946, native courts had been reduced from over 1,300 in 1938 to 122. The fact that the earlier figure was substantially revised, on the grounds that the responsible officials had originally based their calculations on recommendations made to them by the ward chiefs, illustrates the extent to which indigenous leaders and officials were imprisoned in the persistent dual system of administration. The carrying out of both Proclamations was received favourably, compared with the opposition of the Bechuana in similar circumstances four years earlier, not only because of the support which they received from the Paramount Chief, but because of widespread discontent with the chiefs and their arbitrary use of 'placing' power.

These reforms of the native authority were followed over the next few years by a number of institutional innovations: (1) the alteration of the authority and composition of the Basutoland Council; (2) the establishment of District Councils; (3) the appointment of a body of Advisers to the Paramount Chief; and (4) the formation of an independent finance committee for regulating the conduct of the national treasury.

Reform of the Basutoland Council

Changes in the composition of the Basutoland Council were facilitated by the divisions rending Basuto society from 1941 to 1943 over the question of succession to the paramountcy. Chief Griffith had died in

1939 and was succeeded by the young, progressive-minded Chief Seeiso, who commenced a programme of reform by making a series of much needed alterations in Matsieng, the traditional headquarters of the Paramount Chief. Unfortunately, Seeiso died in 1940 and left the succession to his son, an infant, and his senior widow, Chieftainess Mantsebo, was appointed Regent. Mantsebo was unsuccessfully challenged in the courts by Seeiso's half-brother, Bereng, the eldest son of Chief Griffith. Believing that the 'Sons of Moshoeshoe' had cheated him a second time of the paramountcy, the embittered and desperate Bereng, despite his Roman Catholic background, sought to advance his own political interests through the use of protective medicines. These medicines, which required portions of human flesh, resulted in 'medicine' or *diretlo* murder and in 1949 Bereng was executed for complicity in murder.

Unfortunately, however, Bereng's involvement in medicine murder was not unique. Other rivalries, originating from the evils of 'placing' and the multiplication of chiefs, together with administrative changes from the top downwards, had only increased the sense of insecurity and uncertainty of the Basuto without a compensating growth of mass involvement in administration. While losing much of their old culture, they were essentially denied access to another. Thus, relief was sought in ancient Basuto practices.

Although medicine murders had been known among the Basuto since at least 1895, between that date and 1940 no more than twenty-five cases had been reported. After 1940, however, the number rose steadily from three in 1941 to a high of twenty in 1948. As Jones's probing study of the problem revealed, the secondary causes of these murders were almost entirely political, and the piecemeal reforms introduced during the decade and a half after 1939, instead of remedying this situation, intensified it. Thus, while reducing the autocratic power of the paramountcy, greater powers were gained by the principal chiefs, as exercised through the Basutoland Council and the Regent's Advisory Council. At the same time, however, the Paramount Chief was said to have increased his power to control appointments within the wards of the principal chiefs. This was further complicated by the enhanced status of the principal chiefs at the expense of the lesser chiefs and headmen.[11] These criticisms, presented in 1951 with the advantage of hindsight, threw considerable light on the complexity of political reform.

As the Jones report in part revealed, two important elements in the

Basutoland Council combined to strengthen their respective positions, partly at the expense of the Paramount Chief and partly at the expense of the administration. The 'Sons of Moshoeshoe', who were attempting to maintain the position of the chiefs, together with the supporters of the Progressive Association, who were seeking a larger measure of representation in the Council, jointly requested in 1943 a declaration that it would be government policy to consult both the Paramount Chief and the Council before enacting any proclamation affecting the administration of the country. This procedure, they said, should exist until 'the time comes for Basutoland to have its own Legislative Council'. In the same resolution a declaration was requested from the Regent that she would consult the Council before making use of any powers conferred under the Proclamation of 1938.[12] In order to provide a means for consulting the Council when that body was not in session, the appointment of an elected Standing Committee and a Management Committee was recommended.

None of these recommendations, however, was embodied in legislation until 1948. By that time, as a result of additional recommendations from the Basutoland Council, the number of Council members to be elected by District Councils was increased to two per District. This provision was again amended in 1950 and the elected number was increased to four, making thirty-six in all. Provision was made for an additional six members to be elected by the various recognised associations, such as agricultural, teachers, business and servicemen's organisations, as well as the Progressive Association. However cautiously, the Basutoland Council thus became more representative in character as new elements were introduced.

Although these developments would ordinarily indicate an intention on the part of the administering power to confer legislative authority, the British government, despite growing demand, appeared to preclude such a step. As late as 1948, London still seemed to envisage the ultimate union of the country with South Africa. The Union government had carefully watched lest the British government embark upon some perilous advancement in the Territories likely to throw her own policies into harsher light, and the British hesitated to promise political advancement beyond such status as might be compatible with incorporation. Uncertainty about the future of the country naturally had a retarding effect on all schemes, political or economic, and the country continued to stagnate.[13]

Despite Britain's reluctance to extend the promise of self-government to its logical conclusion, the Council did acquire competence over a larger range of matters. As early as 1913, its original purpose, described as 'the discussion of the domestic affairs of Basutoland', had been widened to include the right to discuss any matter arising outside the Territory if it affected the affairs of the Basuto. The power of the Council was further enhanced when, in response to Resolution 7 of 1943, the High Commissioner, Lord Harlech, formally declared in 1944 that it was government policy to consult the Council before issuing proclamations affecting the domestic affairs and welfare of the people, or the progress and development of the Basuto native administration.[14] At the same time the Paramount Chief confirmed: 'It is the policy of the paramountcy to consult the Basutoland Council before issuing orders or making rules closely affecting the life or welfare of the Basuto people and the administration of the Basuto.' Finally, in 1950, the Paramount Chief agreed that no local rate or levy would be deemed valid unless first approved by the Council.

The Establishment of District Councils

The second important innovation was the introduction of a system of District Councils with advisory powers, presided over by the District Commissioners. At its thirty-eighth session in 1943, the Basutoland Council suggested the establishment of District Councils 'in order to provide machinery to enable the people to make their wishes known to councillors'. All principal chiefs and members of the Basutoland Council were to be ex-officio members of their respective District Councils. Other members were to be elected directly by the people. Two main functions were envisaged for the District Councils. First, they were to prepare 'motions' for consideration by the Basutoland Council, and second, in order to make the Basutoland Council itself more representative, the Paramount Chief was formally to nominate one member from each District to the Basutoland Council.

The District Councils began to function in 1945, but became statutory bodies only in 1948 as part of the reorganisation of the Basutoland Council. The average number of members on most District Councils was about thirty, or roughly one member for every thousand tax-payers, together with the principal or ward chiefs residing in the District, and association representatives. Although the Councils started well and seemed to arouse genuine interest among the people, the fact that they were merely advisory induced general apathy towards them.

Only in 1950 did the administration become bold enough to experiment with the principle of secret voting and one of the nine advisory
District Councils was then elected by secret ballot. To its surprise, the
administration found that the people's choice ran contrary to the wishes
of their chiefs. Gradually, and with an extreme caution, this
'dangerous' principle of secret voting was extended to the other
District Councils.[15]

The Appointment of Advisers to the Paramount Chief

The Basutoland Council took advantage of the Regent's embarrassment in 1948, over the scandal involving several chiefs of consequence
in medicine murders, to urge that she accept the appointment of
three Advisers, to be attached to her headquarters at Matsieng. Eventually, she consented and agreed to select three Advisers from a Council-
nominated panel of eighteen drawn from its own membership.
Although this brought some good results, the change was not completely satisfactory. However, it did reveal a growing desire among the
Basuto that their Paramount Chief should function as a constitutional
ruler.

The Establishment of the National Treasury

A major proposal in the government's plans for reform was advanced
in 1942 by the Resident Commissioner, Charles Arden-Clarke,* who
informed the Basutoland Council that the 1938 reforms were incomplete inasmuch as no provision had been made for the exercise of
financial responsibility. The Resident Commissioner regarded the
creation of a National Treasury as vital if the whole system of reform
was to work successfully. As he put it to the Basutoland Council, 'the
best form of education in the art and practice of government is the
exercise of financial responsibility'.[16] Opposition to the proposal was
very strong. Not only did it threaten the income derived by chiefs
from the 'placing' system, but it also involved an increase in taxation
to meet the cost of giving the chiefs a scheduled scale of remuneration.
Owing largely to Arden-Clarke's persistence, the National Treasury
was finally established by Proclamation 11 of 1946. Significantly, the
Proclamation vested the High Commissioner and not the Paramount
Chief with the power to make regulations for its constitution and
management.

* Later Sir Charles Arden-Clarke, the notable Governor of the Gold Coast.

Generally speaking, the reforms initiated over the period 1938–55 succeeded in bringing about a closer integration of the Basuto tribal organisation and the machinery of the administration. Nevertheless, critics could point out that the enactments of 1938 gave little consideration to the possibility of meeting the needs of Basutoland by any method other than the adoption of legislation based on the procedure of indirect rule as practised elsewhere. The distinctive features in the Basutoland organisation, such as the position attained by the Basutoland Council, were not taken into consideration. Moreover, the Paramount's agreement to the reforms appeared to have been secured by concessions calculated to delay for a considerable time any measure likely to give practical effect to their provisions. As late as 1941, for example, discussions in the Council revealed that most members had little idea of the policy change implied in the Proclamations. Subsequent experience also revealed that the forces in Basuto society seeking genuine reform were much stronger than the administration had realised at the time. Administrative reforms which were not linked to the prospect of eventual independence were unable to capture the imagination or the enthusiasm of the progressive-minded. In a general way, the medicine murders of the 1940s pointed up the shortcomings of British policy. Concretely, discontent was expressed in growing opposition to the administration's later efforts to reform local government, set out in the Moore Report of 1954, and eventually convinced the British government of the need to accede to the protracted demand for a real Legislative Council.

Constitutional Discussions, 1955–59

An important step was taken in the direction of acquiring legislative power when, at the fifty-first session of the Basutoland Council (September 1955), a motion was passed requesting 'that the Basutoland Council be given power to make laws in all internal matters, such laws to be confirmed by the Paramount Chief'. In May of the following year, the Secretary of State for Commonwealth Relations indicated his readiness to consider proposals whereby the Basutoland Council should be given such powers, and requested detailed recommendations.

After some consideration by the District Councils, the Basutoland Council established a committee in October 1956 charged with the Cuty of framing a detailed reply. At the same time, however, the douncil declined to accept the Secretary of State's suggestion that its

laws should not affect non-Basuto living in the country. This limitation
would mean separate laws—and presumably privileges—for the
Protectorate's white trading community. Another committee, known
as the Chieftainship Committee, was established in May 1956 to explore
the whole question of chieftainship. When it became apparent that the
tasks of the two committees were intimately related, it was agreed that
they should work together to produce one comprehensive report. The
services of D. V. Cowen, Professor of Comparative Law in the University of Cape Town, were enlisted as constitutional adviser. By June
1958, a draft constitution was ready for submission to the Council.

The report, unanimously approved by the Basutoland Council in
July 1958, was essentially concerned with four questions: (1) advance
in constitutional status; (2) the problem of dualism; (3) local government; and (4) the dilemma of the chieftainship. The report stressed
that it was only 'right and proper that the desire of the Basuto for a
greater share in their own government be satisfied'. Specific proposals
for a Legislative Council and an Executive Council were accordingly
presented. The remedy for the problem of dualism was seen in a
divesting, both of the British authorities and the chieftainship, of certain powers and transferring them to the executive and legislative
bodies, where both interests would be properly represented. Decentralisation of government functions to the District level, including the
establishment of District Treasuries, was advocated as the best means
for releasing the dynamic force of public opinion and local energy.
Finally, the report sought to take account of the fact that while chieftainship would continue as a vital factor in the government of
Basutoland for the foreseeable future, it had to be adapted to fit more
comfortably into the emerging patterns of modern Basuto society.[17]

The Secretary of State for Commonwealth Relations, Lord Home,
thereupon invited the Basutoland Council to appoint a delegation for
discussions in London, commencing on November 18, 1958. After a
month of negotiations, during which Lord Home seized upon Basuto
insistence that the elected membership of the Legislative Council be
confined to Basuto as a pretext for limited jurisdiction, general agreement was reached.[17] In effect, the Basuto put forward a very modest
request, no doubt reflecting an acute awareness that the British government was reluctant to risk South African opposition. Talks on particular points were continued in Maseru the following year and certain
modifications, especially with respect to local government and electoral
methods, were adopted. At last, in September 1959, Orders-in-Council

were promulgated to make the new constitution operational in 1960. The Order-in-Council of February 2, 1884, the fundamental constitutional instrument until 1959, was thus supplanted by the country's first proper written constitution.

A principal feature of the constitution was the establishment of a Legislative Council, to be known as the Basutoland National Council, consisting of eighty members. Of this number, forty were to be elected from the membership of the nine District Councils, which thus functioned as electoral colleges for their respective Districts. The remaining forty members included four ex-officio government officers, twenty-two principal or ward chiefs, and fourteen persons selected by the Paramount Chief. The Resident Commissioner was appointed President of the Council for the first year of its existence.

The Council was empowered to legislate on all matters other than those reserved to the High Commissioner—external affairs, defence, internal security, currency, public loans, customs and excise, copyright and related subjects, posts and telegraphs, telephones, broadcasting, television and the civil service. For legislation within the High Commissioner's competence, the Basutoland National Council was to act as a consultative body. Powers of delay over Bills passed by the Council were granted to the Paramount Chief. An Executive Council was provided, consisting of four senior officials (including the Resident Commissioner as Chairman) and four non-official members of the Legislative Council, one of whom would be nominated by the Paramount Chief with a special interest in chieftainship affairs and local government. The Executive Council was also constituted as an advisory body to the High Commissioner and the Paramount Chief.

The constitution stipulated that District Councils should be reformed as primary organs of local government. Members were to be elected by secret ballot except in so far as they contained a small minority of chiefs enjoying ex officio membership. Apart from their function as electoral colleges, District Councils were also given executive responsibilities, and for the first time were provided with their own Treasuries, thereby inheriting the functions and assets of the Basutoland National Treasury, which was abolished. Although all lands and all rights in respect thereof were legally vested in the Paramount Chief, the allocation of land continued to be governed by Basuto law and custom and was, in effect, delegated to subordinate chiefs and headmen. A College of Chiefs, consisting of all principal and ward chiefs, under the titular presidency of the Paramount Chief, was given the threefold duty of recognising chiefs, investigating complaints against chiefs and adjudicating disputes over succession and boundaries.

The 1959 constitution brought Basutoland to the first stage of the normal colonial self-governing constitution, a preliminary to universal franchise and ministerial responsibility. But Basutoland's position, as an island in South Africa, was recognised in three ways—first, by giving the High Commissioner rather vague but over-riding powers; second, by reserving High Commission matters to the Resident Commissioner; and third, by the statement, a sop to South Africa, that Basutoland 'cannot in the foreseeable future become a completely independent state'. Nevertheless, the form of the constitution was British, and diverged from what Verwoerd regarded as a suitable native authority to run a 'Bantu state'. Development was not ruled out and, indeed, scarcely had the constitution been implemented, than it was taken under review.

4

THE POLITICISING OF BASUTO NATIONAL LIFE

B ASUTOLAND's constitutional evolution has at all stages been affected by a complex of factors which, in the African situation, present a certain uniqueness. The essential elements which can be distinguished are: (1) the paramountcy; (2) the chieftainship; (3) the Roman Catholic Church; (4) the influence of African nationalist parties in South Africa; and (5) the modernists or new elite. All of these factors must be seen, moreover, against the general background of South African designs on the three Territories, together with Britain's ambivalent political and diplomatic response.

As the country's first mass nationalist party developed, it was obliged to take a stand on each of these factors, and, in so doing, provoked corresponding responses, some of which were directly political in nature. The resulting interaction and tension promoted a rapid politicising of Basuto national life which, in turn, facilitated and hastened the constitutional process. It remains to be determined, however, whether the multiplicity and diversity of political groupings in Basutoland is a symptom of national disintegration or a sign of vigorous pluralism.

The Paramountcy

Although Moshoeshoe successfully contained potential opposition and achieved minimal political integration, it was the British administration which finally effected the consolidation of the paramountcy. As all key positions in the country were in time held by the nominees of the Paramount Chief, he could govern more autocratically and with less danger of opposition than Moshoeshoe. In the absence of wars, which traditionally forced an African chief to rely on the wholehearted support of his people, it was no longer necessary to keep in touch with them. Eventually, the Paramount Chiefs and the ruling caste, known as the 'Sons of Moshoeshoe', found it less necessary to summon the national assembly of the *pitso*. The administration-sponsored National Council and the Basutoland Council, presided over by the Paramount Chief, were composed almost entirely of the 'Sons of Moshoeshoe', or men of the house of the Paramount Chief. Although the Council consistently opposed any extension of the powers and duties of the administration, increased pressure from South Africa underscored the necessity of constitutional advancement which would both prevent Britain from transferring the country to the Union and still preserve the entrenched position of the ruling class.

Prince Bereng Seeiso,* one of the best-educated among the Basuto of his generation, returned from Oxford in late 1959, against the wishes of the Regent, and assumed the paramountcy. Bereng's installation on February 7, 1960, raised hopes that his traditional office would be strengthened sufficiently to provide a stable centre from which political participation would be extended.[1] He thereafter sought to place himself in the vanguard of the nationalist movement by seizing the initiative in the independence movement. However, his stay at Oxford did not appear to alter his belief that it was in the nature of Basuto history for the Paramount Chief to rule rather than reign. All of this suggests that the presumed conflict between traditional and modern political elites is more complicated than simple juxtaposition of these two labels.

The Chieftainship

Unlike the monolithic tribal structure of the Swazi, which depends totally upon the Paramount Chief, the paramountcy in Basutoland is clearly a political institution. A single Basuto nation under the hegemony of Moshoeshoe's own clan, the Bakoena, to which all but three of the country's major chiefs belong, was maintained by placing 'Sons of Moshoeshoe' in direct control. Needless to say, a certain amount of resentment was felt by the subordinate chieftainship and many chiefs resisted the encroaching power of the Paramount Chief. The tension between him and the vast numbers of the sub-chieftaincy, who continued to recognise the need for a Paramount Chief, has characterised Basutoland to the present day. But if many chiefs opposed the ruling

---

* Moshoeshoe Bereng Seeiso was born in 1939, son of Paramount Chief Seeiso Griffith by his second wife, Mabereng. He was educated at Roma in Basutoland, at Ampleforth, and at Corpus Christi College, Oxford. Although he had hoped to finish his education and succeed to the chieftancy at the age of twenty-five, growing disputes with the Regent, Paramount Chieftainess Mantsebo Seeiso, led him to demand immediate installation.

house, they also feared, in varying degrees, the curbing of their own powers. Self-rule was recognised as both desirable and inevitable, but they had reasonable fears that rapid political advancement would mean a decrease of power without adequate compensation. With the formation of the first mass nationalist party, it was realised that traditional goals had to be achieved within the context of modern political competition.

The Roman Catholic Church

Just as the Paris Evangelical Mission Society featured prominently in the early history of the Basuto, the Roman Catholic Church assumed great importance after 1913. By 1942 the Catholics numbered about the same as the older French Protestant mission, something in the neighbourhood of 60,000. Expansion of schools, clinics, hospitals and the opening in 1945 of the only institution for higher learning, Pius XII College, testified to the growing power and stature of the Roman Catholic Church. But material growth was a mixed blessing. Because of financial and administrative inadequacies, the Catholics, like most Christian missionaries in Africa, developed, in some instances, a too-intimate partnership with the colonial government. Moreover, the absence of government activity along social and economic lines forced the missionaries to become involved in a multitude of mundane occupations, most of which took on the character of a highly competitive inter-denominational struggle for adherents. Such occupations, however beneficial for the Basuto, allowed little opportunity for detached reflection upon the quickening course of African nationalism. Missionary assessment of events was frequently dependent upon the appraisals of colonial officials who, more often than not, were incapable of sufficient objectivity. As a result, missionaries became virtual prisoners of their long and isolated rural experience. Like the chieftainship and the administration, they were viewed by many nationalists as a pillar of the status quo.

In so far as the Roman Catholic Church seemed to provoke particular resentment on the part of the nationalists, at least part of the misunderstanding can be attributed to the origin, composition and organisation of Catholic missionaries in Basutoland. They were all members of one religious congregation, the Oblates of Mary Immaculate (OMI), a group strongly entrenched in South Africa and drawn for the most part from the Province of Quebec. Consequently, they exhibited an excessively conservative and defensive attitude towards non-Catholics. Over paternalistic towards their flock, and perhaps influenced by South African propaganda—which generally identified all African nationalism as Communist-inspired—the Oblates endeavoured to duplicate the Quebec pattern in Basutoland. Of the ferment stirring in Quebec, in reaction to the hierarchy's exaggerated fear of laicism, the missionaries knew nothing. Even at the university level, many missionaries were unable to establish a close relationship with their students, some of whom became independence leaders in Southern, Central and East Africa.

South African Nationalist Parties

African nationalist currents in South Africa have strongly influenced political developments in each of the High Commission Territories. To varying degrees, political leaders in the Territories have participated in the programmes of South African political parties and have imbibed something of their philosophy. Most of those destined to assume prominence in the Territories attended such institutions as Lovedale, Adams College or Fort Hare, centres of nationalist ferment in South Africa. Some spent many years in South Africa, perhaps with the intention of making their home in that country. Like their South African associates, they absorbed some of the bourgeois standards of a capitalist society. Consequently, their attitude towards politics was more sophisticated than in many parts of Africa. Both Communism and anti-Communism have played a role in this development.

Without tracing the convolutions of South African politics, it is important to note that, since its birth in 1912, two strands have dominated the thinking of African nationalists in South Africa. The dominant strand was moderate, conciliatory and favoured constitutional tactics in the fight for equality; the second favoured a more assertive challenge. For almost half a century, the African National Congress (ANC) was led by Christian middle class leaders and included such a figure as Dr J. S. Moroka, resident at Thaba Nchu, and closely related to many Basuto. With the banning of Congress in 1960, its active leadership fell into more militant hands. Shortly before, in 1958, the more uncompromising or Africanist grouping within Congress broke off to form the Pan-African Congress (PAC). The PAC took strong exception to the participation by Congress in the Congress Alliance consisting of the South African Indian Congress, the Coloured People's

Congress, the Congress of Democrats and the South African Congress of Trade Unions, each of which had a strong Communist orientation. When PAC broke away from the ANC, it claimed that the latter was dominated by the non-Africans in the other congresses, many of whom were said to be Communist. For its part, the PAC advocated a strictly Africanist programme so as to maintain control of the nationalist movement. Whatever the merits of their approach, it frequently happened that the PAC message was understood by the more unsophisticated rank and file as straightforward racism.[2]

After the banning of both parties by the South African government in 1960, their representatives sought to establish strong ties with the political parties just beginning to take form in the Territories. In some cases they would be content with fraternal ideological ties; in others, actual control of the territorial party was desired. On the whole, nationalists in the Territories welcomed these associations. Through their South African connections not only could they gain entrance to the council tables of Africa but they could even secure a world hearing. South African political contacts also meant financial support—from London, Accra, Cairo and Moscow. As South Africa increased its efforts to ferret out nationalist leaders, refugees, some of whom could lay claim to British citizenship, poured into the Territories and proceeded to play an active role in territorial politics.

On general principle, even the more conservative traditional elements in the Territories found it necessary to give succour to the South African refugees. Increasingly, however, these refugees were viewed as a definite threat to the gradual political evolution which the traditionalists hoped to carry through. Eventually, as the prospect of independence came closer to reality, even the more conventional nationalist leaders of the Territories were to feel their own positions threatened. Territorial leaders began to let it be known that they had no intention of permitting their people to be sacrificed for South African liberation, however detestable the apartheid policies of the South African government might be.

The New Elite

As early as 1907, the Progressive Association, formed by a few traders, teachers and clerks, was offering mild criticism both of the British government and the chieftainship. From time to time the Association also criticised the composition and policies of the Basutoland Council, and made what, under existing circumstances, were considered radical demands for the election of commoners to the Council. In time, however, the Progressives 'suffered the fate often in store for the first advocates of African political advancement, who usually come from what, in terms of conventional European categories, would be described as an incipient middle class'.[3] Thus, by the time progressive reforms were being carried out by the administration, the new nationalists or radicals were condemning their elderly forerunners as 'stooges of colonialism'. Notwithstanding these charges, many of the country's nationalist leaders were undoubtedly stirred to action through contact with the Progressive Association.

By 1950, there was a wide range of associations and semi-political interest groups. These included the Basutoland Public Service Native Union, the Native Transport Contractors, the Committee of Educated Natives, the Masite Farmers' Co-operative Association and Mothers' Union, the League of the Common Man (*Le khotla la Bafo*) together with numerous commercial, co-operative, agricultural, religious, educational and ex-servicemen's organisations. Although it is difficult, if not impossible, to assess the relative influence of these groupings in the country's constitutional development, it must have been considerable. The experience of 20,000 Basuto in the African Auxiliary Pioneer Corps during the second world war, under their own warrant officers and sergeants, also facilitated the process of constitutional change. Not only had they seen whites outside the usual colonial context, with all their shortcomings and weaknesses, but experience abroad made them more receptive to new ideas. During the course of the war, British authorities took pains to explain contemplated changes in the government, and the Resident Commissioner himself, Lieutenant-Colonel C. N. Arden-Clarke, journeyed north to discuss with the troops the reduction in number of chiefs and courts.[4] Once the nationalist political movement was set in motion, most of these groupings were regarded as fertile recruitment centres.

Among the best organised of the early popular groupings which took on some characteristics of a political organisation was the League of the Common Man, formed by Josiel Lefela and his brother during the second decade of this century. At first very critical both of the British administration and of the chieftainship,[5] after 1948 the League sought the support of the chiefs by accusing the British of seeking their destruction. The group seemed to be anti-European in its outlook, and, symptomatic of its limited vision, sought a return to the ways of the past. Although the League may have accomplished little in the practical order, it did enjoy considerable prestige and inspired the leadership of the Basutoland African Congress.

The Basutoland African Congress: the Emergence of Modern Nationalist Parties

The politicising of Basuto national life proceeded apace following the formation in 1952 of the country's first modern nationalist party, the Basutoland African Congress (BAC), led by Ntsu Mokhehle. Born in 1918 of moderately wealthy parents, Mokhehle busied himself at an early age with the cause of African nationalism. When only nineteen he was writing about the sufferings of Africans, which he attributed to their condition of political voicelessness. He was expelled from the University College of Fort Hare in 1942 for having planned several strikes. During a brief return to Basutoland, Mokhehle joined the League of the Common Man. In 1944, he resumed his studies at Fort Hare, where he graduated Master of Science in Zoology. He became an active member of the African National Congress Youth League but decided to return to Basutoland in order to play an active part in the political life of his own country.[6] Having first received an Education Diploma, he was well qualified to become the President of the Basutoland Teachers' Association. A Pan Africanist and anti-Communist by political conviction, Mokhehle exhibited a complex personality and proved to possess those charismatic qualities which have distinguished most African nationalist leaders. At the same time, however, these positive characteristics were accompanied by a tendency to abandon tact and give vent to anger and the familiar nationalist tendencies of impatience and exaggeration, especially in the face of unreasonable attack. He was thus subject to misunderstanding, especially on the part of the politically unsophisticated, including numerous chiefs and clerics.

In 1955, the Congress Party sponsored the publication of *Mohlabani* (The Warrior), under the editorship of B. M. Khaketla, a forceful writer both in English and Sesotho. The first issue of the paper marked the beginning of the agitational phase of the Basuto nationalist movement. It argued for equalisation of pay in the civil service, criticised the Moore Report for its inadequate reform proposals, and stressed the importance of education and the state's responsibility for it. The publication's cessation in 1960, after the new constitution had gone into effect, was indicative of the division which had occurred in the nationalist ranks. During its lifetime, however, the effective militancy of *Mohlabani* provoked a strong reaction from the British administration.

The new elite of the BAC pushed its systematic challenge to the authoritarian nature of British rule and criticised the Basutoland Council as a rubber stamp offering no opposition to British dictation. Stung by this criticism, the Council rejected the 1954 Moore Commission Report, which proposed to grant District government to the Basuto without conferring real control over the central power. Indeed, it was the rejection of the Moore Report which forced the British government to appoint instead a constitutional committee in 1955.

British Reaction

British reaction to the leadership challenge thrown up by the Congress Party led to the dismissal in 1955 of three of its prominent leaders, B. M. Khaketla, N. C. Mokhehle and Z. L. Mothopeng (later a member of the national executive of the Pan-African Congress), from their teaching positions in the Maseru Basutoland High School. This futile act of revenge served only to quicken the growth of the BAC and to intensify its campaign for self-rule. The party then proceeded to build itself up into a rival 'government' and set about politicising all student, youth, labour, co-operative and teaching associations.

In its campaign for self-rule, the BAC appealed to the arguments of British liberal democracy. At the same time, however, and to the consternation and alarm of chiefs, clerics and administrators, such militant terms as 'imperialist', 'fascist', 'oppressors' and 'exploiters' were employed against the party's declared enemies. Oversimplified as these nationalist labels may have been, they served as a convenient set of concepts for analysing the existing situation and for justifying rapid economic development. Unfortunately, however, this language seemed adequate proof to the conservative mind that Communism was riding strong within the councils of the BAC. Mokhehle's participation in 1958 in the All-African Peoples' Conference in Accra, and his success in gaining financial assistance from Ghana and Egypt, was further interpreted as proof of the party's 'Communist orientation'. It was perhaps the attempt by Congress to politicise the Teachers' Association, so closely identified with the missionary enterprise, that provoked a serious misunderstanding with the Roman Catholic Church.

The elections of 1960, under the new constitution, further polarised the opposition between the Congress (now called the Basutoland Congress Party) and the Roman Catholic authorities. While pledging itself to respect the individual's right to freedom of worship, the BCP insisted that religion be kept out of the political arena.[7] Considering the religious overtones which the political campaign had acquired, a joint pastoral letter from Basutoland's two Catholic Oblate Bishops, entitled *The Church and Politics: Duties and Responsibilities of Catholics in Basutoland*, seemed a direct attempt on the part of Church authorities to influence the outcome of the election. For, in addition to enunciating traditional Catholic social teaching, the document went on to apply the principles cited by Pope Pius XII when dealing with the electoral situation in Italy in 1948. Emphasis was placed on the Pope's injunction forbidding Catholics to vote for parties which worked 'hand in glove' with the Communists. Critical Basuto Catholics seriously questioned whether the electoral situation in Italy in 1948 was the same as that in Basutoland in 1960. It was also open to question whether the small Communist membership of the BCP and the party's collaboration with individual Communists was the same thing as working 'hand in glove' with the Communist Party. In the charged election atmosphere, however, it was inevitable that many Catholics interpreted this letter as an injunction to vote against the BCP and for the opposition. The BCP, at least, interpreted the letter in that light. The clash between the BCP and some Catholic missionaries was continued after the election, especially in the columns of the Catholic weekly, *Moeletsi Oa Basotho* (Voice of the Basuto) and the BCP publication, *Makatolle*. Although Catholic attacks against the BCP were generally by way of insinuation, the BCP retaliated by exaggerating Catholic attempts to preserve mission schools into a 'world motive to dominate'.[8]

Later in 1960, Peter Khamane, an experienced Boy Scout organiser, founded the League of Thaka Tsa 'Mesa-Mohloane, or, by popular connotation, the Anti-Communist League. Although the constitution of the League claimed that it was not a political or religious organisation, several of the aims and principles acknowledged by the League were religious in content, while activities normally carried out by political parties were undertaken. Many people interpreted the formation of the League as an indirect attempt by Oblate missionaries to oppose the BCP. A usual practice during the League's early days was to follow a public meeting of the BCP with a van-mounted loudspeaker, informing people of the dangers of Communism. Inconclusive evidence indicated that mission funds secured in West Germany were used to finance the League's activities. In any event, after a Catholic mission official arrived from Germany in 1963 to check on expenditure of funds, the League's activities were drastically reduced.

The Basutoland National Party

The Basutoland National Party, founded in 1958 by Chief Leabua Jonathan and G. C. Manyeli, sought to associate itself with the preservation of those values supposedly threatened by the BAC. Chief Jonathan and Manyeli, both prominent Catholics, set themselves up as the antithesis of the Congress leadership. The BNP manifesto went to great pains to indicate the party's acknowledgement and dependence upon God, its support for hereditary chieftainship, and its loyalty to the British Crown. Evidence indicates that Catholic missionaries gave considerable support to the new party, by supplying names of prospective party members[9] and by soliciting funds on its behalf in Quebec and West Germany. A confidential missionary circular analysed each issue of *Mohlabani* so that clerics might point out the journal's 'Communistic statements' to political organisers.

Although Catholic missionaries contributed to the birth of the BNP, criticism of this action both by politicians and by more farsighted priests, some of whom resided at Pius XII University College, gradually reduced such involvement. Further admonitions in this regard were given by H. E. Emmanuel 'Mabathoana, newly appointed Archbishop of Maseru. It would thus be inaccurate to designate the BNP as a Catholic party. Rather, as the embodiment of general discontent among the chieftaincy, the BNP had as one of its primary goals the restoration of 'the ancient democratic relationship of the chiefs and the people'.[10]

As the BNP expanded its grass-roots movement, it also began to imitate the agitational tactics of the Congress. As far as self-government was concerned, the party did not differ fundamentally from the Congress, except perhaps in so far as it seemed to advocate a slightly slower pace, lest British withdrawal lead to difficulties with South Africa. Moreover, with the accession of Prince Bereng to the paramountcy in 1960, a certain coolness between the chieftainship, as represented by the BNP, and those elements supporting a stronger political role for the Paramount Chief came to the surface. This friction permitted the BNP greater freedom of action.

The Fragmentation of Congress: The Marema-Tlou Party

Not all opposition to Congress originated from without. Personality clashes as well as policy differences soon precipitated two significant splits from Congress which led to the formation of the Marema-Tlou or United Party and the Basutoland Freedom Party (BFP). The Marema-Tlou was founded in 1957 by Chief S. S. Matete, an early Congress supporter. For some months, the Marema-Tlou was little more than a caucus of like-minded chiefs, but in 1958 the group officially broke with Congress. One of the original objectives of the group was the installation of the young prince, Chief Bereng Seeiso, in place of the faltering Regent. As a political party, the Marema-Tlou urged that under a new constitution the Paramount Chief should be Head of State and assume all powers then exercised by the Resident Commissioner. Although Matete was not himself of the ruling house, the prominent role which he played in securing Bereng's recognition as Paramount Chief enhanced his position among the 'Sons of Moshoeshoe'. In 1960, Chief Matete was appointed, on the Paramount Chief's recommendation, Member of the Executive Council associated with Chieftainship Affairs and Local Government. Evidence indicated that his party enjoyed at least tacit support from the British administration as well as from the Paramount Chief.

The Basutoland Freedom Party (BFP)

The other breakaway party, the Basutoland Freedom Party, emerged after the country's first elections in 1960. It was led by the Deputy-President of the Congress and editor of *Mohlabani*, B. M. Khaketla. Although his resignation from Congress on December 29, 1960, seems to have been triggered by a minor personal dispute, two factors in his post-election situation undermined his popularity with the party masses. Having been appointed Member of the Executive Council associated with Health and Education, Khaketla was bound by an oath of secrecy. Already known as an 'intellectual', his new responsibilities gave him less time for party affairs and drew him more closely into contact with official members of the government. Khaketla explained his resignation from Congress as a protest against the extreme agitational tactics of the party. In April 1961, Khaketla, together with a number of other ex-Congress members, launched their new party. The BFP revealed itself as a conservative force both in terms of the pace towards independence and the proposed power to be exercised by the Paramount Chief as Head of State.

A Merger of Dissidents: The Marema-Tlou-Freedom Party

Towards the end of 1962, the BFP and the Marema-Tlou initiated merger talks which were successfully concluded in early January, 1963. The BNP, which also participated in these discussions, eventually declined to join the new party. The conference elected Chief Matete as President and Khaketla as Vice-President. Dr Makotoko, a former BFP member, was elected General Secretary of the new Marema-Tlou-Freedom Party.

A statement released by the new party suggested a different policy from that previously followed by either of the merging parties. To attain economic self-sufficiency, the party declared the need 'to revise completely our whole approach to agriculture, land tenure, commerce, industry, education and all other facets of our national existence'. Confirmation of this bid to capture the nationalist leadership was seen in Makotoko's 1963 attendance at the Addis Ababa Conference. He reminded the delegates that Basutoland was totally surrounded by an unfriendly South Africa and needed outside support, a position which brought some public demur from the party Vice-President. After unsuccessful appeals for funds in western Europe and the United States, support was sought from various African states and possibly, too, from the Soviet Union.

The Communist Party and the Nationalist Movement

Apart from some contacts with the League of the Common Man, it would appear that, before the 1940s, the Communist Party of South Africa made very little effort to penetrate Basutoland. A party of the large towns and urban locations, they had no real interest in the native reserves or the High Commission Territories.[11] All of this changed, however, with the establishment of the wartime 'popular front' and the Communist decision to penetrate the African National Congress. To the extent that the Basutoland African Congress enjoyed ANC support, some Communist contact was perhaps inevitable. A few avowed Communists, some being refugees from South Africa, openly joined the Congress. To the Congress leadership, however, the collaboration of African nationalists who happened to be Communists was not at first viewed with alarm. On the contrary, a severe shortage of trained manpower seemed to make any other course impracticable. It was not long, however, until the Communists were challenging the neutralist position endorsed by Mokhehle and the PAC. Mokhehle subsequently denounced the Communists for seeking 'to cripple African nationalism'.[12]

In March 1961, Jack Mosiane, reputedly the Communist Organising Secretary of the General Workers' Union, and a member of Congress, led a strike apparently designed to gain popularity as a preliminary bid to challenge the leadership of Mokhehle. Consequently, on August 28, 1961, Godfrey Kolisang, Secretary-General of the party, issued an open letter tracing in great detail the efforts of the Communist faction of the ANC to take over the leadership of Congress. Another episode in the leadership struggle occurred on October 31, 1961, when Communist elements apparently manipulated a Congress demonstration so as to precipitate a riot and attempted arson against the Roman Catholic Cathedral in Maseru. But this effort to discredit Mokhehle's leadership also proved abortive, since the government was unable to link Mokhehle with the disorders. Another major attempt to unseat Mokhehle was made in December 1962 by Robert Matji, an alleged leftwinger and a Congress member of the Legislative Council. Matji's strategy called for the establishment of a 'National Liberation Front' of all groups and persons striving for independence. Mokhehle, according to Matji, by reason of his 'dictatorial' policies, was an obstacle to the creation of such a front and should be removed from office. This attempt failed and Mokhehle not only won full support at the party's annual conference, but was confirmed in office for another five years.

These unsuccessful efforts to disrupt or capture the BCP from within may have accounted for the formal but secret launching of the Communist Party of Lesotho on May 5, 1962.[13] The proclaimed secrecy surrounding the event was possibly a ruse to conceal the paucity of party membership. John Motloheloa, a former South African trade unionist, was named Secretary-General, and remained the only announced party office-holder. Motloheloa, long regarded as a semi-comical figure on the Maseru streets, hardly seemed to fit the description of a serious Communist leader. It has been suggested that the Communist Party in Basutoland, one of the two legal Communist Parties on the continent of Africa,* is primarily a cover for the South

* The other is in Tunisia.

African Communist Party's activities in the country, especially for the attempted infiltration of the MFP, whose rival, the BCP, had sent a delegation to Peking.[14]

The Basutoland Labour Party—The South African Equation

Further political fragmentation occurred in November 1962, when the Basutoland Labour Party (BLP) announced its formation. The significance of the party lay not in its political manifesto, which virtually coincided with that of the BNP, but in the fact that the party's raison d'être seemed only to be one of maintaining good relations with South Africa, a matter which assumed greater importance as the country moved towards independence. Elliott E. Lethata, the Labour Party leader, ruled out the possibility of Basutoland's appealing to any third party, such as the United Nations Committee on Colonialism. Basutoland's position, he emphasised, meant that 'there can be no room for pressure politics from without' and that 'the Republic and ourselves are fated to remain good neighbours as we have always been'. Although he endorsed the conservative position of the BNP, he pointed out his party's stand against outside political pressure as a basic difference. Lethata's approach to the country's problem was highly approved in South African government circles and every opportunity was afforded the BLP to visit Basuto living within the Republic. Whether motivated or sustained by the South African government, the emergence of the BLP served warning that Basutoland's economic dependence upon South Africa remained a vital political issue.

By the time of the 1960 elections, the nationalist movement had spawned a number of political parties. These parties, ranging from left to right across the political spectrum, took their positions relevant to a host of issues, including the pace towards self-government, the role of the Paramount Chief as Head of State, the place of the chieftainship, ownership of industry and control of concessions, government control of education, Pan-Africanism, and the over-riding issue of relations with South Africa. During the next six years, the political fever would intensify and, under pressure from South Africa, a major political shift would occur.

5

THE ROAD TO INDEPENDENCE, 1960–1966

THE GENERAL ELECTION of January 1960, which followed the promulgation of the 1959 constitution, was the first election based on modern British electoral practice to be held in Basutoland. Although twelve months had originally been envisaged as the shortest possible period required for proper preparations, this period was eventually reduced by half when over-riding political considerations supervened.[1] The majority of candidates (188) for the forty contested seats (the remaining forty being nominated or ex officio) stood as Independents, although most of them probably had party leanings. It was, however, clear indication that the country was not yet used to party organisations and, for many candidates, party identification would have forfeited votes. The next largest group of candidates (125) supported the BCP, the most active and organised party in the field. They were followed by the BNP with 77 candidates, the Marema-Tlou Party with 51, and the failing Progressive Association with 6.

The election campaign was a somewhat dramatic if extended affair, and was generally conducted in an orderly manner. Many candidates promised little more than to represent the best interests of their constituents. Predictably, the Congress Party pressed the campaign most vigorously and demanded immediate independence. Britain was severely castigated and South Africa was condemned for its apartheid policies and designs upon the Territory. Other issues included condemnation of church interference in politics, demands for rapid Africanisation of the civil service, the immediate removal of the Resident Commissioner, A. C. T. Chaplin (a South African), improvement of education, and a thorough investigation of the land tenure system—a suggestion originated by the opposition leader, Chief Jonathan. Congress leaders showed an awareness of the 'objective' primacy of the overlapping economic and external problems of their country, but, as elsewhere in Africa, they denied that there were economic solutions to the problem. Only the development of local industries, they said, could make Basutoland self-sufficient, and this could be accomplished only after the attainment of independence. Once this goal was reached, they said they preferred to industrialise with help from the United Nations and the United States rather than from Britain.[2] On most of these matters party differences lay mainly in personality and approach rather than principle.

To the surprise of the British administration and the chieftainship, the election results gave a dominating position to the BCP, which exceeded most estimates by securing 36 per cent of the popular vote (12,787) and winning 73 of the 162 District Council seats. The distribution of these seats among the 9 District Councils, which acted as electoral colleges, was such that the BCP was able, with a little assistance from the Independent candidates, to control 6 of the Councils and thus elect 30 out of 40 elected members to the 80-seat Legislative Council. This extreme distortion of the popular vote served to minimise the real strength of the BNP. Although generally dismissed as a doomed party, direct elections five years later under a new constitution were to produce vastly different results. The Marema-Tlou Party polled 8 per cent of the votes and won 15 District Council seats. Nevertheless, it received 5 seats in the Legislative Council. The fact that the 51 successful Independents gained nearly as many votes (12,470) as all the Congress candidates together, and yet secured only 4 seats in the Legislative Council, further falsified the political picture. The Paramount Chief somewhat balanced the composition of the Legislative Council by filling the 14 nominated seats with 9 more Independents, 2 BNP members and 3 Progressives.

The official reasons advanced in favour of indirect elections were financial and 'educational'. Not only were election costs considerably reduced under the indirect system but, in the absence of a smoothly functioning party system, it was assumed that the qualifications of candidates could be better assessed by members of the District Councils. However, the disadvantages of the system included not only the distortion of the popular vote, but the difficulty facing National Councillors in fulfilling their obligations to the local District Councils which elected them. In the event that an outstanding candidate failed in the general election, there was no way of getting him into the Legislative Council. Especially dangerous was the importation of national politics into local government matters, a situation which frequently prevented the carrying out of worthwhile projects. The District administrations suffered also from the fact that all the Councils were composed of members who had, in most cases, stood for election hoping that they would go on to the Legislative Council.[3] Provision for proxy voting for those Basuto resident in South Africa was also the subject of criticism. Despite widespread illiteracy among the electorate, voters in South Africa were asked to send their unmarked papers to a friend or relative in Basutoland, advising him into which box his ballot was to be dropped. The system was challenged both by the BCP and the BNP, but the High Commissioner refused to alter the postal voting system on the grounds of expense. As it turned out, postal voting accounted for only two per cent of the total vote.

The New Government Established

The Basutoland National Council assembled in its revised form as a legislature on March 12, 1960. The day was also marked by the formal 'placing' and presentation of the young Bereng Seeiso, under the title of Moshoeshoe II, as Paramount Chief to the High Commissioner, Sir John Maud. The first important action of the legislature was the election of three members to the Executive Council, a task entrusted to the entire Council. B. M. Khaketla of the Congress Party, M. Lepolesa of the Progressive Association and Chief Matete of the Marema-Tlou were elected to the Executive Council, and the appointment of Chief Leshoboro Majara by the Paramount Chief completed the non-official membership of the eight-member body. With the subsequent defection of Khaketla from the BCP, the Executive Council remained a highly conservative force, closely identified with official British policy. As a result, the elected majority in the Legislative Council became the opposition without representation in the 'government', and considerable tension developed between the two. Despite obvious shortcomings and inconsistencies, the new constitutional arrangement at least had the merit of establishing legitimate channels of protest. Compared with the prevailing system across the border, the spirit if not the letter of the constitution was almost radical. Henceforth there could be no doubt that any decision on the future of the country would be subject to the declared wishes of the people. Basutoland thus became the first of the High Commission Territories to be brought into the broad stream of African constitutional evolution.

Demand for Constitutional Review

Almost from the first day of debate, the BCP emphasised its rejection of the constitution and reiterated its call for independence. The Executive Council, somewhat reluctantly, was forced to keep abreast of these demands by moving for a constitutional review as early as September 1961. The motion was proposed by Chief Matete, Executive Council Member associated with Chieftainship Affairs and Local Government. It was a cautious move, designed to placate nationalist feeling while yet affirming the country's dependence upon two traditional pillars—the High Commissioner and the Paramount Chief. The nominated and official majority therefore requested the High Commissioner to invite the Paramount Chief to appoint a constitutional commission, which, after consultation with leaders of all political parties and representatives of the chieftainship and other groupings and organisations, was to review the 1959 constitution. Proposals for its improvement were to be formulated while 'having regard to the responsibilities for Basutoland of Her Majesty's Government and with particular reference to the constitutional position of the Paramount Chief in a responsible form of Government'.[4] The commission's proposals were to be transmitted to the Paramount Chief who would in turn refer them to the Council for approval.

Debate on the method of constitutional review served to crystallise the vital policy differences between the BCP and the majority in the legislature. For the BCP, the real issue was immediate independence and responsible government under a constitutional monarchy as against continued dependence and chiefly dominance. They therefore sought to omit any reference to the High Commissioner or the Paramount Chief which might be construed as admitting a special extra-constitutional power residing in either authority. Rather, the BCP urged the appointment of a Select Committee dependent on the Council, which would consider 'the transference of the Basotho sovereignty from the British Crown to the Paramount Chief, a Legislative Council with a clear majority of elected Members, an Executive Council of Ministers responsible to the legislature with a Chief Minister, direct election to the legislature, the position of chiefs under the constitution and provisions protecting Human Rights and Fundamental Freedoms'.[5] Although various reasons were advanced by the BCP in opposing the appointment of the commission by the Paramount Chief, it was obvious that a constitutional committee dependent on the

Legislative Council would constitute a formidable victory over him and over the chieftainship as a whole. The BCP amendment, while calling for the transfer of sovereignty from the British Crown to the Paramount Chief, implied that the latter's role would be that of a limited constitutional monarch. Although defeated on this issue for the moment, the BCP continued to press for total independence under a constitutional monarchy.

The appointment of the constitutional commission was discussed both by the High Commissioner, Sir John Maud, and by the Paramount Chief at the opening of the second session of the Legislative Council on January 26, 1962. The High Commissioner gave no indication, however, that constitutional review portended any significant change in the basic relationship between Her Majesty's Government and Basutoland. A reference to the need for maintaining cordial relations with South Africa, now no longer a member of the Commonwealth, was his only mention of external affairs. Consequently, the speech from the throne had the effect of stirring strong resentment among the elected members, who again linked the question of independence to internal reform. Inasmuch as the High Commissioner's address made no mention of either question and ignored the effects of South Africa's racial policies upon the Basuto, Sir John's speech was only just acknowledged by a vote of 29 to 26.[6]

Criticism from the Paramount Chief

The address by the Paramount Chief and its reception by the Council stood in remarkable contrast to that of the High Commissioner. In the words of a BCP member, if the words had been used 'by the leaders of the BCP first, you would not be surprised if such a leader were drawn before the law. It would be alleged that by that speech the party was inciting sedition.'[7] Although an exaggerated comment, it did point up a remarkable departure by the Paramount Chief from official policy. In his address he stressed those points which the Congress Party had long advanced: the inadequacy of British rule, the need for responsible government, and the necessity for reform of traditional institutions. His condemnation of 'empiricism' in public affairs left little doubt that past British policy was under attack. He called for a 'national crusade' against 'empiricism' and named it the country's foremost enemy:

[Empiricism] means that decisions are taken on purely short-term grounds, without any clear perception of their long-run implications. Policy is made hand-to-mouth; and when there are no agreed views about the general principles of public policy, the proper role of various organisations and institutions, or the ideal ultimate shape of social and economic relations, these piecemeal decisions are apt to make two malcontents for every citizen. The result is to create frustrated groups. . . . One empirical, ready-made, 'commonsense' decision after another, taken to deal with situations which are seldom foreseen, and carrying consequences which are equally full of surprises; until all too often a once-popular government finds itself grown authoritarian but to no particular purpose; presiding over a stagnant economy, no longer even expecting any enthusiasm among the people, or having any power to mould the future. If Empiricism governed Basutoland in the past . . . we must resolve at once that no such fate could possibly be forecast for Basutoland.[8]

In place of empiricism, a term which so aptly described the existing philosophy of government and its practical effects upon the country, the Paramount Chief called for an 'ideology': 'an analysis of the total social, economic and political situation that exists now, and an attempt to classify and summarise it in a way which exposes its determining features . . . an attempt to imagine and describe the society one really would like to create in place of the present one—how it should be organised, how wealth should be shared, how learning should be carried out, in short, how the happiness of the greatest number can be achieved. . . .' The need for a shared ideology, said Moshoeshoe II, was evident at all levels, and had to come from the government, even under the existing constitution, and 'before the restoration of the heritage of self-rule which the great king Moshoeshoe left us', so that 'the government [be] not only responsive to popular and reasonable demands, but, more important still, [be] in practice, if not in law, responsible to Basutoland and her people'.

Finally, his remarks on the institution of chieftainship served to warn that it must be modified. If traditional institutions, he said, were to remain a living, vital force in national life, they must be willing to 'adapt themselves to the changing circumstances of the times . . . on occasion to modify their form'. Consequently, he noted that during the new session of the Council, it would perhaps be necessary to legislate upon 'certain established institutions'; a statement which later seemed to prompt a chief in the Council to observe that chieftainship was built from bottom to top and not in reverse.

Thus, however cautiously, Moshoeshoe II had succeeded in identifying himself with the new forces of Basuto nationalism without giving himself up to the nationalist politicians. There was ample indication that he hoped to cast the paramountcy in the vanguard of the nationalist struggle, though it be at the expense of the lower chieftainship. It was also evident that political independence and chiefly reform were inextricably bound together and that one could not be had without the other. By adopting this attitude, the paramountcy might now be translated into 'kingship' while retaining various powers absent in the European concept of the constitutional monarchy. The political correctness of the Paramount Chief's position was borne out by the BCP leader, Ntsu Mokhehle, who, at least for tactical reasons, expressed the general feeling of the Council that 'the speech of the Paramount Chief is in principle generally accepted'.[9]

The Constitutional Commission

The constitutional commission, under the chairmanship of Walter Stanford (former Liberal member of the South African Parliament representing Transkei Africans), President of the Legislative Council, included two representatives of the chieftainship and government. The commission's work was seriously under way by May 1962, as it began examining what would eventually amount to over 1,140 written memoranda, a number indicating a very high degree of popular interest and participation. The commission also proceeded to tour the entire country and received testimony on eight vital points: (1) the status of the Paramount Chief; (2) the status of Basutoland; (3) the relationship between Britain and Basutoland; (4) elections, direct or indirect; (5) the franchise; (6) the form of Parliament; (7) the function and future of chiefs; and (8) the future of the Basuto courts.

While co-operating with the commission, the BCP strongly objected to the equal representation given the various political parties. Such a procedure, claimed Mokhehle, merely elevated several parties to a level in the public mind which was not deserved in terms of their support from the electorate. The composition of the commission was denounced by the BCP as undemocratic and unrepresentative—'a direct reflection and repetition of the mockery representation in the Legislative Council'—and proof that the Paramount Chief was being used by the British as a tool.[10] Throughout the commission's hearings, the BCP continued to press for complete independence.

This demand was supported simultaneously on the international level as Mokhehle, together with K. T. Motsete, President of the Bechuanaland Peoples Party, and J. J. Nquku, President of the splintered Swaziland Progressive Party, appeared before the United Nations Special Committee on Colonialism. Consequently, support was received from that body when, by resolution of June 7, 1962, the Committee recommended that elections be held in each Territory on the basis of direct universal adult suffrage and that a constitutional conference of elected political leaders be convoked to establish dates for the independence of the three Territories.[11] The issue was also pressed before the second conference of the Casablanca Powers meeting in Cairo from June 15, 1962. There the existing constitution was denounced, together with 'the protracted constitutional negotiations then in progress'. Although the territorial leaders hardly expected any dramatic assistance or intervention, the object of focusing wider attention on the subject so as to hasten constitutional advance was clearly served. As the only delegation direct from Southern Africa to attend the February 1963 meeting of the Afro-Asian Peoples' Solidarity Conference in Moshi, Tanganyika, the BCP was able to capitalise on the conference's concern with the non-independence areas of Africa.

Political Crisis: Basutoland and South Africa

Throughout 1962 and 1963, an air of urgency was given to the constitutional discussions as a result of a change in relations with South Africa, now no longer a Commonwealth member. The necessity of redefining the relationships between the High Commission Territories and South Africa was further complicated by the growing number of South African political refugees escaping to Basutoland. British authorities were especially embarrassed by the presence of Patrick Duncan, a prominent Liberal Party member under South African restriction, and Potlako Leballo, the top-ranking exiled member of the Pan-African Congress. The latter's claim, in March 1963, to have some guiding influence over Poqo, a secret revolutionary movement in South Africa, gave South Africa a pretext for imposing severe border restrictions. Even the BCP, however, was fearful of South African refugees becoming involved in the politics of Basutoland or straining relations with South Africa. A pointed warning in this regard was issued as early as February 19, 1962.[12]

Thus, from both the British and the Basuto points of view, independence seemed more realistic. On the one hand, it would relieve Britain of the unpleasant task of taking up every irritant which might arise between Basutoland and South Africa. At the same time, the expectation that the Basuto would act in accord with their economic dependence on South Africa, and thus themselves impose restrictions upon possible revolutionary activity, seemed a realistic assumption. On the other hand, events had demonstrated that the British were not prepared to react forcefully to South Africa's new border restrictions and that they were unwilling to elevate the difficulty to the full international level. The elimination of passenger train services to Maseru, imposition of air flight restrictions, ill-treatment of Basuto, collusion between South African and expatriate Basutoland police—on none of these issues did Britain take a resolute stand. Moreover, Britain seemed determined to prevent United Nations involvement, a lever which an independent government might exploit.

The hardening of Basuto opinion on the existing political situation, together with British ambivalence, were apparent with the opening of the third session of the Legislative Council on August 20, 1963. The speech from the throne, delivered in the name of the new High Commissioner, Sir Hugh Stephenson, by the Resident Commissioner, A. F. Giles, made only a slight reference to the constitutional commission and dealt sketchily with external affairs. Even in June, shortly after taking office, Sir Hugh had recognised 'the legitimate Basotho desire for internal self-government' but made no mention of full independence. Further, he had stressed that Basutoland could not afford trouble-makers or differences if the country's destiny were to be realised,[13] an assertion which, however correct, seemed unsatisfactory in the context. Consequently, throughout the debate on the speech from the throne, members repeatedly criticised the High Commissioner's assurances that he was protecting Basuto interests vis-à-vis South Africa. As a result, for the first time in the history of the Territory's Council, the speech from the throne was decisively rejected, by 22 to 7. Even the nominated half of the Council for the most part abstained or were absent. The Paramount Chief, in contrast, noted that Basutoland was 'on the threshold of a new stage in its constitutional development' and he called upon Britain to protect the interests of the Basuto. His address was accepted without difficulty by the Council.

Amid obvious discontent with British rule and after demonstrating that South Africa could both hinder and promote the interests of the

Basuto, the South African Prime Minister, Verwoerd, found it opportune to offer to 'guide' the Protectorates in their economic and constitutional development. Undoubtedly, the offer was calculated to take advantage of events more in Swaziland than in Basutoland, but, hopefully, it could also attract the Basuto. Generally, however, Verwoerd's offer fell on deaf ears in Basutoland since no political leader could believe that the Prime Minister would be willing to meet the Basuto on equal terms. And on this condition all Basuto were unanimous.

The Report of the Constitutional Commission

The anxiously-awaited report of the constitutional commission, which had sat for eighteen months, was released in early October 1963. The report made five major sets of recommendations: (1) rapid transition to independence in 1965, with separate citizenship, national flag and anthem, renaming the country Lesotho, and membership in the British Commonwealth; (2) establishment of a constitutional monarchy under Moshoeshoe II, who would retain special powers over land allocation and the institution of chieftainship; (3) creation of a bicameral National Assembly, comprising a lower house of 54 to 60 elected members and an upper house, which would have only delaying powers, composed of the country's 22 principal chiefs and 11 persons nominated by the King; (4) a cabinet on the British model, collectively responsible to the National Assembly; and (5) universal franchise, in place of the existing system of male suffrage.

The commission recommended that Basutoland should be accorded the official status of a Protected State during the transitional period, rather than continue its existing colonial status. The control of defence, external affairs and internal security would be shared during the pre-independence stage by the British and Basuto governments, with carefully defined powers of veto and certification remaining temporarily in the hands of Britain. The existing grant-in-aid system for bolstering the Basutoland economy would be replaced by two separate block grants from the United Kingdom, one for the ordinary expenses of the country and one for defence, external affairs and internal security. The disposition of the second grant could be supervised jointly by the British and Basuto authorities.

The British Adviser, suggested the report, would henceforth serve as representative of the Queen, not as the local head of government, and would be responsible directly to London rather than to a regional

High Commissioner. According to the commission's recommendations, the British Adviser would also serve as a member of the Lesotho King's Privy Council during the pre-independence period. This body, which would include the Prime Minister, the Principal Legal Adviser to the government, a nominee of the King, and possibly two co-opted members, could be chaired by the King if he so desired, even though he was not formally to be designated as a member of the Council. It also recommended that necessary arrangements be made, even during the transitional period, for independent Lesotho diplomatic representation in the Republic of South Africa, and perhaps in other countries. In South Africa, the Lesotho diplomatic representative should, it was suggested, be accommodated in the British Embassy.

The report reflected the widespread conviction that independence was both desirable and somehow feasible. A majority of politically-conscious Basuto felt confident that independence would release latent energies, promote a wider range of outside interest, and even permit a more realistic bargaining with South Africa in terms of contemporary political forces shaping modern Africa. Only through real independence was it seen possible to reconcile traditional authority with modern currents of political and economic life. Rightly or wrongly, the report genuinely reflected the common opinion that, while independence might involve risks, these risks demanded immediate confrontation. The argument that economic viability was a prerequisite for independence was thus rejected by virtually all segments of public opinion.

British and Basuto Response

Confronted with the challenge to stand up against the diplomatic pressures of South Africa and grant the Protectorate the normal right of progress towards self-government, the British government seemed to waver. A preliminary indication of Whitehall's views on the sweeping constitutional recommendations was released in London on November 12, 1963. While recognising 'that attainment of independence was a natural and legitimate aspiration of the people of Basutoland', and welcoming the commission's 'general proposal that the people of Basutoland should assume a much greater responsibility for the administration of their country', the British government expressed specific doubts on four of the commission's proposals: (1) the British government 'could not accept continued responsibility for internal security, defence, external affairs and financial support, unless it is assured of the constitutional means to discharge them' (in London's view, the commission's recommendations did not assure the means); (2) the proposal 'that an executive public service commission should be introduced at once with a full compensation scheme for expatriate officials' was regarded as premature; (3) Britain could not accept, at that stage, the loss of its power to amend the constitution; (4) the British government did not consider that the 'headship of the state' should yet be changed.

British hesitation was not based on any desire to turn back the clock in Basutoland, but rather reflected a fear that new responsibilities and problems could arise for London with the establishment of a virtually independent British-protected enclave in the heart of South Africa. A fully self-governing Basutoland close by South Africa's first Bantustan, the Transkei, would invite comparisons of real and sham independence and further complicate British-South African relations. If South Africa decided to deal with a challenge from Basutoland by imposing an economic stranglehold, a strong case could be made for United Nations intervention. Considering British economic and historic ties with South Africa, such a possibility led the British government to pause and consider the apparent dilemma at hand. Still, the ultimate necessity of moving forward was inescapable. Any other course of action would only precipitate those very consequences which British policy sought to avoid at all cost in the High Commission Territories—violence and outside intervention. The reaction of Basuto political leaders to British hesitation was immediate and unanimous. On December 11, the leaders of the three major parties—Ntsu Mokhehle (BCP), Chief S. S. Matete (MFP) and Chief Leabua Jonathan (BNP) issued a vigorous statement reaffirming their acceptance of the constitutional commission's report as a basis for negotiation. The three leaders, in an unexpected show of unity, jointly charged that the effect of the preliminary observations made by the Secretary of State for Commonwealth Relations and Colonial Affairs, Duncan Sandys, was 'to give encouragement to traditional holders of power who desired to resist change and to cause general confusion'. Further, they suggested that the timing of the statement, prior to debate on the report in the Legislative Council, was 'to say the least, mischievous and premature'.[14]

Whatever the immediate tactical objective, the Sandys statement did serve to provide various chiefs with tangible objections which otherwise might not have been marshalled. When the Legislative Council met to consider the report on November 25, two nearly-equal factions emerged. Most of the elected members and a minority of the nominated members favoured the report, whereas the majority of nominated members, apparently prompted by the lobbying British officials, and led by Chief M. J. Qhobela, urged a postponement of a decision until the proposals could be advanced anew to the people for their approval. The prospect of constitutional delay brought a threat of mass resignation from the Legislative Council. Mokhehle informed the twelfth annual conference of the BCP in late December that rejection of the constitutional proposals by the Legislative Council would result in the resignation of all BCP members. If that happened, said Mokhehle, a special conference would be called to consider methods of 'positive action' for gaining independence. In the end, however, the Legislative Council approved the report on January 31, 1964, with several amendments. These amendments, as proposed by the chiefs, would entrench the chieftaincy and give more power to the Paramount Chief, who would have the right to assent to or dissent from Bills. For the moment at least, the political leaders were willing to accept these amendments. Then, in order to facilitate the expected constitutional change, the government secured a one-year extension of the life of the Legislative Council, due to expire on March 11, 1964.

Constitutional Agreement

Having agreed on general demands and strategy, a ten-man Basutoland parliamentary delegation, headed by the Paramount Chief and including all members of the constitutional commission, left for London in early April. Constitutional talks were under way by April 20, but within a few days it was apparent that an impasse had been reached. Difficulties arose on the status of the civil service, the responsibility for internal security and foreign affairs, the relationship between the Paramount Chief and the Queen's Commissioner, and the timing of independence. The BCP officially charged, through its London representative, that the attitude of the British government was 'diametrically opposed' to all its utterances on the subject of Basutoland's independence made in the United Nations. 'The real activation behind this attitude of the British government', said a Congress Party statement, 'was the protection of a thousand-odd million pounds invested by British capitalists in the Fascists' Republic of South Africa.' At the same time, however, lest the question of relations with South Africa be used as an excuse to delay independence, the BCP declared that its first loyalty was 'not to Africa—nor for that matter to South Africa—but to ourselves'. All of the delegation agreed that it was necessary for Basutoland to 'live in complete harmony with the South African people'.

After several weeks of heated debate, in the course of which Britain admitted her inability even at the moment to defend Basutoland militarily against South Africa, agreement was reached on all major points. The result was a decided victory for the Basuto point of view. Although the Paramount Chief was not recognised as King, he was commissioned under the style of 'Motlotlehi' (a recently-coined title, approximating to 'His Majesty' without implying sovereignty) to perform his functions in the name of the Queen. It was recognised that he would have the right to be kept informed and to be consulted by his Ministers on matters of government, and to enjoy full immunity. He would take precedence over all other people in Basutoland. The constitution would establish the office of the British government's Representative, who would retain responsibility for external affairs, defence and internal security but have the power to delegate any part of those responsibilities to a Minister of Motlotlehi's government designated by the Prime Minister. Any such delegation of responsibility could be revoked, however. The Representative was entitled to immunities and privileges similar to those enjoyed by a diplomatic envoy accredited to the Queen.

Parliament, as suggested by the commission, was to be bicameral, comprising a Senate of 33 members and a National Assembly of 60 elected members, with full power to legislate in all fields other than those reserved to the Representative. Bills, to become laws, would have to pass through both houses and be assented to on the Queen's behalf by Motlotlehi. Members of the National Assembly would each represent a single-member constituency and be elected on a franchise based on universal adult suffrage. The Senate was to be empowered to refer Bills back to the National Assembly with amendments, but had no power to initiate legislation. Should the Senate fail to pass a Bill within a specified period, the National Assembly could then on its own submit the Bill for assent. The usual procedure for the selection of a Prime Minister and cabinet was provided, and agreement was also reached on the appointment of an Electoral Commission, a High Court, enforceable safeguards for human rights and provisional arrangements regarding extradition. For certain purposes there was also a Privy Council and a College of Chiefs. Despite British reluctance to set a date for independence, a compromise solution provided that twelve months after the holding of elections under the new constitution, independence would be granted upon request. Every effort was to be made to hold elections before the end of 1964, or, at the latest, by early 1965.[15] A final technical anachronism was corrected after the conference on July 31, when it was announced that the office of High Commissioner for Basutoland, Bechuanaland Protectorate and Swaziland had been abolished, and the Resident Commissioner was made directly responsible to the Secretary of State as Her Majesty's Commissioner for Basutoland.

A Shift in Political Allegiances: BCP Decline

With independence thus assured, the various political parties stepped up their efforts to win the support of the electorate. At the same time, however, the Basuto were forced to reassess the probable consequences of independence upon vital 'bread and butter' issues arising from the country's economic dependence on South Africa. During 1963, for example, some 52,000 Basuto labourers working in the South African gold mining industry had earned approximately £4,000,000, of which £377,655 went directly to their relatives and families in Basutoland. As thousands of women totally dependent upon menfolk in South Africa would, for the first time, exercise the franchise, their attitude towards immediate economic issues assumed vital importance. Women were also of great political significance inasmuch as they were traditionally the strongest church supporters among the country's 430,000 Christians, and extremely sensitive to real or implied threats against religion. The formation within the Republic in November 1964 of a Basuto organisation known as 'The Sons and Daughters of Moshoeshoe' was also symptomatic of increasing concern to maintain good relations with South Africa. Formed by Elias Letele of Bloemfontein, the organisation pledged 'to promote peace, to support the laws of South Africa and to oppose Communism'—a programme in complete harmony with South African policy.

Despite the danger signals, the dominant BCP maintained its strong ideological attachment to Pan-Africanism and reiterated its opposition to the apartheid policies of South Africa. This did not mean, however, that the BCP leadership intended to provoke the Republic after independence. On the contrary, Mokhehle stressed his party's desire 'to negotiate on an equal footing with the Republic on matters of common interest'. But in the public mind, both through a certain ineptness on the part of BCP spokesmen and as a result of a concerted effort by party opponents to frighten the electorate, the BCP was identified with violence, the Chinese Communists, anti-white, anti-Church and anti-South African programmes.[16] From the latter part of 1964 down to the elections on April 29, 1965, South African newspapers, the BNP and numerous Catholic missionaries strove successfully to implant this image. In a futile effort to redress the balance, the BCP executive issued in October 1964 a strong denial that visits by party leaders to China had 'placed the party or any of its members under any obligation to foster Communist aims', and assured the people that the party remained free 'from any political philosophy propagated by any party or country overseas'.[17] The party statement also endorsed the constitutional clauses relative to human rights and freedom of worship. Fearing that the postponement of elections to early 1965 would only assist the opposition, the BCP leadership flew to London and pressed unsuccessfully for immediate elections. Delay, said Mokhehle, could only make it possible for South African pressures 'to play as big a part as in the recently held Swaziland elections'.[18]

The BCP also suffered from its past associations with the PAC of South Africa. Although Mokhehle had warned PAC refugees that he could not tolerate interference in Basutoland affairs, his basic Pan-Africanist commitment ruled out any decisive break. The activities of Potlako Leballo, and the violence aimed at him by rival South African refugees, did not improve the position of the BCP. Bombings, shootings and arson came as an embarrassment to the Basuto, and seemed to put the BCP under a cloud. Although Leballo left the country in August 1964 on a 'safe conduct' arranged by the British Embassy in South Africa, the arrest of seven PAC members on charges arising from the Prevention of Violence Abroad Proclamation revived the real or imputed danger that refugee activity posed for Basutoland. As early as January 1965, there were strong indications that a big shift was occurring in Basuto allegiances. It was assumed, however, that any loss in BCP support would be to the advantage of the Marema-Tlou-Freedom Party, now led by Dr Seth Makotoko, which enjoyed the backing of at least eighteen of the country's twenty-two principal chiefs,[19] all of whom were entitled to seats in the Senate.

Makotoko's MFP: BCP Contender

Makotoko's rise to power as President of the MFP was a result of the unworkable merger of Chief Matete's Marema-Tlou and the Freedom Party, a union brought about in January 1963. The strains in this somewhat unnatural union were especially evident after the June 1963 Addis Ababa Conference, which Makotoko attended as MFP General Secretary. It was subsequently alleged by Chief Matete, party President, that Makotoko had received Communist assistance to attend the conference and that his memorandum on South Africa was prepared by a Communist element in Maseru.[20] In sharp contrast, Chief Matete announced that he would propose a discussion at the next party meeting on the merits of inviting Verwoerd to explain his recent offer to the Protectorates.

By early 1964, the MFP was clearly split into two factions, the major one being loyal to Makotoko. He was subsequently elected party President, an action which Chief Matete charged was unconstitutional. Although Matete was granted a provisional interdict by the High Court forbidding Makotoko's group to function as the party's executive, the order was discharged in July and Makotoko was recognised as President of the 'legal' wing of the MFP. According to Chief Matete, the party cleavage was promoted by Joseph Matthews, a noted left-wing political refugee (son of the famous Professor Z. K. Matthews of Fort Hare), who publicly favoured the MFP. Matete thereupon revived the Marema-Tlou Party and stressed his determination to fight Communism. Lacking any real support or party platform, his party had little prospect of capturing significant electoral support.

Makotoko's active political involvement had begun about 1944. After taking his medical degree in 1953 from the University of Witwatersrand, he worked in South African hospitals prior to his appointment in 1955 as a Basutoland government medical officer. An early member of the BCP, Makotoko objected to Mokhehle's leadership and left the party. As General Secretary and later President of the MFP, he proved something of a pragmatist, broadly motivated by socialism but undogmatic in tactics. He was also able to achieve rapport with Pan-African circles. Under Makotoko's leadership, the MFP seemed to differ little in ideological matters from the BCP. Its demand that greater powers be exercised by the chiefs was possibly designed to capitalise upon the influence which the chiefs exercised over their people and also to win the backing of the Paramount Chief. With respect to

South Africa, the party advocated a strictly neutral position of mutual non-interference and co-operation on matters of common interest. Because of Mokhehle's rebuff to the South African Communists—presumably enjoying Moscow's backing—the MFP became the beneficiary of the dispute. Evidence seemed to indicate that the construction of the new headquarters, and its several heavy duty vehicles, were at least in part paid for with Soviet funds. Until late 1964, it was generally believed that the MFP had fairly even chances with the BCP of winning the elections. But the killing of four BCP members by a group of MFP supporters at Rothe on October 18 also associated the MFP with violence. One of the alleged murderers was a successful candidate who won his election from jail.

Improved Position of the BNP

The real beneficiary of the violence and ideological imputations which marked the electoral campaign was the BNP, led by Chief Leabua Jonathan. In contrast to the somewhat grudging recognition given by the BCP and the MFP that proper relations would be required with South Africa, Chief Jonathan came out forcefully, in October 1964, for the strongest possible economic ties with the Republic. The Republic, he said, would be given first preference to establish industries in Basutoland so that water, the country's 'white gold', might find a market in South Africa. Although opposing South Africa's apartheid policies, which, he said, could not continue indefinitely, he expressed his firm hope that Basutoland might become the first black African state to establish diplomatic relations with the Republic. One of the points he hoped to negotiate immediately was the easing of travel to Basutoland, a subject of grave concern to most Basuto, and the improvement of wages for Basuto working in South Africa. Significantly, the BNP was the only party permitted by the South African government to send its representatives into the country to prepare for the election campaign. Chief Jonathan was at the same time critical of British 'unwillingness' to build up the economy of the country, a development, he said, which would come only with independence. He deplored the growing spate of violence and the murders at Rothe which, he claimed, were provoked by the militancy of the BCP and because of the associations of both the BCP and the MFP with non-Basuto ideologies. He apparently considered that his greatest strength lay in the fact that neither Mokhehle nor Makotoko, both banned in South Africa, would be in a position to negotiate with the Republic.

The BNP's strong denunciation of Communism won it the slightly concealed support of the Roman Catholic Church and the South African government. The Roman Catholic Church, with its 215,000 adherents and its extensive school system, was particularly sensitive not only to the Communist issue but to the implied threat against its schools. Although a pastoral letter from Archbishop 'Mabathoana did little more than point out the duties of rulers and ruled alike, many of his priests actively supported the BNP campaign and apparently established profitable financial contacts for the party in West Germany. While denying that any approach was made to the South African government for financial aid, Chief Jonathan stated that individual South Africans had been requested to contribute so that his party might combat Communism. Notwithstanding an official government admission that none of the contesting parties was Communist-dominated, the BNP successfully capitalised on the Communist issue. With regard to the Paramount Chief, Chief Jonathan denounced the personal attacks made on Motlotlehi's integrity but did call for a clear declaration from Moshoeshoe II deploring the action of certain chiefs supporting the MFP who forbade political rallies in their villages. He also called on the Paramount Chief to repudiate claims that he personally supported the MFP. Aided by a South African helicopter and a fleet of sound trucks, Chief Jonathan proved a forceful campaigner. Six weeks before the election, he drew the largest crowd of the campaign when an estimated 40,000 persons heard him read the party manifesto in Maseru; it was a sure sign that the political balance was shifting.

Elections under the Pre-Independence Constitution

More than two hundred candidates entered the election lists to contend in single-member constituencies for the sixty parliamentary seats. Government information teams covered the entire Territory explaining the identification of symbols with political parties—BNP, a cow; BCP, a knobkerrie; Marema-Tlou, an elephant; MFP, an open hand—and general election procedures. Some 75,000 leaflets and 25,000 posters were distributed. Although postal voting was originally provided for Basuto workers in South Africa, at the request of all four parties the government reversed its decision and required that all wishing to vote must return to Basutoland. Eventually, some 300,000 persons were registered, or approximately 90 per cent of the qualified adult voters. This figure included about 900 whites and a small number of Indians. The campaign was marred by a number of acts of violence and some intimidation. During the first four months of 1965, over 273 persons were arrested for carrying firearms. As a precaution, two RAF Pioneer planes were flown down from Aden to increase the mobility of the security forces, and the Lancashire Regiment in Swaziland was alerted as election day approached.

Early lowlands returns from the two day election, April 29-30, indicated a definite trend towards the BNP, a pattern repeated in the mountain regions. Of the 100,000 voters working in South Africa, only some three or four thousand returned to vote, a factor which made the women's vote decisive. The final election tally gave the BNP, with 108,162 votes (41·63 per cent), 31 of the 60 seats in the National Assembly; the BCP, with 103,050 votes (39·66 per cent), took 25 seats; the MFP captured only 4 seats although it received 42,837 votes (16·49 per cent). The Marema-Tlou failed to gain any seats and received only 5,697 popular votes (2·19 per cent). Independents, in striking contrast to the previous election, received only 79 votes. Four constituencies were won with majorities of less than 100 votes and the smallest was 17. Surprisingly, however, Chief Leabua Jonathan and his party's General Secretary, Charles Molapo, were both defeated, as was MFP leader, Makotoko. According to figures released by the Chief Electoral Officer, some 62·32 per cent of the total registered electorate (including Basuto working in the Republic) of 416,952 exercised the franchise. Excluding those in the Republic, the percentage poll for voters in Basutoland was over 90 per cent.

The BNP victory was generally seen as a triumph for the Roman Catholic Church, whose support was especially evident in the rural areas where the party had done little or no pre-election campaigning. According to Makotoko, his party's defeat could be attributed to the fact that the MFP 'had not reckoned with the earnestness with which the Roman Catholic Church would come out against us; and the degree to which it would influence our own supporters to vote against us'. This charge and similar allegations by the BCP were vigorously denied by Archbishop 'Mabathoana, who termed it a slander similar to that made by the Nazis in Germany.[21]

Predictably, the BNP victory was also hailed as a significant triumph for the Nationalist Party of South Africa, and seemed to bring closer to reality Verwoerd's proposed association of independent states 'linked with the Republic and with the Bantu states of South Africa in a consultative body dealing with mutual political interests'. In a post-election speech, Chief Jonathan reaffirmed his desire to initiate conversations with Verwoerd. He also announced that, so long as he was directing the country's affairs, he would not allow into Maseru 'a single embassy of any Communist country or of countries who are sympathetic to the aims of communism'. Ghana and Tanzania, along with the Arab countries, were placed in this category. The BNP leader also ruled out the possibility of Communist financial assistance and indicated his keen interest in Verwoerd's proposal for a Southern African common market. Many of these sentiments were repeated by Motlotlehi when he addressed the new National Assembly and Senate on May 13.

The day following the elections, Sir Alexander Giles relinquished his post as the last Resident Commissioner of Basutoland and Moshoeshoe II was sworn in as Her Majesty's Representative. On May 7, Basutoland's first Prime Minister, Chief Sekhonyane Maseribane, deputy leader of the BNP, took the oath of allegiance to the Queen. This followed a BNP decision that Maseribane, a descendant of Moshoeshoe, an ardent Roman Catholic and prominent business man, would serve as interim Prime Minister until Chief Jonathan had an opportunity to win a seat in the National Assembly through a by-election.

The narrow margin of BNP victory, while obviating the need for a parliamentary alliance, gave little assurance of political stability. The election probably settled little more than who was going to be Prime Minister and choose the first cabinet. The traditional balance of power reflected in the old constitution, between the legislature, Paramount Chief and Resident Commissioner representing the British government, was essentially maintained under the new constitution—though concealed amid 50,000 words and ninety-two printed pages of a complicated constitution. The combination in Motlotlehi of political power with functions comparable to those of a British monarch provided abundant possibility for conflict. Although reserve powers retained by the British government's Representative might prevent any serious conflict from arising during the pre-independence period, it remained problematical whether this nicely-balanced constitution could survive the withdrawal of British power from the country.

In exercising his prerogative to nominate eleven members of the Senate, Motlotlehi attempted to increase its prestige by including a number of prominent political figures from all parties. The MFP, which gained 16.5 per cent of the popular vote but won only four seats in the Assembly, was compensated with the appointment of five members to the Senate, including Seth Makotoko and J. Mokotso, the party's General Secretary. The two BCP nominees were G. M. Kolisang, General Secretary, and K. Chakela. The defeated Secretary-General of the BNP, Molapo, and Chief Quobela, a BCP dissident, were also appointed. Makotoko was subsequently elected President of the Senate.

Ntsu Mokhehle, the only party leader returned to the National Assembly, quickly asserted that the narrow BNP victory made it impossible for the new government to enjoy the nation's confidence, especially since at least four results were to be challenged. The BCP leader therefore proposed the creation of an interim all-party government under Chief Maseribane and the holding of fresh elections, a proposal immediately rejected by the BNP. The BCP repeated its claim that the administration had purposely left known Congress supporters off the voters' roll, that ballot boxes had been tampered with aboard RAF planes, and that missionaries had improperly influenced their communicants.

The BNP government comprised mostly unknown and inexperienced persons and drew strong fire from the opposition parties as a government 'of shepherds and herdboys'. Apart from Chief Maseribane, who had some official court experience and sat as a nominated member of the last National Council, only Patrick 'Mota (Health), Anthony Manyeli (Education) and Selborne Letsie (Agriculture) had relevant education or experience. Chief Peete Peete (Deputy Prime Minister and Justice), Benedict Leseteli (Finance), Setho M. Letsie (Public Works) and Matete Majara (Local Government) rounded out the cabinet. Of all the cabinet members, only Manyeli possessed a university degree.

By-Elections and Grain Gift: BNP Government Under Attack

According to plan, a by-election was brought on by the resignation of John M. Mothepu, the sitting BNP member for the 'safe' mountain constituency of Mpharane, who stepped down to permit Chief Jonathan to contest the election announced for July 1. As a member of the Assembly he would then become Prime Minister. Although Chief Jonathan won the election as expected (2,873 votes, to 1,055 votes for the BCP candidate Philip Lebona), and was accordingly sworn in as Prime Minister four days later, his pre-election appeal on June 9 to Verwoerd for famine relief brought considerable criticism. In Pretoria, the British Embassy reported that it had not received any urgent appeal for help and it was assumed that conditions were much as usual. More-over, the gift, totalling some 100,000 bags of grain worth over £150,000, was made over personally to Chief Jonathan as the leader of the BNP by the South African government. Khaketla, deputy leader of the MFP, denounced the arrangement as 'a cheap political trick intended to buy support for Chief Jonathan and his National Party', and Congress saw it as proof of a 'sell-out' to South Africa. Leaflets distributed with the grain proclaiming 'Leabua is feeding the people' did not make the BNP disclaimer any more credible.

Continued controversy about the motives behind the grain gift led to an uproar in the National Assembly, which opened its second session on July 12. When the Prime Minister praised South Africa's action as a 'generous gesture' and then announced that he was donating the grain gift to the government for completion of distribution, the sharpness of the opposition's attack resulted in scuffles and police intervention. Support for the belief that the gift was politically moti-vated came from D. J. Swart, an auctioneer and brother of the Republic's State President, who claimed that the gift was a political gesture and totally unnecessary. The fact that only 6,854 of the 100,000 bags of grain had even been moved into the Territory, and that only 5 per cent of this had been distributed, made Jonathan's plea that the Basuto were 'on the verge of great starvation' at least suspect. But if Chief Jonathan's motives were clouded, it was quite clear to the South African press that the grain was intended to guarantee the future of a friendly politician in a neighbouring black state.

Although South Africa had indeed acted to win Basuto friendship, it was obvious that its acts of friendship were selective. The funda-mental question of transit rights was brusquely dealt with in late May when ten Basuto students touring independent African states under BCP patronage were refused permission to continue their journey from Johannesburg. Although Chief Jonathan also protested against this action as prejudicial to the establishment of friendly relations and contrary to Basutoland's national rights, neither his protests nor the polite requests of the British government impressed the South African government. This was followed by the refusal of transit rights to several American academics (including the author, despite official

Basutoland entrance permission and representations by the US Department of State). Of special significance was the refusal in October to permit Makotoko, President of the Senate, to attend the OAU conference in Accra. Earlier, the refusal of service to the interim Prime Minister, Chief Maseribane, at a leading Bloemfontein bank, underscored the basic problem of relations with South Africa.

Straining under its narrow electoral victory and under strong attack on the grain gift, the government's position was rendered more precarious when the Chief Justice ruled in favour of two petitions brought against BNP members from the Masemouse and Qaqatu constituencies. With these seats declared vacant, the government majority was reduced to nil. Meanwhile, rather than risk further danger, the Prime Minister secured, on July 28, the adjournment of the Assembly *sine die*, a move designed to ensure government survival until at least the September by-elections (set for September 9 and 23) which the BNP confidently expected to win. The adjournment was denounced by Khaketla as a retrogressive move and the BCP brought an unsuccessful petition calling upon Motlotlehi to protect the constitution in the absence of a parliamentary majority.

The government's position had already been saved, however, by the action of a MFP member, Chief Mapheleba, who announced his support for Chief Jonathan. His action pointed up a new cleavage opening within MFP ranks under the impact of the BNP victory. Increasingly under pressure to support either the BNP or BCP, the traditionalist-modernist alliance showed signs of dissolution. Although Khaketla, as Deputy Leader, had re-emphasised in early August that the MFP, having been spurned by the BNP immediately after the election, could not enter a coalition, the national executive did not unanimously support this opinion. A statement by the party's General Secretary, Senator J. T. Mokotso, urging co-operation between the MFP and the BNP, led to his expulsion on September 4 and his immediate appointment as Assistant Minister of Interior and Exterior Affairs. Matters were further complicated when Makotoko returned from a trip abroad and urged a common front with the BCP. This suggestion, which seemed to contradict the statement of a few weeks earlier that the BCP was only 'a short cut to Communism', also met with stiff resistance. Another telling blow to MFP fortunes was delivered in early October when twenty of the Senate's twenty-one principal chiefs pledged their support of the government. Inasmuch as eighteen of the principal chiefs had openly favoured the MFP before the election, their support of the government assured it a working majority in both houses.

Meanwhile, the BCP pressed its opposition to the new government both within and outside the Assembly. In May, Mokhehle proposed a motion of no confidence but it lost by a 32-23 vote. Pointing out that in the April elections more people voted against the BNP than for it, the BCP announced its opposition to independence in 1966 unless preceded by a general election or a referendum. From time to time over the next few months there were protest marches through the streets of Maseru and these gave rise to fears of an open clash liable to upset independence plans. At the same time, South Africa placed severe restrictions upon the organising activities of the BCP in the Republic and several party leaders, long resident in South Africa, were expelled.

The gradual worsening of drought conditions towards the end of the year caused the government additional worry. Reports of stock losses were staggering and, in the Qachas Nek district alone, it was estimated that more than 12,000 animals had died as a result of snow and drought. Imports from South Africa, paid for with remittances sent home by relatives in the Republic, increased rapidly as the effects of the worst drought in thirty years became critical. An unprecedented rush of men from the mountain areas to join the South African mines underscored the seriousness of the problem.

Amid these generally depressing events, the discovery in September of a 527-carat diamond in the Letseng-le-Terai diggings, which sold for £58,000, produced high hopes of unexploited diamond potential. This sum represented more than the total worth of all diamonds produced the previous year by some 1,200 diggers. Eugene Serafim, a noted diamond authority, suggested that the government should encourage thirty times the number of diggers to take up shovels and seek diamonds in the Leribe, Butha Buthe and Mafeteng areas. The type of diamonds, he said, which were found in Basutoland, were generally of a poor quality and eminently suited to 'a shovel and muscle' approach. But even a major concentration on diamonds, as with other potential developments, seemed to depend on greater powers in the government's hands.

Negotiations on the Reserved Powers

Britain's reserved powers and the inability of Basutoland to negotiate directly with South Africa thus became vital issues for the new government, which insisted that even the delivery of milk to Maseru involved foreign relations. Flying to London in late August, Chief Jonathan insisted that additional powers were necessary to get on with the job of preparing for an orderly transition of power in 1966. A meeting in London with the South African Ambassador, Dr Carel de Wet, and the strict silence maintained by South African authorities on the visit seemed to indicate a rift with the Colonial Office. This difference of opinion was much in evidence after the Prime Minister's return to Basutoland. Whereas Chief Jonathan insisted that the way had been cleared for him to negotiate directly with South Africa on such vital issues as transit rights, diplomatic representation, economic matters, and the ten stranded Basuto students, the Colonial Office continued to claim full responsibility in matters of external relations. Charges of British prevarication were heightened with the news that London had attempted to impose her own appointee as principal legal adviser to the Basutoland government. But faced with the adamant resistance of the Prime Minister and his cabinet, the British government finally appointed to the position Professor Denis V. Cowen, long associated with the country's constitutional development and the nominee of Chief Jonathan.

An announcement by the British Embassy in Pretoria that negotiations had already been initiated with the South African government on important aspects of relations between the two countries, and that Basutoland government association with these negotiations would be acceptable, did not receive an enthusiastic response in Pretoria. South Africa thus reinforced Chief Jonathan's belief that any talks should be bilateral, precluding a British presence. British reluctance to withdraw, it was assumed, was motivated by the sting of Chief Jonathan's earlier approach to Verwoerd on the grain gift, a step which had presented Britain in a bad light. Of even greater importance, however, was the likelihood that BCP charges, accusing Britain of driving the Protectorate into the arms of South Africa, might be taken up by the Afro-Asian members of the Commonwealth. Already embarrassed by the escalating Rhodesian problem, Britain felt little inclination to see negotiations begin prior to formal independence. Indications that the South African government had given a 'co-operative' reply to cautious British feelers and indicated its willingness to deal directly with the Basutoland government served to strengthen Chief Jonathan in his bid for control of the reserved powers and for greater authority over matters of finance and the civil service. The latter question especially

nettled the government, since the bulk of the civil service supported
the opposition and a number of confidential documents and letters had
appeared in BCP newsletters.

Accompanied by the Minister of Justice, Chief Peete Peete, and
Professor Cowen, the Prime Minister again flew to London and began
conversations with the Colonial Office on November 22. During these
talks, the Prime Minister confirmed that his government would ask
for independence immediately after April 29, 1966, and Eirene White,
Parliamentary Under-Secretary of State for the Colonies, accepted
his assurance that the stipulated conditions for independence were
likely to be fulfilled. This guarded phraseology seemed to mean that
independence would be granted provided chaos did not occur in the
meantime. The Basutoland delegation obtained most of what it
wanted. Provided that the British government be kept informed,
Basutoland was given permission to open direct negotiations with
South Africa on transit rights and the right of entry into and exit from
the country, extradition, labour and employment, cultural matters,
the Ox-bow project, diplomatic representation after independence, and
commercial matters—all with the proviso that no binding agreements
could be concluded without British consent. Britain also agreed to
grant immediate authority for Basutoland to apply for membership
of specialised agencies of the United Nations, of regional African
organisations, and to make cultural or technical agreements arising
from such membership.

A major exception, however, debarred the Basutoland government
from opening negotiations on revision of the customs union agreement, since the question of redistribution of customs revenue was in
an advanced stage of negotiation. As events soon proved, these negotiations drastically altered the apportionment of the 1.31097 per cent
of South African customs revenues among the Territories. For Basutoland, the agreement meant a loss of £450,000, thereby bringing the
country's total deficit to about £2,350,000, which the British government had to make good. Although there was some justice in the
redistribution, South Africa's keen desire to see a reapportionment of
shares only slightly concealed the Republic's desire to make Basutoland more vulnerable to pressure. The Basutoland delegation unsuccessfully protested that the new share was objectionable, economically and legally.

Preparations for South African Negotiations: The Refugee Problem

Chief Jonathan announced his intention to seek discussions with Verwoerd on the basis of equality early in 1966. This meeting, said the Prime Minister, would be strictly a 'head-of-state to head-of-state talk' and he emphasised that he would 'not accept an inferior position', since he was 'not a Mantizima'. He also told the welcoming crowd of some 3,000 that he would insist on the right of all Basuto to freely return to their own country, a direct reference to the question of the stranded students. His air of toughness was balanced with a strong statement on refugee activity, a matter of prime importance to South Africa. While prepared to give asylum to genuine political refugees as opposed to criminal fugitives, he insisted that his government would not permit refugees to interfere in the internal politics of the country or act in a subversive manner against any other government.

The question of political refugees, which attracted considerable attention in early 1963 in conjunction with statements of P. K. Leballo, had occasioned increased concern thereafter. The problem had become an election issue, as various refugees were arrested on charges of conspiracy. In May, two Johannesburg Africans were charged with illegal possession of arms and various PAC presidential council members were charged with conspiracy to commit acts of violence against South Africa. In July, a reported assassination plot against Chief Jonathan by outsiders closely associated with suspected underground activities heightened alarm. Also in July, six PAC refugees were sentenced to a total of eleven years when found guilty of a conspiracy to abduct white children for ransom and to commit sabotage and robbery within the Republic. Although their conviction was set aside by the Chief Justice, who asserted that nothing other than training in guerilla warfare had been proved, police authorities increased their surveillance of approximately 130 refugees.

In early December the Basutoland government spelled out the implications of Chief Jonathan's declaration with a circular letter to all political refugees in the country. Signed by the Permanent Secretary for the Ministry of Internal and External Affairs, the circular stated that, while the government was sympathetic towards their plight, they would not be permitted to use their status as 'an umbrella for criminal activity within the country, or for active participation in local politics, or for subversive action against other governments'.

Refugees were required to conform with these regulations and report to the police by February 1, or face deportation 'with consequences which you can best assess'. In January, to guarantee complete control over the refugees, they were fingerprinted and photographed. Behind closed doors, security police required refugees to give full personal details under oath about their political activities in South Africa. Whether or not there was any guarantee that this information would not be transmitted to South Africa, it was bound to please that government and was roundly applauded in the South African press. About the same time, the Republic announced that, as of February 1, the police would take over full border control from immigration authorities, ostensibly to check gun-running, an activity considered a threat to both governments.

BNP *Government Gains and Consolidation*

As a result of Basutoland's greater control over finance, prospects of foreign aid increased. Hopes of improving the country's highways, as a step towards converting from subsistence to cash agriculture, were given a boost with the announcement in February 1966 that the International Development Association, an affiliate of the World Bank, had approved a credit equal to £1,435,000. This credit is to be used to improve a seventy-six mile section of the main north-south road and a seventeen mile feeder road. The agricultural area likely to be affected by the road is estimated at about 450,000 acres, somewhat less than half Basutoland's arable acreage. Conversations with representatives of the Bank of England and Germany's Deutsche Bundesbank, covering prospects for a separate currency, a central banking system, credit facilities and membership in the International Monetary Fund, were also welcomed. The Japanese Consul-General in South Africa announced that he had recommended to his government the favourable investigation possibility of future trade with Basutoland. In addition, the United Nations General Assembly adopted a recommendation of the Fourth Committee on December 16, 1965, that a special fund for the development of the Territories, on the basis of voluntary contributions, be set up under the direction of the Secretary-General. Although Britain objected to several references in the resolution, it did not vote against the resolution since all aid was said to be welcome.

Despite various setbacks, including the breakaway in September of a splinter group called the Lesotho Unity Party—which especially objected to the appointment of a large number of chiefs to senior posts—and a lower percentage poll than anticipated in the September by-elections, the seven months following the election seemed to show up the leadership of Chief Jonathan to greater advantage than had been expected. Whereas many had assumed that the BNP government would not see the New Year, the fiasco of the grain gift and negotiations with London gave the Prime Minister greater knowledge of practical politics and made him a positive force in his own party. Reversing an earlier position that he could not bring himself to sit down with 'a dictator such as Nkrumah', Jonathan cordially accepted an invitation to attend the OAU October conference in Accra as the 'special guest' of the President. Since the Prime Minister was already scheduled to visit London, however, he requested that Albert Mohale and Senator E. D. Letele be received in his place. Acceptance of the invitation held out the possibility not only of improving his government's image abroad, but of undermining the BCP, which had long enjoyed the patronage of Ghana. Although the BCP was successful in gaining continued recognition, the fact that the BNP delegation received every consideration was something of a setback for the opposition. The Prime Minister's announcement that he would seek official membership for Basutoland in the OAU was denounced by the BCP as an attempt to gain a 'listening post' in that body for Verwoerd. But despite these attacks, Chief Jonathan's international position was enhanced.

While BNP successes could at least in part be attributed to the skill of the party leader, the opposition saw a better explanation for government survival in assistance which it allegedly received from South Africa. It was increasingly charged that Chief Jonathan was becoming a dictator with South African support and was bent on stifling dissent under the pretext of guaranteeing public peace. Although it had long been charged that Chief Jonathan would lead the country into a Bantustan status, the intensity of this conviction became more evident.

A number of events seemed to bear out the feeling that the government was seeking to consolidate its position at any cost. Announcement in January that students wishing to study abroad would henceforth be 'screened' by a special committee prior to the issuance of passports appeared as a strong restriction on the opposition. A continued civil service shakeup caused much resentment and led at least one high ranking civil servant to return his MBE to the British government's Representative. Following the delegation of more powers to the Basutoland government, the Prime Minister assumed responsibility for External Affairs, Defence and Civil Service; in addition, the portfolios of Information and Broadcasting, Economic Planning and Development, the Department of Labour and the Rand Agencies, the Bureau of Statistics, tourism, commerce, licensing industrial development and water resources (including the Ox-bow project) all fell under his office.

The strengthening of the Prime Minister's office, accompanied by severe restrictions on refugees, was carried further with the suspension of all nine District Councils and their replacement by forty-nine persons appointed to exercise local government powers. Significantly, these appointments conferred power upon all the principal and ward chiefs. Although there had indeed been ample room for criticising the District Councils, it was generally assumed that the government had acted to avoid embarrassment by District Councils which for the most part were dominated by opposition parties.

The arrival on February 21 of a British Gloucestershire Company from Swaziland seemed designed to reinforce internal security, despite official announcement that the visit was purely a routine one. The opening of the fourth meeting of the first session of the National Assembly was marked by the presence of armed guards inside the Assembly chamber and brought strong denunciation from the opposition. While the government officially denied that there was any unrest in the country, prominent BNP leaders, such as Chief Leshoboro Majara and Senator Molapo, urged that the government prepare itself 'for any eventuality'. But despite such signs of alarm, a White Paper was issued in early March setting October 4, 1966, as the provisional date for independence—an indication that Whitehall either believed Chief Jonathan's government strong enough to carry Basutoland through to independence or was prepared to make it equal to the task.

6

THE ECONOMY OF LESOTHO
by Dr H. George Henry

THE FORMER High Commission Territories may be described as traditional societies[1] in the sense that the volume and quality of economic activity are greatly influenced by such institutions as chieftainship and the land-tenure system. They are traditional also in that the capital and technology used by the great mass of the labour force, representing up to nine-tenths of the total, are of a primitive type. In each, the infrastructure which is a prerequisite for economic development—roads, railways, telegraph, telephone, radio, water supply, electricity or other source of power—is strikingly inadequate.* The skeletal banking and other financial institutions are concerned primarily with siphoning off savings for outside investment. Africans' opportunities for obtaining high grade skills, and the possibilities for employing such skills by the very few who do acquire them, are severely limited by institutional factors, customs, laws, traditions, politics and social sanctions.

Both the natural and the human resources of the former Territories are underdeveloped, and any meaningful economic programme for them must not only develop natural resources but also provide industrial skills and economic opportunities for the Africans. The proportion of skilled to unskilled members of the labour force must be progressively increased from the current low figure of under five per cent of the total force until it approaches the levels obtaining in developed countries. The human aspect is emphasised by Myint: 'The problem of the so-called underdeveloped countries consists not merely in the "underdevelopment" of their resources in the usual sense, but also in the economic "backwardness" of their peoples. Where it

* Swaziland is moving ahead of the other two countries in its provision of the infrastructure, chiefly because of its better endowment with natural resources, including iron and coal, and the establishment of closer operational relationships with the government and the financial interests of South Africa.

exists, the underdevelopment of natural resources and the backwardness of people mutually aggravate each other in a vicious circle.'[2]

Agriculture

Out of a total area of 11,716 square miles, between two-thirds and three-quarters of Lesotho is mountainous country.[3] The total cultivated area is estimated at roughly 950,000 acres,[4] excluding communal grazing lands in the villages and in the highlands and the cattlepost country of the mountain areas. Total arable acreage is estimated at 1·2 million acres or approximately one-sixth of the area of the country. There are few trees and soil erosion is widespread. Limited efforts to control erosion were introduced by the British administration after 1936, and were slightly intensified after the second world war, but these fall short of what is required. Grass strips planted by government agencies to control erosion 'have been narrowed by the plough so that they are now ineffective in controlling surface wash ... diversion furrows have not been kept open and thus have settled and become functionless, while many of the trees established have not been cared for nor ... protected against the depredations of livestock'.[5] This apparently irrational behaviour is partly the result of non-economic factors, including attitudes and values. A colonial government which decides what is best for the people without fully permitting them to share in the decision-making process frequently fails to get a high level of co-operation, and this kind of approach sometimes even breeds malicious opposition.

Another handicap is the land-tenure system, which represses the instinct of self-interest. If the seasonal or temporary land rights now enjoyed by the Basuto farmers were converted into land rights of a more permanent nature, a much more 'economising' attitude would be fostered. It would then be possible for the Basuto to recognise that better husbandry, greater care and attention bestowed on animals, trees and buffer strips bring increased rewards. Under the existing land-tenure system, some Basuto have snatched what short-term advantage there is in such activities as allowing their animals to destroy trees. The system lacks incentives and fosters traditional subsistence farming. Now that the Basuto enjoy independence, they can reorganise the land-tenure system themselves so that it encourages the most efficient use of the land.

The average annual rainfall of 29·26 inches[6] on the lowlands, the main crop-producing areas, is considered sufficient for agricultural production, but, unless this is favourably distributed over the planting and growing season, the crops suffer. Thus periods of above average rainfall may result in very poor crop production, while periods of less than average rainfall may produce good yields (see Table I). From September 1950 to December 1951, a rainfall nearly 33·3 per cent above average had a damaging effect on crops, to which the swollen imports of maize, the staple foodstuff, bear witness. On the other hand, a slightly less than average rainfall, properly distributed, from September 1952 to December 1953, resulted in good crop production. Rainfall in the mountain areas is greater and believed to be in the vicinity of 40–60 inches per annum.

Lesotho's agricultural capacity is also affected by occasional destructive hailstorms in summer, and occasional-to-frequent droughts. But

TABLE I
RELATIONSHIP BETWEEN RAINFALL AND CROP PRODUCTION

Period	Total Rainfall (inches)	Annual Average for over 3 decades (inches)	Deviation	Crop Production	Net Maize Imports (£000)
Sept 1950–Dec 1951	38·23	28·87	+9·36	Poor	£257
Sept 1951–Dec 1952	27·85	28·78	−0·83	Poor	£273
Sept 1952–Dec 1953	28·00	28·76	−0·76	Very Good	£73
Sept 1953–Dec 1954	25·74	28·68	−2·94	Good	£99
Sept 1954–Dec 1955	34·80	28·84	+5·96	Very Poor	£395
Sept 1955–Dec 1956	33·28	28·95	+4·33	Poor	£252
Sept 1956–Dec 1957	39·67	29·92	+9·75	Good	£114

Source: Compiled from Colonial and Department of Agriculture Annual Reports.

this perversity of climatic conditions could largely be offset by development of water resources. The country possesses the most important
watershed in Southern Africa, and there is an obvious need for harness-
ing the water for irrigation and other purposes. Today, only primitive
forms of irrigation exist, far from adequate even for the needs of
agriculture and livestock raising. Plans for implementing the recommendations of the Morse Report of 1959 for developing water
resources are still in an embryonic stage, because an accommodating
and lenient British colonial policy failed to resist political and ideological pressure coming from South Africa.[7]

Minerals

The nature, quantity and value of the mineral resources of Lesotho
are a source of controversy. The Basuto believe that there are deposits
of diamonds, gold, coal and iron—whether in commercial quantities
or not is another matter. After two geological reconnaissance surveys,
the British administration reported that the country was unlikely to
have any valuable mineral deposits other than diamonds.[8] Since the
reconnaissance surveys were neither comprehensive nor conducted in
sufficient detail, they did not provide conclusive answers; but unfortunately some British officials—or so the Basuto think—circulated the
notion that no valuable minerals were to be found in the Territory.
In the light of recent developments, this has been interpreted by the
Basuto to mean that the British do not want to exploit the mineral
resources, but prefer to have the Basuto largely dependent on the sale of
their labour to the farms and mines of the Republic. The most recent
report on the mineral potential seems to support the position of the
Basuto, specifically as regards the existence of diamond-producing ore.

In 1955, in keeping with traditional colonial policy, the monopoly
right of prospecting and mining for diamonds in Basutoland was given
to a citizen of South Africa, Colonel Jack Scott. This monopoly right
ended after five years. In 1961, the right to prospect for and mine
diamonds in the Letseng-le-Terai area was reserved exclusively for the
Basuto, but participation of non-Basuto in the mining industry is not
ruled out. They can, as partners of a Mosuto, contribute capital, entrepreneurship and technology, but the regulation makes it clear that the
right to use the land for mining purposes must be vested in a Mosuto.
According to available records, mining by the Basuto in this area has
turned out to be the most profitable venture so far. In less than two

years, the Basuto, using extremely primitive tools and methods of recovery, have been able to produce diamonds valued at 127 per cent more than were mined in a five year period by Jack Scott who 'procured the services of the technical personnel of the Anglo-American Corporation' and used superior technology. But the great disparity in the quantity and value of the diamonds raises doubts as to the accuracy of the figures taken from the official report and shown in Table II. It is unlikely that the major divergence in the value of the diamonds mined during the two different operations can be fully accounted for by differences in prices or quality. It is possible that more careful records were made of the Basuto mining than of the Scott mining.

TABLE II
RECORDED ESTIMATES OF PRODUCTION OF THE
TWO MAIN DIAMOND MINING SCHEMES, 1955–1963

	Quantity Produced (carats)	Quantity Sold (carats)	Estimated Value
Jack Scott's Operations* (1955–59)	18,930	£17,559	£140,373
Basuto Operations, Letseng-le-Terai, Sept 1961–June 1963	9,489	9,489	£179,339

Source: Confidential Report of the Director of the Geological Survey and Mines Department of Swaziland, based on his visit to Basutoland, February 5–8, 1962.

The British administration took no steps to ensure efficient exploitation of the diamond industry, maintenance of reasonable living and working conditions in the mining area, or the introduction of controls against diamond smuggling. Although the product of this enterprise should have been used to develop capital or to contribute towards improving the skills of the Basuto, the government allowed it to be used mainly for conspicuous consumption.

The most recent official report[9] confirms the Basuto belief in the diamond-bearing potential of Lesotho, for it states that the country

---

* No records were available of the output or value of the mining operations of Jack Scott for the period 1959–63.

is a kimberlite province. Kimberlite is the ore that must be processed to produce diamonds. Up to April 1960, some 15 major kimberlite pipes and 109 kimberlite fissures had been located. Where exploration has been most extensive, as in the Scott block, economically profitable diamond pipes have been discovered, and detailed exploration of the rest of the country is warranted. The report also confirms the presence of minor quantities of gold in the Morija area and adds that the possibility of the discovery of gold in commercial quantities should be explored. Finally, the report refers to the discovery in the area between Leribe and Butha Buthe 'of a substance which had a certain amount of phosphate in it'.

Although the diamond mining industry is new and small-scale, it is providing much-needed incomes, employment and government revenue. But government action is needed to reform the inefficiency and wastefulness of the process in the most profitable mining area, the lack of security measures and the low level of capital and technology. The policy of the colonial administration was to leave the industry to a large extent under the control of traditional institutions, which were hopelessly inadequate and unsuited for dealing with the problems connected with diamond mining. For example, the chieftainship did not have the decision-making authority necessary to invite in external capital and technology; the land-tenure system lacked the incentives and security necessary to attract long-term investment. Whereas the British followed a laissez-faire policy or deliberately supported non-progressive traditional institutions, an enlightened Basuto government can initiate positive action in all areas of development.

Water

Given the present state of knowledge on the natural resources of Lesotho, its water supply is its most abundant and most valuable resource. The whole of the upper catchment of the country abounds in streams and springs, most of which are normally perennial. The Orange river, one of the largest in Southern Africa, has its source high in the mountains of Lesotho. The tested physical and chemical purity of the water makes it especially suitable for domestic and industrial purposes. However, in spite of the abundance of water resources, the country suffers from irregular to fairly frequent droughts and, consequently, from periodic food shortages; supplies have then to be imported from South Africa.[10] There is practically no irrigation.

There are records of some fifty-five boreholes, most of which are situated on the smaller government stations.[11]

Three professional reports on the country's water resources have been made since 1951. The first two put forward very similar proposals for the construction of dams and for power development. The third (the Shand Report) is much more ambitious in scope and emphasises development. It makes 'proposals for diverting the flow of the upper tributaries [of the Orange river] westward by tunnels into the steep river valleys ... thus making use of the very great fall available for generating hydro-electric power and making it possible [in the case of highest development] to deliver pure water into the Orange Free State'.[12] Three schemes were suggested by the Shand Report: (1) the Ox-bow scheme, (2) the Kau river scheme and (3) the Semena river scheme. The Ox-bow scheme, which has been considered in greater detail than the others, could be developed in five stages to supply water and electricity to Lesotho and the Orange Free State: a three-stage completion would provide sufficient water and electricity to satisfy the needs of Lesotho for some time. The additional two stages of construction would be necessary if water and electricity are to be exported to the Orange Free State as well. If the five stages of the Ox-bow scheme are completed, the Shand Report estimates that 'over 350 million kilowatt-hours of energy could be generated per annum, and a steady flow of pure water of 100 million gallons per day delivered at rates highly competitive with those ruling in the areas of supply at the present moment.

In none of the three reports was any doubt cast on the feasibility or viability of any of the development schemes. The Shand Report was quite explicit on this question: 'The essence of the conclusion reached is that it is economically feasible to develop regional schemes in the uplands of Basutoland for the supply of water and power both to western Basutoland and the Orange Free State.' The complete five-stage Ox-bow scheme is estimated to cost about £15 million[13] and would benefit not only Lesotho but also the Orange Free State, where already there is a strong demand for water and power from the scheme. If further industrial development is to take place there, the demand will increase. With ever-growing pressure on the resources of the Vaal, Lesotho water could become indispensable to South Africa's economic existence. The current Orange river scheme (see below, p. 105), impressive as it looks in blueprint form, cannot solve the mounting water problem facing the northern provinces.[14]

The economic arguments for the Ox-bow scheme may be summarised as follows: (1) great potential demand for water and electricity exists in the country and even more so in the external market of the Orange Free State; (2) Lesotho has the potential capacity for meeting the combined demands of the domestic and external markets; (3) professional investigation affirms that water and electricity produced by the Ox-bow scheme could be supplied at highly competitive rates; (4) the cost of undertaking the scheme is relatively low; (5) the scheme, which was given priority by the Morse Report, is financially self-liquidating; (6) agricultural and industrial development of Lesotho is dependent on, and impossible without, adequate supplies of water and electricity, which the scheme could provide cheaply; (7) the development of the water resources of Lesotho would be of mutual economic advantage to Lesotho and the Republic of South Africa. In view of the strong economic case for developing the country's water resources, earlier hesitancy can be explained only in political and diplomatic terms.

The Ox-bow scheme, strongly recommended in the Morse Report of 1959, was delayed chiefly because of the colonial status of Basutoland, which deprived the Basuto of decision-making power, its poor and ambivalent diplomatic representation and the hostile political attitude of South Africa. The colonial administration's inaction over the scheme has been attributed to Britain's realisation that the Republic might not like to be dependent on a small country for the supply of vital industrial resources.[15] Indeed, South Africa has blueprinted and already taken the first steps towards carrying out the Orange river project in order to reduce its dependence on a Lesotho scheme. But the South African scheme will take some twenty-five years to complete and will cost over £450 million.[16] Meanwhile, the three-stage version of the Lesotho project, estimated to cost only £5,370,000, was pigeonholed. It is noteworthy that the international character of the Orange river is readily invoked to remind the Basuto that consultation and agreement with South Africa are inviolable prerequisites for implementation of Lesotho's Ox-bow scheme, and this is often suggested as the reason for its indefinite postponement. But, in contrast, the Republic has initiated its Orange river development without a protest on behalf of the Basuto.

The development of the country's water resources is a prerequisite for economic progress: no other known asset has the necessary economic potential. Water and electricity are indispensable for industrialisation and, among the many important secondary benefits, hillsides could be irrigated, opening up large tracts* of arable ground which would otherwise be condemned to dry farming methods.[17] Other important secondary effects would include the use of the remarkable climate and scenery of the country in the development of a tourist industry and the introduction of fish farming.

Human Resources

The productivity of the human resources of any country depends on the level of nutrition, the standard of literacy and the quality of its industrial skills, as well as incentives and opportunity. By these standards, Lesotho is very backward, even taking into account its relatively high rate of 60 per cent literacy. For this literacy is primarily of the elementary or trade school level and is not of the quality that can make any appreciable contribution to economic development. The standard of 90 per cent of the literates is not high enough to produce efficient teachers of elementary or secondary schools, farmers, accountants, typists, stenographers, middle-rank civil servants, technical assistants or any of the other middle-level skills so indispensable to efficient production and industrialisation, let alone high-grade skills.

Of a population of about 975,000, 90 per cent or more of the labour force is engaged in subsistence agriculture. At any given time, over 100,000 of the able-bodied men are engaged in unskilled jobs, mainly in the mines and on the farms of South Africa. The cash wages of these migrant workers, far higher in the mines than on the farms, reach a maximum of sixpence per hour. In some mines, the social costs involved in supplying the Republic with labour far outweigh the benefits received. The incomes earned by migrant workers do little other than contribute to the maintenance of subsistence standards of living in Lesotho and depress the wages of African workers in South Africa. A nutrition survey conducted by the World Health Organisation found that 85 per cent of Basuto families consume unbalanced diets, and that more than 75 per cent suffer from diseases due to malnutrition.[18] The very low level of the administered wages paid to the migrant workers contributes to the maintenence of infra-subsistence agriculture and perpetuates migrant labour and human backwardness. However, unless the government launches a comprehensive develop-

* The *Morse Report* expresses the less optimistic view that 'the areas which are irrigable in Basutoland are not likely to be large'.

ment programme, up to 60 per cent of Lesotho's able-bodied males have no alternative to work in South Africa at non-competitive rates.

Less than one-quarter of one per cent of the population is provided with commercial and industrial skills and about one-half of one per cent has professional skills in the fields traditionally open to Africans under British colonial rule: teaching, medicine and nursing, law and lower-echelon jobs in the civil service. The first Basuto civil engineer entered the Public Works Department in 1963.

Basuto education has been provided mainly by missionaries since the first group, the Paris Evangelical Missionary Society, was invited into the Territory by Moshoeshoe I. The Roman Catholics (who assumed ascendancy), the Anglicans and the African Methodists have also made important contributions to Basuto education; unfortunately, their denominational outlooks and long-standing rivalries tended to discourage intelligent leadership.

The key to change in developing the human resources lies in the decision-making institutions.[19] Now that the most important of these have been handed over to the Basuto, they have the opportunity and the authority to broaden the goals of the economy, to create new and relevant value systems, to work out new relationships that will offer free scope for reducing human backwardness and for exploring and exploiting the natural resources of the country.

High among their priorities must be a reappraisal of the position held under the colonial administration by the chieftainship. All land in Lesotho is allocated by the chieftainship—a bureaucracy of headmen, sub-chiefs and chiefs, at the apex of which is the Paramount Chief, now King of the Basuto nation—and the land-tenure system has been its principal source of strength. The over-riding principle which governs the distribution and use of land is that it is owned collectively by the nation, not by individuals. This means, technically speaking, that it is not the ownership of the land but the right to use it that is allocated. In theory, each household should have three good units of land of approximately equal size for growing wheat, maize and sorghum (kaffir corn).[20] These three units are exclusive of a garden plot near the home, where the grantee may plant any crop he pleases.

The granting of land rights is conditional on the individual's giving allegiance and showing subjection to his chief. A man may forfeit his land through failure to cultivate it or because of disloyalty to his chief, an offence described in No 9 of the Laws of Lerotholi, 1922, as 'turning the door to the house against his chief, and looking up to another chief'.[21] There have been many complaints that 'chiefs do, on occasion, abuse their power of recovery of land from individuals'.[22] The grantee, in turn, becomes liable for payments in cash and in kind and for rendering labour services to the chief.[23] These labour services were commuted only in 1950. Moreover, chiefs 'are entitled to larger and more numerous lands than commoners'.[24]

Two kinds of rights of use of land are allocated: semi-permanent rights and temporary or seasonal rights. Semi-permanent rights are granted to schools and initiation lodges, the British administration, churches, traders, and for housing, gardens and playgrounds, and, since 1961, to the Basuto for diamond mining. Temporary or seasonal rights are given to the Basuto only for the express purpose of growing the traditional crops. An individual finds that, after he has harvested his crops, his individual rights to the land are superseded by the communal rights of all the stockholders of that community. In other words, the rights of use of agricultural land do not persist throughout the year, although they normally carry over from one year to the other.

The main principle guiding distribution of land rights is that every Basuto family is entitled to a share of land rights, based on the assumption that every household must produce its income, wholly or in part, directly from the land. Given this assumption and the discouraging effects of the system on capital improvements and capital accumulation, mere subsistence agriculture is a natural consequence. Because of custom, tradition and social sanctions associated with the land-tenure system, the use of any of the two or three units of land allotted to an individual for production of alternative crops, cash crops or even for setting up a dairying industry, is forbidden. The Basuto are expected to plant only the traditional crops; as these are one-season crops, they fit neatly into the concept of communal ownership of land. After the grantee has harvested his crop, his right goes into abeyance and is over-ridden by the community's right to turn its stock to feed on the remains of the harvest. Thus the planting of certain cash crops would interfere with communal rights. For example, potatoes would be planted in the late winter–early spring season, the period when the cattle, most of them down from the mountain cattleposts to avoid the bitterness of winter in the higher altitudes, would customarily be turned loose to feed on the remains of the maize or sorghum harvests. Livestock owners would therefore object to such a cash crop. Custom and tradition forbid the use of fences because they violate communal rights and interfere with footpaths and shortcuts as the peasants move between fields and villages. Fences could impose tremendous physical burdens on peasants, who must cover, mainly on foot, many miles per day between scattered fields and villages, but they would free 66,000 herdboys, whose occupation deprives them of education and training in industrial skills. Moreover, fencing could contribute to better pasture management and control of arable lands.

The land-tenure system has developed as a result of the impact of western institutions on the traditional system. In addition to its traditional functions, it is also a reaction to the plundering and expropriation of land by Europeans in the imperial era. It embodies the reaction of the traditional society to the racial attitudes and political principles of the Europeans, especially of the South Africans with whom they came in contact. It enshrines the dignity and proud spirit of the Basuto, who have never been subdued by the Europeans; it is a symbol of their independence and nationhood. All this is to be understood in the cold candour of Moshoeshoe's announcement that 'there is no place belonging to the whites in my land'.[25]

The British administration, utilising the economy of indirect rule, gave support to these growth-inhibiting institutions. Thus, their overriding power and authority contributed to the backwardness and underdevelopment of Basuto agriculture. Independence requires the final reconciliation of traditional authority with modern currents of political and economic life. Left to themselves, the Basuto will have to remodel the role of chieftainship so as to eliminate its paralysing effect on the administration and use of the land.

PART II

FROM BECHUANALAND
TO BOTSWANA

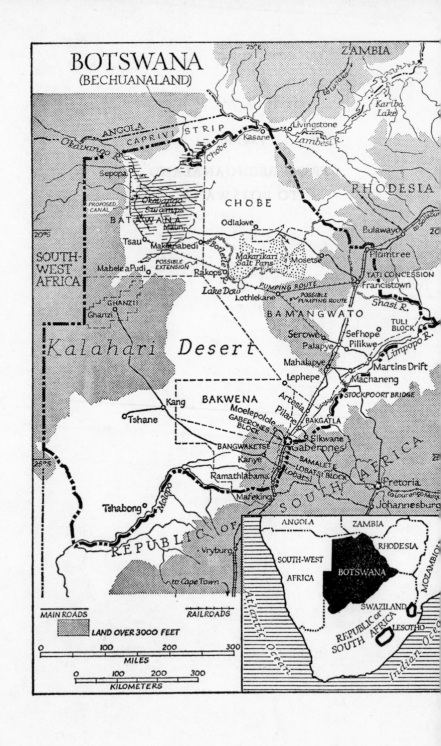

THE ESTABLISHMENT OF THE
BECHUANALAND PROTECTORATE

B Y ORDER-IN-COUNCIL dated January 27, 1885, the British
government provided for the establishment of civil and criminal
jurisdiction in Bechuanaland. Some historians have described this
move as a turning point in the history of Britain's South African
policy, inasmuch as it constituted a recognition of her responsibilities
in the region. Whether this view is justified or not, there can be little
doubt that the British objective of establishing firm control over the
'Road to the North' was thus achieved. At the same time, the acknowledged primacy of this goal was destined to have the unfortunate effect
of retarding the social and economic advancement of the indigenous
population and of delaying the Territory's political and constitutional
evolution.

The declaration of the Protectorate also had other important effects
since it brought together under British rule a large number of peoples,
generally of Batswana stock ('Bechuana' is a corruption), but historically divided into eight principal tribal groups, each occupying
its own territory and governed by an hereditary chief, and perhaps a
dozen or more related or subjected peoples. Of the eight 'independent'
tribes, the Bamangwato is the largest, having about one-third of the
total population of the Protectorate and occupying an extensive area of
44,941 square miles in the east. The Bamangwato capital of Serowe,
with its population of more than 40,000, is the largest tribal capital,
closely followed by Kanye and Molepolole in the south, capitals of the
Bangwaketse and Bakwena respectively. The other ruling tribes, with
their capitals, are the Bakgatla (Mochudi), Bamalete (Ramoutsa) and
Batlokwa (Gaberones), all to be found in the south-east, and the Barolong in the extreme south-east. Divided between Bechuanaland and
South Africa, the Barolong have their capital at Mafeking in the
Republic. The Batawana (Maun) border South-West Africa. The
related or subordinate tribes, which do not possess demarcated lands,

had either voluntarily surrendered their independence to one of the stronger tribes or had lost their lands through conquest. Of the 220,000 square miles contained in the Protectorate, 107,497 square miles were declared tribal territories.

Apart from the Batswana,* numbers of alien Africans reside at towns such as Lobatsi and Francistown, which are outside the tribal areas. In the Tati District, the Tati Federated tribes have an area of approximately 320 square miles, for which the government pays an annual rent to the Tati Company. The Kalahari Desert still remains the home of the dwindling number of nomadic Bushmen or Masarwa who owe only tenuous allegiance to any outside element. After the turn of the century, many Herero seeking refuge from the Germans in South-West Africa also settled along the western borders.

The absence of a homogeneous population, such as exist in Basutoland and Swaziland, inhibited a strong sense of national consciousness. The lack of homogeneity also encouraged the development and expression of divergent views and interests on all levels of political life and gave a distinctive character to the country's constitutional and political situation. Lacking a centralised tribal authority for the whole Protectorate, local tribal authorities could have greater freedom in their dealings with District Commissioners. Decentralisation also facilitated a certain amount of experimentation and the testing of political innovations.

In addition to the African tribes, the Protectorate also includes small, concentrated groups of whites, today numbering about four thousand. About 70 per cent of the whites are Afrikaans-speaking farmers and ranchers, who have occupied approximately 7,500 square miles. Most of the white areas, located in the eastern fringe of the country, were ceded to European companies in the early days of the Protectorate—the Lobatsi, Gaberones and Tuli blocks, which were originally acquired by the British South Africa Company from various chiefs, and the Tati or Francistown District. The Tati District (2,062 square miles) is owned by the Tati Company, which has full power to sell or lease any portion except the area leased for Africans, although the government has the right to acquire sites for public buildings. The whole of the three blocks and part of the Tati District are divided into farms and, until recently, were held under restrictive title which barred owners from selling to non-whites. Some 104,069 square miles

---

* Batswana, referring to the Bechuana people, is not to be confused with Batawana. Botswana is the name of the country.

of Crown lands remain 'unalienated' with the exception of nearly two hundred farms in the Ghanzi district and a dozen or so in the Molopo area, as well as certain areas recently leased to the Colonial Development Corporation.

Missionaries and Boer Trekkers

The political fortunes of the Batswana, like those of the Swazi and Basuto, were intricately bound up with the divergent policies of the British and Boers competing for dominance in Southern Africa. Although much of the early history of the Batswana tribes is shrouded in legend, during the first quarter of the nineteenth century their history was linked with a number of recorded events in the history of South Africa, including the expansion of the Zulu under Shaka. Amid the tumult and confusion created in the region after 1817 by the Zulu warriors or by those tribes fleeing in their path, European missionaries and traders were making their first cautious expeditions north from the Cape and into the territory of the southern Batawana. In 1820, Robert Moffat of the London Missionary Society established his mission at Kuruman, in the country later to become British Bechuanaland and now incorporated in the Cape Province of South Africa. There he was able to wield a unique influence over the breakaway Zulu chieftain, Mizilikazi, who, as leader of the Matabele, ordered the plundering of the Batswana tribes. Although Moffat's influence was able to secure protection for those persons in the vicinity of the Kuruman mission, he was unable to deter Mizilikazi from his attacks. Only the strong action of the migrating Boers, who defeated Mizilikazi in 1837, could urge him on to the north. Even then, he preyed upon the weaker Batswana tribes as he moved towards the Bulawayo region and only the Bamangwato people gave any significant resistance.

The years between 1820 and 1870 were years of chaos and anarchy, of internecine quarrels and struggles, complicated by the impact on the southern and eastern Batswana borders of the Boer trekkers who had departed from the Cape Colony in 1837, determined to preserve their loose form of government, isolation and religious exclusiveness. At a time when the whole trend of British colonial policy was strongly against expansion, there was much hesitation whether the British government should assert its sovereignty over the emigrant Boers north of the Vaal river. Although the independence of the Transvaal from the Cape Colony was conceded in 1852, and the independence of the Orange Free State two years later, the claim of the Transvaalers to a western boundary which included the missionaries' 'Road to the North' and the tribes along it brought them into conflict with one or the most remarkable missionaries sent to Africa—David Livingstone. The missionaries and the Voortrekkers were bound, in the nature of things, to be mutually antipathetic.[1]

The Transvaal Boers' concern over their western border was increased, late in 1866, after the reported discovery of gold in the Tati area, land claimed by the Bamangwato. Previously, the Boers had been more concerned with consolidating their position in the High Veld and extending their authority over Natal and the eastern coast rather than acquiring territory in Bechuanaland. Even so, they had made occasional attacks on the Bakwena (among whom Livingstone was residing), who accordingly, in 1852, made the first futile attempt to obtain British protection from Cape Town. Stimulated anew by the prospect of gold and the possibility of closing the northern road, the Transvaal proposed establishing a protectorate over the Bamangwato. Without awaiting a reply from Chief Matsheng, the Transvaal annexed the Tati area and thus closed the northern road.

On the advice of the able British missionary, John Mackenzie, Chief Matsheng, without going so far as to request total British jurisdiction, appealed to the British Governor of Cape Colony to occupy the Tati area.[2] The Governor, Sir Philip Wodehouse, took no action on the request and in all probability would not have been too concerned at the closing of the road had it not been for the fact that the Transvaal was, at the same time, proceeding to annex a strip of land in the east, leading down to Delagoa Bay on the Indian Ocean, thus ignoring both British and Portuguese claims. The government of Natal protested vigorously and London consequently refused to recognise either annexation.[3] Shortly thereafter, the discovery of diamonds prompted the British government, in 1871, to annex Griqualand West, an area inhabited by the Barolong in what came to be known as British Bechuanaland, but the tribes of northern Bechuanaland were not touched.

Khama Appeals for British Protection

By 1876, one of the most remarkable Africans of his time had acceded to the chieftainship of the Bamangwato tribe. This was Khama III, son of Sekgoma I. During the first years of his reign, he enhanced the standing of his tribe until the Bamangwato were recognised as one of the more prominent tribes in Southern Africa. To Khama, more than to any single factor, must be attributed the territorial unity of Bechuanaland. He was a skilled strategist and his well-trained army earned the respect of Lobengula, the son of Mizilikazi, who ceased to attack this formidable enemy. Khama became a rigid adherent of Christianity and introduced many reforms into the life of the tribe, one of the most important of which, at least in Khama's mind, was the total prohibition of alcoholic liquor. Along with his fear of the effects of liquor, Khama correctly perceived the potential danger of European settlement. He thus accorded his royal favour to only a few whites and generally stipulated that settlement grants were not permanent.[4] He also firmly set himself against the granting of mining concessions o any kind.

Under Khama's domination, some stability and order had come to prevail by the mid-1870s, not only among the Bamangwato, but among the Batswana tribes in general. But amid this increased security from inter-tribal conflict, the Batswana began to feel the effects of forces which were to alter their lives profoundly and remould their destinies. Hitherto they had seen little of the white man. A few traders and hunters had penetrated their territories, but these expeditions had been few and far between. Only in a few centres were permanent relations established, and the few whites who had really lived among them were extraordinary missionaries like Robert Moffat, David Livingstone and John Mackenzie. Therefore, when a large group of Boer families trekked through his country in 1873-4 to South-West Africa, Khama was much disturbed, and appealed to the British government for protection. Some of these trekkers settled at Ghanzi, where their descendants remain to the present day. At this stage, however, Khama was probably seeking little more than imperial assistance. Because of general lawlessness which had spread to southern Bechuanaland from Griqualand, the British did despatch a small force in 1878. But when it was withdrawn in 1881, the region was again plagued with anarchy. However, the British government was little disposed to do more than fix a boundary between Bechuanaland and the Transvaal in terms of the Pretoria Convention of 1881. These terms were on the whole more favourable to the southern Bechuanaland tribes than the Boers would have accorded. At the same time, the British laid down for the northern Batswana tribes a line which more or less coincides with the present southern boundary of Botswana along the Molopo river, and splits the Barolong. Following the conclusion of the convention, the British withdrew the few representatives who had been sent into the country, and the area again became 'the abode of anarchy, filibustering and outrage'.[5]

Cecil Rhodes and the 'Imperial Factor'

In 1883, the establishment by dissident Boers from the Transvaal of the 'republics' of Stellaland and Goshen in southern Bechuanaland made a British challenge inevitable. Apart from the manner of their founding, which was indeed contrary to the Convention of 1881, the two republics were a serious threat, for they lay right across the vital northern road. Graver still, they seemed bound in due course to be incorporated in the Transvaal. Cecil Rhodes, then leader of the opposition in Cape Colony, was especially emphatic in his condemnation of this threat to what he described as 'the bottleneck to the north'. But Rhodes's thinking was even more pregnant with meaning, inasmuch as it foreshadowed some of the basic contradictions of British policy towards the Protectorates in Southern Africa. He was convinced that, in dealing with the Bechuanaland problem, the 'imperial factor' must be removed, by which he meant government from London. Only then, he argued, could 'judicious compromises' be made which would ensure a united South Africa with Boers and Britons living together in amity and exploiting in their chosen ways the wealth of Southern Africa. 'It was, therefore, above all, necessary that the Boers should not be antagonised, whether by zealots in Africa, or by interfering busybodies in London. In the policies of Mackenzie, first and foremost an apostle of the rights of the native, he saw the very antithesis of his own views, and he realised very clearly that with Bechuanaland governed from London (by a government which he thought weak and vacillating), and an Exeter Hall regime in force in the new Protectorate, the Boers, both in the Cape and in Bechuanaland, not to mention the Transvaal, would be alienated, and no union such as he dreamed of could ever be brought about. Bechuanaland must therefore be governed by the Cape Colony, with no interference from London, while the burghers of Stellaland and Goshen must be conciliated and the Government of the Transvaal, in the person of Kruger, very sensitive to events on the frontier, must be diplomatically and tactfully handled.'[6]

Renewed British Interest

While Rhodes urged his view in Cape Town, John Mackenzie returned in 1882 to England, where he pressed for a British protectorate over Bechuanaland on moral as well as political grounds. Meanwhile, opinion in England was reacting strongly in its turn: the 'scramble for Africa' had by then become an open source of contention in European politics. Thus, despite President Kruger's protestations, the bi-lateral London Convention of February 27, 1884, which laid down the boundary between the Transvaal and Bechuanaland, was, with few modifications, a repetition of that of 1881. It definitely excluded from the Transvaal the greater part of Stellaland and Goshen and purposely drew the Transvaal boundary line to the east of the trade route, thus preventing any closure of the northern road. It also checked a possible linking up of the Germans, who had declared a protectorate over the Namaqua–Damaraland coast in 1884, with their Boer friends in the Transvaal. The British government thereby showed itself at last convinced that some form of protection must be extended over the country of the Bechuanaland chiefs and that the Transvaal must be held directly responsible for preventing border encroachments.

Even before the Convention was officially signed, a commission was issued to the Governor of Cape Colony, by which, as High Commissioner, he was placed in direct relationship with Africans outside the boundaries of the Transvaal and Orange Free State. He was subsequently authorised to appoint Deputy, Resident or Assistant Commissioners. It was as Deputy Commissioner that John Mackenzie returned to Bechuanaland in May 1884, and unsuccessfully attempted to establish a British protectorate in the disputed area—a step apparently viewed with as little enthusiasm by Cape Colony as by the resident Boers. But a renewed incursion by the Boers, this time at Mafeking, where the republican flag was hoisted, was more than London could tolerate. Sir Charles Warren was therefore sent as Special Commissioner with a strong force of troops 'to remove the filibusters from Bechuanaland, to restore order in the territory, to reinstate the natives in these lands, to take such measures as may be necessary to prevent further depredations, and finally to hold the country until its further destination be known'.[7] These instructions also clearly envisaged the ultimate taking over of Bechuanaland by Cape Colony.

The Protectorate Established

On March 11, 1885, Warren arrived at Mafeking where he received a telegram informing him that Germany had been officially notified that 'Bechuanaland and Kalahari, as limited by first section of Order-in-Council of 27 January, are under British protection'. He was directed to communicate this message as soon as practicable to Chiefs Sechele and Khama 'and take care that no filibustering expedition takes possession of the country, more especially Shoshone'.[8]

The idea of a protectorate was, of course, nothing new to the chiefs. So when Warren, together with Mackenzie, left for the north, they had every reason to expect a good reception. As Warren moved north, Khama decided that the best hope for the preservation of the Bamangwato lay in a British protectorate. In May, when Warren met the three principal chiefs of upper Bechuanaland—Sechele of the Bakwena, Gaseitsiwe of the Bangwaketse, and Khama of the Bamangwato—the latter proposed that the British accept his whole country, which, according to him, extended as far as the Chobe and Zambezi rivers in the north, and the Tati area and beyond in the east, reserving for himself only the 20,000 square miles around Shoshone. But while Warren had the authority to grant protection to the Bamangwato, he could not accept such a vast area (whose ownership was debatable) without first consulting London. Extension of British protection into the vast unmapped region to the north would have meant giving protection 'that would have cost England more trouble than it was worth, and all she was concerned with at the moment was keeping open the corridor to the great north of Rhodes's dreams; and so, while the southern Bechuanaland of the filibusters became a prim and proper crown colony, the northern Bechuanaland of King Khama and half a dozen other rulers of equal and lesser status evolved into a British protectorate'.[9] Thus, Warren read out the boundaries established by the order-in-council which set the northern boundary at 22° s and the western at 20° E. Between 1892 and 1899, these boundaries were subsequently placed further north to include all of the Bamangwato country. The southern part of the Territory, meanwhile, had been annexed as a British territory (September 30, 1885) subject to the Governor of Cape Colony but not incorporated into that colony.

The Implications of the Protectorate

Khama, in contrast to the other chiefs, appeared more aware of the consequences which might follow the declaration of a protectorate over the Territory. He emphasised that he did not desire to be:

> . . . baffled in the government of my own town or in deciding cases among my own people according to customs, but again I do not refuse help in these affairs. Although this is so, I have to say that there are certain laws of my country which the Queen of England finds in operation, and which are advantageous to my people, and I wish that these laws should be established and not taken away by the Government of England. I refer to the law concerning intoxicating drinks, that they should not go into the country of the Bamangwato, whether among black people or white people. I refer further to our law which declares that the lands of Bamangwato are not saleable.[10]

Khama also realised that the grant of protection inevitably involved the possibility that whites would seek grants of land directly from the protecting power. A considerable area of the country was therefore proposed for occupation, with the stipulation that all colonists should be approved by an officer of the Queen. Chief Gaseitsiwe of the Bangwaketse had somewhat similar views, while Chief Sechele of the Bakwena doubted that he needed protection at all and was soon inquiring what a protectorate meant. Warren's own conception of the implications of 'protection' was somewhat vague and he had to be reminded by the High Commissioner that the position of the Crown in Bechuanaland would not amount to sovereignty.[11]

The declaration of the Protectorate in 1885 was not accompanied by any enactment providing for the extension of it to a regular system of administration. Government policy was to allow the chiefs the maximum internal independence and all that was asked of them was to do their best to maintain law and order. This policy meant a total rejection of Warren's proposal that the whole of the Protectorate, including southern Bechuanaland, should form a crown colony under the High Commissioner but not in any way under the orders of the officer administering the government of Cape Colony. His suggestion, calling for a staff of magistrates and professional and technical officers as well as police forces, was dismissed as impracticable. Warren's proposal to limit colonists to Englishmen also seemed unsuitable, since it would have serious political consequences in South Africa. In brief, the Warren plan would have put an end to the prospect of the annexation of Bechuanaland by Cape Colony, an eventuality which seemed politically desirable. Thus, the country north of the Molopo river was administered, in so far as it was administered at all, by the High Commissioner through a Deputy Commissioner for the Protectorate.

An order-in-council of May 9, 1891, gave some precision to the nebulous control exercised over the Territory by conferring certain specific powers on the High Commissioner. Acting under this order-in-council, the High Commissioner issued a proclamation on June 10, 1891, providing machinery for the appointment of officials and the establishment of courts, the legalisation of marriages, the regulation of trading and the levying of taxes. The proclamation also laid down that the jurisdiction of the courts should not extend to cases where natives only were concerned, except in the interests of peace and good order. If a case where natives only were concerned should come before the court, then native law and custom should usually be followed. It also provided that chiefs might be appointed to exercise jurisdiction (but not over Europeans), that claims to land by Europeans were valid only when approved by the High Commissioner and that concessions given by chiefs were valid only when approved by the Secretary of State.

A New Threat Withstood: The British South Africa Company

The whole course of the Protectorate's history was nearly altered with the formation in 1889 of the British South Africa Company, of which Rhodes was the founder. Even before the granting of the charter, which described the Company's principal field of operations as lying north of British Bechuanaland and the Transvaal and west of the Portuguese possessions, Rhodes offered to contribute £4,000 a year for the maintenance of an imperial officer in the Bechuanaland Protectorate. From the very outset, there could be no question that it was the intention of the Colonial Office that the Company should eventually take over the control of the Protectorate and thereby relieve the British government of the expense and responsibilities of administration. Rhodes himself was particularly set on achieving that goal and constantly reminded the Secretary of State of this understanding.

The Batswana chiefs, however, reacted unanimously in rejecting a transfer of the Protectorate to the Chartered Company and were supported by the then High Commissioner, Sir Henry Loch, who told the Secretary of State that to hand over Khama and his people to a commercial company would be 'a breach of faith such as no government should commit'. Chiefs Sebele, Khama and Bathoen even journeyed to London in 1895 to press their case. It was at last agreed that the chiefs would assist in the plans of the Company for the extension of the railroad under construction, by ceding to it a strip of land running along the 'northern road'. The Colonial Secretary, on his part, agreed that each of the chiefs should have 'a country in which to live, as before, under the protection of the Queen'. The chiefs had gained their point and were not to come under the administration of the Company; but this decision applied only to the areas within their own jurisdiction and it was made clear that the tribal lands would be further demarcated. However, the whole question of transferring any authority to the Company was virtually rescinded in the Proclamation of February 3, 1896, which postponed *sine die* the transfer of the Protectorate. This decision was a direct result of the ill-fated Jameson Raid upon Johannesburg, which was staged from the Protectorate and had the backing of Cecil Rhodes. It was thus made clear that the imperial government must exercise authority in the region, especially since the Bechuanaland Colony had been transferred to Cape Colony the previous year. Further delay could only give rise to the possibility of the imperial government's losing all control over the course of events in Southern Africa. Following this decision, the Protectorate's administration was moved north from Vryburg to Mafeking, still outside the boundaries of the Protectorate but considerably better situated for administrative purposes. Never again was the Company able to press for the right to administer the Protectorate, despite the fact that its legal rights presumably persisted until the termination of its charter in 1923.

The end of the first era of the Protectorate's history was now reached. The people were assured of their land and there was no danger of incursions by filibusters. The days of migration were over, and the fear of the Matabele, which had overshadowed the life of the Batswana tribes for over sixty years, was a thing of the past. Increasing stability brought an end to internecine war and the Protectorate settled down to the difficult task of defining tribal boundaries, demarcating the land set aside for the construction of the railroad to the north, and, finally, accepting the legal implications of protectorate status.

8

THE PROTECTORATE ADMINISTRATION,
1885–1961; NATIVE AUTHORITIES AND REFORM

THE BECHUANALAND PROTECTORATE was acquired by the British government with reluctance and after much hesitation. Consequently, the original plan for its administration was very limited in scope and reflected the narrowness of British interest. In 1885, the High Commissioner defined the role of the British government thus:

> We have no interest in the country to the north of the Molopo, except as a road to the interior; we might therefore confine ourselves for the present to preventing that part of the Protectorate being occupied by either filibusters or foreign power, doing as little in the way of administration or settlement as possible.[1]

The early stages of British rule therefore saw the maximum regard for the customary authority of the chiefs. Unfortunately, however, by backing the chiefs, the administration tended to weaken old tribal checks and to make the chiefs' rule autocratic.

The Nature of Indirect Rule

However much the British government wished and tried to leave the internal administration of the Protectorate alone, the very fact of a British presence compelled a change in policy. A short time after this policy was enunciated, the Deputy Commissioner and his assistants found themselves intervening in tribal affairs. Boundary disputes, dynastic quarrels which threatened civil disturbances, incidents involving neighbouring governments, land and mineral concessions, all claimed the attention of the imperial representatives. Moreover, when these representatives had a strong sense of responsibility towards the protected tribes, as frequently occurred, they perhaps unconsciously tended to extend the British commitment through their own personal involvement. The fact that the Protectorate was in the middle of aggressively expanding Boer communities and on the direct trade route to the interior also necessitated a deeper involvement than was originally intended.

The order-in-council of May 1891, which empowered the High Commissioner to appoint a Resident Commissioner over the Territory, provided that, in issuing any proclamation under the order, he should 'respect any native laws and customs by which the civil relations of any native chiefs, tribes or populations under Her Majesty's protection were at the date of the order regulated, except in so far as the same might be incompatible with the exercise of Her Majesty's power and jurisdiction'.[2] Despite this injunction, changes were gradually introduced which limited the jurisdiction of chiefs and simultaneously increased the power of the protecting authorities. In all of these changing relationships, there was considerable lack of precision, and the whole constitutional position of the Protectorate became increasingly obscure. Whether this was simply the result of a policy of drift or, as some critics charged, an attempt 'to disguise the change in its position' by asserting that it could not do otherwise 'without a change in the legal status of the Territory',[3] the effect was to complicate and retard rational political reform.

In 1904, the Resident Commissioner described the system of rule in Bechuanaland as based on the policy of permitting 'a very wide latitude to the Paramount Chiefs in the management of their own people'. This observation applied in particular to those areas set aside in 1899 as tribal reserves: the Bamangwato, Bakwena, Bangwaketse, Bakgatla and Batawana.* The remaining lands, which, had there been no Boer war, would have been handed over to the Chartered Company, were declared Crown lands. By an order-in-council of May 16, 1904, Crown lands were defined as all lands 'over which the rights and jurisdiction had been abandoned by the Chiefs Khama, Sebele and Bathoen', and this in effect was taken to mean all lands lying outside the areas demarcated in 1899 as tribal reserves or the lands held by the Tati Company. Of the lands ceded in the east by the chiefs, the Gaberones, Lobatsi and Tuli Blocks were created in 1904, and these, together with Tati and Ghanzi, constituted the areas of white settlement.

---

* The Tati, Bamalete and Batlokwa reserves were established, respectively, in 1908, 1909 and 1933.

Bechuanaland and South Africa

So long as the British administration made no overt moves with respect to the Protectorate's internal or external political relations, Bechuanaland remained tranquil. The events of the Boer war did not greatly disturb the Protectorate since the chiefs were told that it was no concern of theirs. But when, as a result of British desires to conciliate their former opponent, it seemed that Bechuanaland and the other High Commission Territories were to be included within the terms of the 1909 draft Act of Union, the Batswana chiefs expressed their united opposition.[4] With one voice they spoke against any schemes which would bring the Protectorate under the rule of the proposed Union of South Africa. Protests from the Protectorates, combined with the force of liberal British sentiment, were at least sufficient to preserve the separate identity of the Territories and bring the nebulous promise that 'the wishes of the inhabitants would be ascertained and considered before any transfer took place'.[5]

The South African Act did not include the Protectorate within the Union of South Africa, but the preamble ominously said: 'It is expedient to provide for the eventual admission into the Union, as Provinces or Territories, of such parts of South Africa as are not originally included therein.' When addressing the chiefs at Mafeking in March 1910, Lord Selborne informed them that the transfer to the Union government would not take place in the immediate future, 'but in the natural course of things it would take place some day'.[6] Constant pressure throughout the years by South African Prime Ministers for the transfer of the Protectorate tended to fix the chiefs in their opposition to administrative changes. With the threat of incorporation always a distinct possibility, the safeguarding of chiefly sovereignty appeared essential to avoid the disruption that had come to tribes in the Union.[7]

The Development of Councils: The Native Advisory Council

It was not until 1920 that the administrative unity imposed in terms of the British Protectorate found a parallel support in the creation of a Native Advisory Council. Its function was 'to discuss with the Resident Commissioner all matters affecting native interests which the members desired to bring forward'. While in principle the selection of representatives to the Council rested with the tribal *kgotlas* (councils), in practice the choice was usually exercised by the chiefs. To that extent the effort to constitute an institution providing popular representation probably failed. Nevertheless, in the absence of a monolithic traditional structure, more interplay of diverse opinion occurred. Whereas in Basutoland and Swaziland 'only one official native viewpoint [could] be expressed . . . in the Bechuanaland Protectorate each chief or Native Authority could express his separate opinion, so that the Bechuana [spoke] officially with divided voices'.[8]

Whatever its weaknesses, the Council did afford a most useful link between the administration and the recognised voice of the people, and thus laid the groundwork for constitutional advance. Meeting once a year, the Council became the embryo of a consolidated constitutional authority. At first only the six southern tribal areas sent representatives. However, by 1931, the Batawana were participating, and at last, in 1939, the important Bamangwato became full members. Membership on the Council was roughly proportionate to tribal population with from two to eight representatives per tribe. In 1940, the title of the Council was changed to that of the African Advisory Council and it continued under that name until 1951 when it was renamed the African Council.

The African Council was composed of the Resident Commissioner as President and had a maximum of seven other official members. The chiefs of the eight 'independent' tribes were recognised as permanent ex officio members. Thirty-two members were elected by tribal meetings or by the tribal or district councils. Not more than two non-official members could be appointed by the Resident Commissioner. The composition of the African Council was thus decidedly different from that of the Swazi National Council and bore considerable resemblance to the Basutoland Council. It differed from the latter, however, inasmuch as the Basutoland Council was the ultimate and sole recognised authority for the expression of opinion within the territorial limits of the country. The Bechuanaland African Council, on the other hand, was limited in its discussions to matters affecting Africans. Perhaps the most important function of the Council was its responsibility after 1950 to act as an electoral college for the purpose of selecting eight African members for the newly created Joint Advisory Council, a function exercised until 1960.

The European Advisory Council

In addition to the creation of the Native Advisory Council, the Protec-

torate also deemed it necessary to constitute a European Advisory
Council (EAC). This body, which held its first meeting in 1921, came to
exercise great influence in the affairs of the Protectorate. At the outset,
the European Advisory Council had six members elected from the six
electoral areas into which the Territory was divided. In 1947 it was
established on a statutory basis and consisted of eight elected members
and seven official members. It was laid down that the Council's function was to advise the Resident Commissioner on matters directly
affecting the European residents of the Territory, but that neither the
High Commissioner nor the Resident Commissioner was obliged to
accept its advice. Since the Council's scope did not extend to matters
falling in the category of 'native affairs', there was always a section of
the Council which did not conceal its belief that the European
farmers would have secured better treatment from the Union government. As early as 1923, in fact, a section of the Council advocated
closer association with the Union, if not actual incorporation.

The Pim Report: Reassessment of Dual Rule

In the early thirties, the whole of the organisation of government was
reviewed by Sir Alan Pim, who had just completed a similar review for
Swaziland and Basutoland. Although one of the main purposes of his
enquiry was to study the means of re-establishing the financial stability
of the Protectorate, his report contained much that directly concerned
the organisation of the native administration. Generally speaking, Pim
found that the administration of the Protectorate had been conducted
on the principles laid down in 1895, which were designed to maintain
the position and power of the chiefs. At the same time, no attempt had
been made to define their powers or formally to harmonise administrative procedures between appointed civil servants on the one hand and
native authorities on the other. Referring to the administration of
justice, Pim argued that the practice of leaving this responsibility in
the hands of tribal authorities was 'almost equivalent to saying that it
remained in the hands of the chiefs, because by existing custom among
Batswana tribes the Chief is much more independent of the advice and
consent of a tribal council than is usual among Bantu tribes . . .' The
result, said Pim, 'was that a practical autocracy [was] developed by a
number of strong chiefs of whom Khama is best known'.[9] The Pim
Report also referred obliquely to a situation having serious consequences for political development in each of the High Commission

Territories—the practice of selecting South Africans for administrative positions. Inasmuch as the Territories had come under the Commonwealth Relations Office, the services of South Africans could be enlisted without legal impediment. Little concern was felt that these administrators might have no inclination to advance the well-being of the Territories. Without probing deeply into the implications of this practice, Pim did suggest that the linking up of the service of the three High Commission Territories with that of the colonies might bring great advantages.

While the observations and recommendations of the Pim Report had some notable effect on the economy of the Protectorate, the report's impact on native administration was less direct. By the time it was issued in 1933, the discussion of reform proposals suggested by the government had already reached an advanced stage. Following the publication in 1922 of Lord Lugard's *The Dual Mandate in British Tropical Africa*, the problems and implications of native administration began for the first time to receive systematic consideration. The urgency of reform was further demonstrated by a series of incidents which drew attention to the standards of tribal justice operating in the reserves. There was also disquiet over Bamangwato treatment of servile tribes like the Masarwa and the lack of supervision over large sums collected by the chiefs in their political and judicial role. Resentment also mounted over the power of native courts, and their lack of records, which tended to nullify the effect of appeals to the magistrates. As a result, after 1922 there was less tendency to acquiesce in a system dependent upon the authority exercised by chiefs and closed to any vigorous programmes of economic, social or political reform. The need for a new policy was also apparent as the older chiefs—those who had helped to develop the personality and maintain the identity of the tribes—were giving way to a new order, better educated and more acquainted with European ways, though for this reason perhaps less closely associated with the masses.

Tshekedi Khama: Conflict and Administrative Reform

The whole course of administrative reform and political development in Bechuanaland was vitally influenced by the activities of Tshekedi Khama, generally recognised as one of the most impressive modern African chiefs. As the first modernising force among the traditionalists, Tshekedi was destined to play a decisive role both at the tribal and territorial levels. Tshekedi came to power in January 1926 because of the infancy of his nephew, Seretse Khama, the heir apparent of the Bamangwato. From the outset of his reign, the Chief Regent was determined to preserve the chieftainship intact for Seretse and to conserve the best in traditional African life through progressive education. As the leader of the largest and most important tribe in the Territory, his efforts as a moderniser had a forceful impact on all the Batswana tribes. While not opposed to reform, he saw the Bamangwato traditions being undermined and weakened by the imperial authority and thus found himself in continuous conflict with the British administration.

The Regent's conflict with the imperial authority was dramatically illustrated in September 1933 when, as the result of corporal punishment administered under his authority to a white morals offender, the Acting High Commissioner, Admiral Evans, ordered a naval detachment up from Simonstown. Tshekedi was briefly suspended from office, a move not only reflecting the Admiral's sympathies with the racial policies of South Africa, but one which was probably designed to break Tshekedi's resistance to the draft Proclamations then about to become law.

The Proclamations of 1934: Resistance from the Chiefs

Proclamations had been drafted both in Basutoland and in Bechuanaland with the intention of defining the powers of the chiefs, so as to bring them under control and to prepare for new developments of indirect rule.[10] This new concept of indirect rule was cautiously applied to the Protectorate through the Native Administration and Native Tribunal Proclamations of 1934. While providing for the legal recognition of chiefly authority, these measures were designed not so much for the purpose of using indigenous institutions as agencies for local government but rather as a means of preventing the misuse of power by the chiefs. It was in this spirit that tribal councils were required to be formally constituted and judicial tribunals were given a fixed composition.[11] Chiefs were legally obliged to obey the instructions of the Resident Commissioner, and become responsible for promoting the social and economic welfare of the people as directed by the administration. In addition, chiefs were forbidden to demand tribal levies without the Resident Commissioner's approval, which would be given only if the *kgotla* approved. The *kgotla* was also replaced as a judicial body by a tribunal of limited membership and well-defined jurisdiction. These developments did not fail to capture the attention of the Union government which was distressed by the accompanying authoritative statement on the importance of African interests, a statement not in accord with the trend of legislation in South Africa.

Neither did the new policy commend itself to old-fashioned chiefs, who were accustomed to look to the Protectorate administration to uphold, rather than control, their own privileges. To the embittered chiefs, the Proclamations of 1934 appeared as an abrupt departure from tradition. In an attempt to remove their apprehensions about the purpose of this legislation, the Proclamations were accompanied by a Memorandum in which the High Commissioner insisted that it was not the intention of His Majesty's government to interfere unnecessarily with the chiefs, who resented these measures with their portents of official intervention in the selection of advisors and counsellors. The people also saw them as a menace to a system of trial to which they were deeply attached, and a relegation of the *kgotla* to a subordinate position. Because the government had given no sign during the previous forty years of its intention to make any substantial change in the procedure initiated by the Proclamations of 1891, some provisions of the Proclamations of 1934 seemed so wide a departure from custom that they were difficult if not impossible to operate in practice.

Although some of the chiefs accepted the innovations contained in the Proclamations of 1934 and attempted to put them into operation, Tshekedi, together with Chief Bathoen II of the Bangwaketse, also a moderniser of sorts, opposed them. The decision of Tshekedi and Bathoen to sue the High Commissioner was based on their belief that the Proclamations infringed the internal sovereignty reserved to them by treaty, and contravened native law and custom.[12] While the chiefs were perhaps fearful of losing some of their personal powers and prerogatives, essentially their opposition was considered a continuation of their ancestors' efforts to safeguard the constitutional integrity of their tribes. In the event that sovereignty over Bechuanaland should pass to South Africa, the only defence left to the tribe would be the traditional authority. South Africa could no longer be opposed on the field of battle but it could be challenged indirectly in the courts of the imperial government. The British government was therefore petitioned to examine thoroughly the constitutional position of the Territory.

The validity of the Proclamations of 1934 was tested in a Special Court of the Protectorate in 1936. But when the Court applied to the

Secretary of State for a decision as to the nature and extent of British jurisdiction in the Protectorate in terms of the Foreign Jurisdiction Act, it was laid down that His Majesty's Government had 'unfettered and unlimited power to legislate for the government and administration of justice among the tribes of the Bechuanaland Protectorate and that this power was not limited by Treaty or Agreement'.[13] Having lost the legal case, which left them totally subordinate to the protecting power, a general effort was made by the chiefs to carry out these and future Proclamations.

A New Approach to Administrative Reform

The whole sphere of local government was vastly improved after the appointment of Charles Arden-Clarke first as Government Secretary (in 1936) and then as Resident Commissioner (1936–42). The first Bechuanaland official with previous knowledge of native administration, Arden-Clarke brought his sixteen years of experience in Nigeria to tackle the problems of the Protectorate. After observing that Tshekedi was the key to the country's advancement, he thereafter sought Tshekedi's advice and criticism. However, the appointment of Arden-Clarke also brought a protest from the South African Prime Minister, General Hertzog, who complained that an official 'more conversant with South African problems' was required.

Previously Tshekedi and Bathoen II had been rebuffed in their efforts to set up proper treasuries and were told that their people were not ready for such innovations. But with Arden-Clarke's co-operation, the finances of the local tribal treasuries were regularised through the Native Treasuries Proclamation, No 35 of 1938. Chiefs were given a fixed stipend and thirty-five per cent of the tribal collection of native tax was credited to these treasuries, while, after 1940, monies provided under the Colonial Development and Welfare Act also became available for developmental purposes. The effect of this reform was to give the chiefs and their newly established finance committees responsibility in such fields as education and agriculture—a move which softened their objections to the new system and made for more harmonious relations. Thereafter increased attention was given to education, the cattle industry and agriculture. Tshekedi was especially preoccupied with the founding of the country's first secondary school, a dream eventually realised in 1949 with the opening of Moeng College.

As a result of his study of Lugard's *The Dual Mandate*, Tshekedi

expressed a willingness to co-operate with Arden-Clarke in reorganising the tribal administration established by his father and half-brother
and joined the African Advisory Council, with the agreement of the
kgotla. When, in 1940, the administration proposed a number of
amendments to the 1934 Proclamations, they were exhaustively discussed with the native authorities. Many valuable comments were
offered by the chiefs, and particularly by Tshekedi. Aided by his old
friend and legal adviser, Douglas Buchanan, Tshekedi produced the
drafts of almost entirely new proclamations. The final results of these
joint deliberations were Proclamations 32 and 34 of 1943, which consolidated, repealed or superseded certain aspects of the Proclamations of
1934.[14]

A point of special importance in the new Proclamations was that the
Tribal Council, for which provision had been made in 1934, practically
dropped out of the picture and the *kgotla* re-emerged as the main
consultative body of the tribe. Similar changes occurred in the judicial
sphere and the traditional practice of 'trial by *kgotla*' reasserted itself.
Despite these concessions granted in deference to the wishes of the
chiefs, the advice of District Commissioners and technical officers of
the central government was made more systematic and had greater
effect at the 'grass-roots' level. Matters which in Bechuanaland were
dealt with between the District Commissioner and the local tribal
authority, were discussed in the other Territories at the level of Paramount Chief and Resident Commissioner. However modest the
improvements, the foundations of government were notably strengthened.

A Renewed Challenge by Tshekedi

In 1946, Tshekedi again demonstrated his determination to oppose
South African policies, and to do so in the face of British opposition.
As the likelihood of South Africa's incorporation of the mandated
territory of South-West Africa appeared imminent, Tshekedi cabled
the newly formed United Nations, urging that such a step be prevented.
Tshekedi had a special interest in the question inasmuch as many
Herero, fleeing German savagery in South-West Africa in 1905, had
received sanctuary from Chief Khama. His memorandum, which
received the endorsement of other chiefs, called the attention of the
Trusteeship Committee to the fact, frequently repeated in subsequent
debates, that the object of the Mandate was to promote the moral

well-being and social progress of the inhabitants. This charge, originally granted to His Britannic Majesty, had been conferred on His
Majesty's Government in South Africa, which had not fulfilled its
obligations. Despite many efforts to place the question of South-
West Africa before the United Nations in person, the British government prevented Tshekedi from undertaking the journey on the grounds
that it was not a matter of concern to Bechuanaland.[15] Still determined
to press the issue, Tshekedi enlisted the support both of notable
Africans in South Africa and of the Reverend Michael Scott, who
thereafter ceaselessly pursued the question of South-West Africa
before the United Nations.

The Seretse Khama Marriage Dispute

Tshekedi's most serious clash with the British government was a by-
product of the marriage of his nephew, Seretse, to an English girl.
Having matriculated at Tigerkloof and Lovedale in South Africa,
Seretse graduated with a Bachelor of Arts degree from Fort Hare in
1944 at the age of twenty-three. Wishing to continue his education,
Seretse secured a postponement of his official accession so that he might
study at Oxford. In London he met and became engaged to Ruth
Williams, and, in spite of opposition from Pretoria, Salisbury, Whitehall and his uncle the Regent, Seretse was married in September 1948.

In Tshekedi's view, his nephew's marriage spelled doom for the
tribe. The marriage of a sovereign, he contended, was the concern of
the people, who must be consulted if feuds were to be averted. This
seemed doubly dangerous, since the Union government might seize
upon disturbances in Bechuanaland as an excuse for intervention.
Tshekedi therefore informed Seretse, who had returned in October
1948 to press his case, that if the tribe were not unanimous in any of its
decisions, he himself would leave the Bamangwato country. However,
even before Seretse returned to England in early January 1949 to re-
join his wife and resume his studies, there were strong signs that the
sentiment of the tribe was turning in favour of Seretse. At the same
time, it was rumoured that Tshekedi was himself seeking the chieftainship—an unlikely proposition but indicative of the tribe's concern
for their rightful chief.

In June 1949, a *kgotla* endorsed Seretse as their rightful chief and
accepted 'the white queen' rather than suffer further inroads upon the
tribal system. By this time, however, the British government was

inclined to bow to pressure from the South African government, which feared the unsettling example on the borders of the Republic of a white woman married to an African chief. While strongly opposing Seretse's action as a serious violation of tribal custom, Tshekedi also feared that the government might act arbitrarily to prevent Seretse from ever becoming chief and so resigned the chieftainship. Meanwhile, Ruth Khama had arrived in August 1949 to settle down while a government commission, sitting in Bechuanaland, unsuccessfully tried to come to a decision on whether Seretse would be recognised as chief.

Seretse was officially invited back to London in February 1950 for conversations with the Secretary of State for Commonwealth Relations to discuss 'the future administration of the Bamangwato'. Although his wife was also invited, Seretse correctly suspected a plan to prevent her return to the Territory, and, as a precaution, Ruth remained in Serowe. The Secretary offered Seretse £1,000 a year tax free if he would live in England and renounce all claim to the chieftainship. But Seretse refused to give in to this pressure and was therefore exiled from the Protectorate and then deprived permanently of the chieftainship in 1952. At the same time, Tshekedi, whom the government insisted on viewing as a contender for the chieftainship, was also exiled 'while the chieftainship [was] in suspense', a decision only slightly mitigated in its harshness by the fact that the Regent had already gone into exile in the Bakwena reserve. His exile was officially justified on the grounds that his presence was inimical to peace and good order. The District Commissioner of the Bamangwato, it was announced, would rule over the tribe as 'a purely temporary expedient'.

During a brief return permitted Seretse in mid-1950 to put his affairs in order and collect his family, Tshekedi advanced a proposal that Seretse join with him in renouncing the chieftainship and requesting permission to return as private citizens to participate in the life of the Bamangwato. The government's case, he suggested, would thereby be demolished, while they would be free to sit in tribal councils. In principle, they agreed that a federation of tribes in the Protectorate should be considered, a decision reflecting Seretse's earlier doubts about the merits of chieftainship and Tshekedi's serious misgivings regarding the status of African chiefs in the colonial context. Although a technical difficulty prevented this plan from being advanced and meant further estrangement between Tshekedi and his nephew, these terms were ultimately to be adopted as conditions for the return of both.

Tshekedi Promotes Political Reform

Tshekedi, in exile, continued to press the administration to set up tribal councils which would give the people a greater understanding of the aims of the government. All these suggestions, however, were ignored, even though official attempts to introduce reforms were not particularly successful. The government unconvincingly explained that Seretse and Tshekedi had been exiled so that local councils could be formed, an assertion contradicted by the fact that not only was Tshekedi the leading spirit seeking administrative reform, including the establishment of a Legislative Council for the Protectorate, but he was the first person to submit a scheme to implement local councils. While claiming that tribal reform and progress was the administration's foremost concern, the exile of Tshekedi cut off one of the most important growing points in Bamangwato tribal society, for Tshekedi's pioneering efforts were vital factors in the social and economic development of the Territory.

In the absence of a properly constituted tribal authority, disorders among the Bamangwato continued to plague the administration. Although the exile order against Tshekedi was revoked in August 1952 (while still banned from participating in politics inside the Bamangwato reserve), it was not until the appointment in May 1953 of Rasebolai Kgamane, third in line of succession and an uncle to Seretse, as African Authority in place of the District Commissioner, that a gradual restoration of orderly tribal life was brought about.

As a member of the African Advisory Council, having been appointed one of the regular representatives of the Bakwena by Chief Kgari Sechele, Tshekedi was joined by Chief Bathoen II, another long-time supporter, in arguing for the political advancement of the Protectorate. The government's argument that the time was not ripe for the creation of a legislative council was attacked as a concession to South Africa, which feared such development for Africans. Whereas the guiding principle of British policy in colonial areas was said to be the aspirations of the people, the chiefs contended that in Bechuanaland the government seemed concerned only with the aspirations of official bodies which did not confide in the people, such as the Colonial Development Corporation. Despite the opposition of the Resident Commissioner, Tshekedi continued his fight in the Joint Advisory Council for a legislative council.

The creation of the Joint Advisory Council in 1951 reflected government awareness that the existing system of African and European Advisory Councils was both cumbersome and unprofitable. Such a division made it impossible for the government to respond quickly and efficiently to the economic and social needs of the Territory. As a result of conferences held in 1949, representatives of both bodies agreed on a scheme for a Joint Advisory Council. It comprised eight members appointed from the European Advisory Council and a similar number from the African Advisory Council, together with four official members. Thereafter it was the custom to meet twice a year, under the presidency of the Resident Commissioner.

Malan's revival in 1954 of South Africa's claim to the High Commission Territories stirred Tshekedi to address himself more vigorously to the question of political reform. While Sir Winston Churchill, the British Prime Minister, had rejected Malan's request and reiterated the government's position that the Territories could not be transferred until the inhabitants had been consulted, Tshekedi pointed out that there was no effective body to express the views of the people of Bechuanaland at such time as consultation might take place. Neither the chiefs nor the *kgotlas*, he said, could any longer represent the peoples' views and the system of dual administration further complicated the matter. In a pamphlet prepared for the Africa Bureau in London, *Bechuanaland and South Africa*, Tshekedi argued that no time should be lost in advancing the political development of the Territory through local, legislative and executive councils. He pointed out that the High Commission Territories were virtually the only British dependencies where legislative councils had not yet been established. Administration claims that local councils were a precondition for the establishment of a legislative council meant a complete reversal of usual practice, and could be explained only in terms of the British government's timidity about South Africa.[16] This departure from practice, said Tshekedi, was deliberately followed so that the inhabitants of Bechuanaland 'should not appear to be enjoying political rights which African people in the Union have been denied'.[17] He further pointed out that local councils were nothing more 'than what the Union of South Africa is attempting to establish today by the Bantu Authorities Act, 1951', the only difference being one of degree inasmuch as British policy was influenced by the liberal policy of the British Parliament.[18] These councils, he claimed, could never be a substitute for a legislative council capable of negotiating effectively with the British government. Only after the status of the Protectorate was clarified would real economic and political progress be possible.

The Return of the Khamas: Politicising of Tribal Life

The Bamangwato refusal in 1955 to discuss a mining agreement unless both Khamas were present undoubtedly influenced the British government to review the bans imposed. Meanwhile, the Labour Party, now out of office, promised to rectify its earlier action against the Khamas if returned to power. When Tshekedi arrived in London in July 1956, he reiterated his belief that the only way to achieve tribal unity, to establish councils, and achieve settled conditions in which mining negotiations could be concluded, was for the government to permit Seretse and himself to return as private citizens to participate in tribal affairs. Considering that Tshekedi had renegotiated a mining concession in 1932 with the British South Africa Company, his presence among the Bamangwato became imperative for any new discussions. Having effected a reconciliation with his nephew and after eliciting Seretse's consent to the formula earlier advanced, that both should renounce the chieftainship and return as private citizens, Tshekedi laid their joint appeal before the Secretary of State. Confronted with this powerful appeal and prompted by public demands for justice, the British government announced on September 26, 1956, that both Khamas were free to return as private citizens and participate in the affairs of their tribe. Simultaneously, a tribal council of an advisory nature was announced for the Bamangwato, with Rasebolai Kgamane as Chairman.

The return of the Khamas the following month meant not only the healing of the schism which had rent the Bamangwato for eight years, but the acceptance of new realities involving the politicising of traditional life. Constructive efforts to improve the conditions of the tribe were opened on three fronts—economic, political and administrative. Tshekedi himself proposed Seretse as Vice-Chairman of the Council, a move unanimously supported by Rasebolai and the other members. Seretse, in turn, proposed Tshekedi as Secretary of the Tribe, an appointment he eventually took up in September 1958 over the objections of the High Commissioner and Resident Commissioner. The local councils set up by the Bamangwato in late 1957, which brought chiefs and tribesmen into closer co-operation, were quickly duplicated by the other tribes. Parallel with these administrative reforms, agreement was reached with the Rhodesian Selection Trust on terms for mineral exploitation. The cattle industry was also strengthened when the Colonial Development Corporation agreed to public participation in its projects.

Constitutional Advancement: A Legislative Council

But the major political objective was the establishment of a legislative council for the Protectorate. In 1958, Seretse and Tshekedi, supported by the Chairman of the European Advisory Council, Russell England, initiated a motion in the Joint Advisory Council calling for the establishment of a legislative council. Tshekedi noted that both Africans and Europeans had realised the need for this step and urged that Bechuanaland develop its own political ideal. This involved further consideration of the merits of federation as opposed to a unitary state, and questions involving whether there was to be one nation with a common citizenship taking no account of race. A proposal for a separate Governor, directly responsible to London, was also advanced.

Meanwhile, the British government was at last moving towards a positive policy for the three High Commission Territories. The breakdown of the old-style authority within the Bamangwato and the weakness of authority in other tribal areas demanded attention. Constitutional talks taking place in Basutoland with the objective of forming a legislative council, and a programme of economic development announced for Swaziland, encouraged similar consideration for Bechuanaland. Moreover, under the spotlight of world opinion and amid growing reaction to the increasingly intolerable policies of a succession of South African Prime Ministers—each introducing harsher measures than his predecessor—British rule in the adjacent Territories was subjected to closer scrutiny. The appointment in 1959 of Sir John Maud, a distinguished scholar and firm supporter of self-government, as High Commissioner, marked the adoption of a constructive and more definite policy towards the Territories. The arrival of a new Resident Commissioner, Peter Fawcus, also brought a breath of fresh air into the administration at Mafeking.

In this new atmosphere the Joint Advisory Council set up a Constitutional committee to frame the Protectorate's first constitution. The committee proposed an executive council and a legislative council, the latter consisting of 31 to 35 members, with the Resident Commissioner as President. In addition to three ex officio members, there were to be 7 appointed official members (white), 2 appointed un-

official members (white), and 10 members elected by the white population. With 2 appointed and 10 elected African members, plus 1 Asian,
the total would come to thirty-five, of which the Africans would
comprise something like a third. The election of the African members
was to take place through the African Council meeting as an electoral
college. Thus, after a decade or more of tireless effort on the part of
'traditionalist modernisers' such as Tshekedi Khama, Bechuanaland was
started on the road to responsible government.

9

POLITICAL PARTIES AND CONSTITUTIONAL
ADVANCEMENT, 1961–1966

BRITAIN's decision to advance the constitutional position of the Protectorate coincided with the rising tide of modern Batswana nationalism. Unfettered by traditional ties of loyalty and respect for the imperial protector, new leaders with radical ideologies were seeking the peoples' affections. Rejecting political structures that would incorporate racial or tribal divisions, the new nationalism took its cue from the political ideologies being generated in South Africa, which, after the Sharpeville shootings, had become increasingly militant. From 1960 to 1964, over 1,400 South African refugees entered the Protectorate and, through numerous contacts and discussions, played a decisive role as a catalyst in the development of modern Batswana nationalism. Here, as in the other High Commission Territories, Pan-African Congress (PAC) and African National Congress (ANC) refugees assisted the political parties then being organised under the twin banner of Pan-Africanism and militant opposition to the apartheid policies of South Africa. Although these new nationalist forces were not yet a threat to the traditional and moderate leadership, there was a distinct possibility that a combination of political skill and daring might enhance their chances of winning popular support. Unless the drawing up of a non-racialistic constitution were hurried along, the initiative might be lost. With the lines thus drawn, the British government fairly rushed the Protectorate along the road towards ultimate independence.

The Bechuanaland Peoples Party: Leadership Rivalry

The vital inter-relationship of constitutional evolution and political development was effectively demonstrated in Bechuanaland on December 6, 1960, a date memorable both for the government's announcement that a Legislative Council would be established and for the birth of the Bechuanaland Peoples Party (BPP), the Territory's first formal political party. Drawing its membership primarily from the urban areas of Francistown, Palapye, Mahalapye, Gaberones and Lobatsi, and supported by immigrants or refugees from South Africa, the BPP announced its firm opposition to the proposed 'racialistic' constitution. The party's declared aim was 'to organise the political consciousness of the people', to abolish discrimination, to protect the citizenship rights of Bechuanaland nationals 'against foreigners and immigrants', and to promote the integrity and security of the Territory. While not dismissing the past 'good and opportune services rendered by the ancient institutions of chieftainship', the BPP flatly opposed nomination of chiefs to representative bodies.[1] A new period in the Protectorate's political history was thus reached and over the next few years the British government would be pressed to substitute modern constitutional principles for the outmoded ideas of 'the dual mandate'.

The founder and President of the BPP was Kgeleman T. Motsete, a soft-spoken, self-effacing intellectual and educator-turned-politician, the embodiment of the old school of Africans in public affairs. Holding London University degrees (BA, MA SOC.), he was a pioneer of secondary education in Bechuanaland, and had held various educational posts in South Africa and Nyasaland. As a prominent member of the Bamangwato, he had represented the tribe before the Commission of Three Observers in support of Seretse Khama in his celebrated marriage dispute. Motsete was also chosen to be the first Secretary of the Bamangwato Tribal Council. His decision to enter the political arena arose from what Motsete considered to be the unprogressive policies of the authorities and government ineptitude in the development of the Territory.

Almost from the birth of the BPP, a dynamic if not rival element was present in the person of the party's Vice-President, P. G. Matante, a Francistown businessman and strong PAC figure in South Africa. Matante's involvement in South African politics was a crucial factor in the development of the BPP as a modern nationalist party. The party's Secretary-General, Motsamai Mpho, a former South African 'treason trialist', and closely associated with the South African Congress of Democrats and the ANC, sought to check the PAC influence and gear the party according to the ideological aims of the ANC. The force of this internecine rivalry, rooted in the competition of South Africa's banned political parties, continued to plague the BPP and deflected its potential impact. In July 1962, eighteen months after the party's birth, Mpho was expelled, along with six of his prominent supporters, for allegedly attempting to stage a leadership coup with Communist backing.[2] This schism was not to be the last and two years later, in March 1964, Motsete was removed from office and replaced by Matante.

Agitation for Constitutional Change

Political rivalry did not prevent mass demonstrations and protests against the racially-balanced Legislative Council which had been established in June 1961. The BPP Vice-President was commissioned to testify before the United Nations Committee on Colonialism in April 1962. Matante's denunciations of racialism and British colonial policy were at least unsettling and undoubtedly influenced the decision of the Legislative Council to establish a Select Committee for the purpose of examining all racially discriminatory laws and practices. So alarmed was the government by these developments that in early August 1962, the Resident Commissioner, Peter Fawcus, announced that, instead of the original plan calling for a constitutional review in 1968, such a review would take place in 1963.

The reaction of the BPP to this announcement was a call for mass demonstrations to urge immediate scrapping of the existing constitution. Political tensions reached a climax on August 18, when Motsete led a group (numbering more than eight hundred) to the High Court in Lobatsi. During the next few days, police and demonstrators clashed 333 miles to the north, in Francistown, where more than two thousand protested against the trial of seven persons accused of intimidation. Authorities were shaken by the strength of the crowds and police reinforcements were rushed in from other districts. Tear gas was finally used to disperse the crowds, sometimes swollen to four thousand, which P. G. Matante, then BPP Vice-President, had addressed. Mass arrests and the temporary banning of all gatherings of twelve or more people in Francistown provided a momentary respite for the beleaguered Protectorate authorities.[3] Matante's departure for a second United Nations appearance, while relieving tensions in Francistown, served notice that the time available for reaching a fundamental agreement was growing short. Not only was the attention of the world body an embarrassment but also the growing strength of the BPP, with its seventeen territorial and five Johannesburg branches, hovered over the administration as a threatening spectre.

Seretse Khama and the BDP

The British administration was not alone in its fear that the BPP constituted a radical threat to planned constitutional evolution and existing harmonious relations with South Africa. Early in 1962, Seretse Khama, the representative of the Bamangwato tribe on the Legislative Council, announced the formation of the Bechuanaland Democratic Party (BDP) which drew its strength primarily from the Bamangwato. Even before the BDP had been officially constituted, representatives of the BPP had been unable to secure permission from the Bamangwato Tribal Authority to hold public meetings, its leaders being regarded as 'corrupters of the youth'.

During the years of Seretse's banishment, the Bamangwato had refused time and again to elect another chief in his place. After his return in 1956, Seretse worked quietly with Rasebolai Kgamane and Tshekedi in the administration of the tribe. But after Tshekedi's death in June 1959, Seretse began to play a more active political role. Already, as Secretary of the Tribal Council and then as Bamangwato representative to the African Council, Seretse had made his mark on the modern political scene.[4]

Under the constitution of 1961, Seretse was elected to the country's first Legislative Council. Having been brought fully into the Territory's political structure, Seretse's good relations with the government were sealed when he was named in 1961 as the senior of two Africans on the governing Executive Council. He was also made a member of the Order of the British Empire. The wheel of fortune had thus turned full circle for Seretse, inasmuch as the deposed chief was once more a considerable power as plain Mr Khama. While enjoying all the charismatic attractions of chieftainship, he had all the political advantages of being free from ceremonial and uninvolved in the usual petty disputes which so complicate the life of a chief. Indeed, his removal from the succession facilitated his acceptance as a modern political leader of a country-wide party. Moreover, he could disavow rigidly traditionalist decisions by chiefs without being disloyal to the institution of chieftainship,[5] and could thus compete with the growing BPP.

Supporting Seretse Khama as his deputy was Quett Masire, a younger man widely known for his keen intellect and powers of debate. Although a member of Chief Bathoen's Bangwaketse tribe, Masire had frequently clashed with his Chief and was consequently deprived of most of his land. Only pressure from Seretse Khama and the British government prevented his banishment to a remote part of the reserve. Masire's role within the BDP was enhanced by the frequent illness of the party leader.

Recognising a threat in the BPP, Seretse proceeded inside and outside the Legislative Council to organise a counter-force. The result was a somewhat conservative party making a conscious appeal across tribal lines to traditionalist sentiment. Of special importance was his alliance with Chief Bathoen II, who, while not a reactionary, was strongly inclined to maintain chiefly authority. To the extent that tribal lines were crossed, the BDP became cautiously nationalistic and thereby reduced the danger of a total political-tribal confrontation. Also, by defending the right of white settlers, whatever their citizenship, to participate in constitutional discussions, Seretse placed his party in solid opposition to the demands made by the BPP for their exclusion. His appeals to whites to remain and help make the Territory a model of multi-racialism won him the sympathy and active political support of many white settlers. But Seretse's basic strength was provided by the Bamangwato, a tribe which included about twenty-five per cent of the country's entire population. Within the Legislative Council, the African members gradually associated themselves with Seretse's BDP, thereby making it a quasi-government party.

The declared programme of the BDP called for one man, one vote, and an African majority in the Legislative Assembly by the time the 'next' elections would be held. Full internal self-government based on a ministerial system was called for by the 'following' elections. Inasmuch as the 'next' elections and the 'following' elections were understood to refer respectively to anticipated elections in 1965 and 1970, it followed that independence would come about after 1970. Such at least was the party's programme at the time of its foundation. By May 1963, however, Seretse asserted that these aims referred to the same elections—in 1965. Still, at the party's annual conference, it was not thought necessary to remove the ambiguity. This led to the criticism that the BDP was deliberately speaking with two voices; one to pacify vocal African opinion favouring immediate independence; the other to soothe the fears of white settlers and to gain favour with the British government.[6]

Constitutional Review: The Lobatsi Conference

In keeping with the promise made by the Resident Commissioner, it was announced that constitutional talks designed to give the Territory internal self-rule would begin at Lobatsi on July 1, 1963. The BPP, meanwhile, was maintaining its pressure by demanding that before June 1963 a date be set for the Protectorate's independence. Suddenly, on the eve of the scheduled constitutional talks, Motsete, the BPP President, made a policy retreat. Possibly fearing that his party was becoming too radical in its demands, Motsete defied his national executive and called for the retention of the existing government in modified form for another four years. Motsete's about-face touched off a wave of anger and attacks upon his leadership. Although he withdrew the document under pressure, thereby allowing the party majority proposal, which called for a parliamentary-cabinet system, to stand, Motsete's position was seriously undermined. Eventually, a full party split occurred in March 1964, as both Motsete and Matante claimed the party leadership. Each proceeded to 'expel' the other and thus gave the advantage to Seretse Khama's BDP. Subsequent efforts to merge all 'modernist' parties, a move counselled by Harold Wilson, British Labour Party leader, proved abortive.[7]

Following the preliminary discussions of July 1 between the Resident Commissioner, representatives of the political parties, the chieftainship and the European community, it was agreed that so far as possible the review would be by way of a joint consultation between the Resident Commissioner and the representatives of the various parties and groups meeting together. The BPP, the BDP, the chiefs and the European members of the Legislative Council were each permitted to choose three representatives. Full and formal consultations began on August 21, and were completed by November 18, after only six days of actual discussion.

The results of the constitutional consultations were announced by the Queen's Commissioner (title of the Resident Commissioner, changed in preparation for constitutional transition) to the Legislative Council on November 18, 1963. In place of the existing racially-based constitution, unanimous agreement was reached on a constitution which, in terms of representative procedure, was probably one of the most advanced proposals yet submitted in British Africa. With official blessing, Bechuanaland thus achieved something, at least in the preliminary stages, rare in the history of African decolonisation—constitutional reform by general consent of blacks and whites.

The constitutional recommendations provided for a considerable measure of self-government. It was agreed that the Legislative Assembly would be constituted largely on the basis of universal adult suffrage open to all British subjects or British-protected persons resident in the Territory. Of its proposed 38 seats, 32 would be elected on a common roll, 4 reserved for prominent figures whom Parliament itself would wish to elect, and 2 for officials. The British government would retain responsibility for external affairs, defence, internal security and the public service. The exercise of these reserved executive powers by the Queen's Commissioner would be with the advice of the cabinet, except in extraordinary cases. The cabinet would consist of the Prime Minister and five other Ministers, all drawn from Parliament.

The all-party talks were free from conflict on two questions which presented serious problems in one or both of the other High Commission Territories—the position of the chiefs and their tribal authority, and safeguards for white interests. The chiefs were offered, and their representatives accepted, a House of Chiefs separate from the unicameral Legislative Assembly, with special responsibilities on chieftainship and tribal matters. Under the proposed constitution, legislation relating to tribal matters would be referred to the House of Chiefs at least thirty days before presentation to the Legislative Assembly, and that presentation would be accompanied by the comments or resolutions of the House of Chiefs.

The whites had no seats set aside specifically for them and instead settled for a Bill of Rights in the constitution; the only way a white man could be elected to the Assembly would be through association with one of the African-based political parties. White leaders thereby agreed to recognise that racialism, in however mild a form, could no longer receive official sanction. Rather than endanger prospects for continued co-operation, the white representatives chose not to oppose the non-racial constitution which had been endorsed by all contending political factions.

White Dissent: The South African Factor

The official concurrence of white representatives at the Lobatsi Conference did not mean, however, that they had acted out of conviction or that they were supported by the Protectorate's white settlers, most of whom were Afrikaner farmers. While the constitutional talks were still in progress, approximately twenty Afrikaner farmers decided to appeal for the independence of the Tati District 'so that our land will not be handed over to the natives'. The farmers' spokesman, Louis

Mynhardt, a local farmer and one of the three white representatives on the constitutional committee, was commissioned to submit this appeal —one which evoked a stern warning from Seretse Khama that no fragmentation of Bechuanaland would be permitted. Mynhardt also objected to the decision that only those persons possessing British citizenship would be given the franchise. Like most other whites in Bechuanaland, Mynhardt hoped to see the Protectorate patterned after the Transkei, somehow permitting 'multi-racialism' or 'race-federation', but not 'integration'.

Preferring to risk the ill-will of the Africans at this crucial stage of constitutional development, the Tati whites stepped up their demands for secession. In February 1964, a petition sponsored by 320 whites, more than 90 per cent of the Tati farmers, asked the administration for independence or self-government or, alternatively, permission 'to merge with a friendly neighbouring white state'. Basing their claims on the concession granted in 1880 by King Lobengula of the Matabele to the Tati Company, which ante-dated Protectorate status and the subsequent incorporation of the Tati area in 1899, the farmers made known their intention of appealing, if necessary, to the International Court. Although the Queen's Commissioner, Peter Fawcus, agreed to discuss the matter on condition that the decision of the British government would be accepted as final, the whites refused to bind themselves. Instead, a Tati delegation visited Pretoria where an appeal was made to the South African cabinet 'not to leave them to the mercy of the Seretses and new Shakas which the British government would let loose upon them'. The Protectorate's race policies, it was claimed, could only lead to a decline in the position of the whites until eventually they would 'have to give way altogether'. Finding a lack of enthusiasm among the South African Ministers for their project, the white delegation resolved to draw up a petition for independence and negotiate with the new government of Southern Rhodesia.[8]

Semi-official intimations that some of the activities of the white farmers might amount to high treason under the provisions of the British constitution did not deter them from their 'fight to the death' decision. In June 1964, a Tati representative set off on a futile trip to the United Nations to seek that organisation's unlikely support. The net result of this comical but provocative action was to stir African demands for a total return to African ownership of the 200 by 6 mile Tuli Block, long occupied by whites and including extensive holdings of two South African Cabinet Ministers, Le Roux and Serfontein.

Mpho, now heading the Botswana Independence Party (BIP), demanded that all white-owned land in the Territory be taken without compensation, and promised that such would be the case if his party came to power.

Already compromised in African eyes for having suggested that Verwoerd be invited to lay his views on the future of the Protectorate before the Council, many whites gave further evidence of their lack of good faith by opposing the government's decision to introduce integration in the Territory's schools in 1964. The most hostile response occurred in Ghanzi, where the whites chose to withdraw their children from an ultra-modern school rather than see one African student admitted. Strong white demands, both inside and outside the Legislative Council, for stricter immigration control was also generally viewed as another effort to bolster their entrenched position and curry favour with South Africa. Whether the white populace can yet enter fully into the Botswana political structure is open to question. A sincere effort by whites to implement the Race Relations Bill of March 1964 may offset anti-white sentiment. The passing of the General Law (Removal of Discrimination) Bill in late 1964, which removed all remnants of racial legislation, may also help to bridge the gap.

Implementation of Constitutional Proposals: Election Preparations

The speed with which the Lobatsi Conference wanted the terms of the constitution implemented was somewhat unexpected. It was urged that the new government be set up by the end of 1964 but, in any case, no later than the first quarter of 1965. To meet this deadline, the administration embarked immediately on a national census, a preliminary requirement for the delimitation of thirty-two election districts. A pilot census in the Francistown area revealed the possibility of fifty per cent more people in the Protectorate than was previously estimated, or something more than half a million persons.

Even before the proposed constitution could be submitted for London's approval, it was generally assumed that final acceptance would follow as a matter of course. Any form of intermediate political advancement could only lead to a lack of stability and public confidence. By anticipating African desires, on the other hand, the government clearly hoped to avoid suspicions of British policy. Moreover, early independence for Bechuanaland posed less of an immediate problem for

British-South African relations than such a step in Basutoland. Since no militant nationalist party yet commanded widespread Territorial support, constitutional delay could only assist the 'extreme' nationalists.

However, even the likelihood of a moderate government in Bechuanaland under the formula of majority rule involved a crucial decision for British policy towards South Africa. In the past, as the Queen's Commissioner pointed out, the policy of the Protectorate was one of strictest neutrality. For Verwoerd, however, neutrality was not enough to outweigh the imagined dangers inherent in any non-racial state bordering South Africa. Britain's declared intention of leading the Territories to complete independence seemed to confront Verwoerd with the prospect of a straight showdown over his own alternative of a Bantustan federation of Southern African states. Thus, on September 3, 1963, at the very time when each of the High Commission Territories was entering some new phase of constitutional evolution, he challenged the British government to hold a plebiscite in the Territories so as to permit a choice 'between economic prosperity in union with South Africa or economic decay' under Britain. Bechuanaland's reaction to this proposal was a solid condemnation by African politicians and chiefs, who saw in it a veiled threat to annex the country. These denunciations in the Legislative Council contrasted sharply with that body's endorsement a few days earlier of the proposed constitution which would carry the Protectorate to independence.

As expected, the British government announced on June 2, 1964, its acceptance of the slightly-revised constitutional proposals. Replying to questions in Parliament, Duncan Sandys, Commonwealth Secretary, stated that general elections under the new constitution would be held in March 1965 as a step towards independence. To this end, registration of voters was scheduled to get under way by September, followed by nominations in February 1965. Eventually, some thirty-one constituencies were delimited.

To implement this decision, donkeys, horses and even camels were pressed into service to carry potential voters to 215 registration points scattered throughout the country's vast 220,000 square mile expanse. As expected, the greatest activity centred on Serowe and Francistown— respective headquarters of the BDP and BPP, and symbols of opposing African political philosophies. Many Africans living near the South African border were refused registration on the grounds of not meeting residence requirements (one year of previous residence unless born in the particular voting constituency). The highest registration was reported in the Bamangwato Reserve, Seretse Khama's stronghold, and final figures indicated that well over 80 per cent of the estimated 222,000 eligible voters had registered. Seven mobile film units and two information vans assisted the registration process, and voters were instructed in the party symbols and colours—a red motor-car jack for the BDP, a black cow on green for the BIP, two white stars on black for Motsete's BPP and a black star on yellow for Matante's BPP.

As Bechuanaland moved closer to independence, the government acted to maintain a vigorous if not dictatorial control over events. In late March 1964, the Legislative Council voted in a penal code which gave the government comprehensive powers covering all crimes ranging from running a betting house to subversion. The Queen's Commissioner was given unprecedented authority to declare as unlawful any society 'dangerous to peace and order'. Stiff penalties ranging up to seven years' imprisonment were provided for learning the use of firearms or practising military exercises. The police also undertook to increase its force by 118 men and control of assemblies was rigidly decreed in several urban areas. According to Matante, the new penal provisions constituted a direct threat to the election campaign, and in November 1964 he appealed to the Commonwealth Relations Office to send a representative to assess the situation.

In other respects, however, government preparations for independence were substantial and constructive. Announcement of a £10 million development plan designed to jerk the country out of its economic rut heightened the significance of the constitutional proposals. Spread over five years, the plan was intended to touch every aspect of the Protectorate's life. A key role in the development programme was assigned to technical and other agencies of the United Nations. Considerable strides were made in postal and telegraphic communications to bring far-flung outposts into contact with each other. An experimental radio station, broadcasting from Lobatsi, was established as a pilot project for a contemplated 10-kilowatt station to broadcast from Gaberones. Measures for improving and increasing teacher facilities, reorganising the secondary school system and promoting adult education were laid down in a White Paper. The need for a critical assessment of the country's education system was underscored by the fact that pupil wastage in primary and secondary schools exceeded 80 per cent. Plans were also formulated for the opening of a Cadet College for Adult Education and Training in Serowe, with the object of providing a ten month leadership-training course.

On the governmental level preparations also proceeded apace. It was announced that the Legislative Council would be dissolved on January 21, 1965, in preparation for nominations on February 6 and elections on March 1. The African Council had its last meeting in June 1964. Almost unprecedented in Africa was the announcement, in November 1964, that the public service in all but the most senior posts would no longer be open to people from outside Bechuanaland. Africanisation of the civil service would particularly affect white South Africans who occupied most of these jobs in the Protectorate. The formation of shadow ministries as prototypes of the new government departments (Home Affairs; Labour and Social Services; Local Government; Mines, Commerce and Industry; Works and Communications; Finance); the moving of the capital, after eighty years, from Mafeking in South Africa to the new capital of Gaberones; the extension of provincial recognition to the consular representatives of the United States and Norway: all provided substantial proof that Bechuanaland would be free, within the bounds of economic necessity, to steer its own course and develop its own policy towards South Africa and the outside world.

Elections under the Pre-Independence Constitution

Seretse Khama's BDP, as generally predicted, scored an overwhelming electoral victory by capturing 28 of the 31 parliamentary seats. Matante's BPP won the remaining 3 seats; neither Motsete's BPP nor Mpho's BIP won any seats. Khama made a remarkable personal showing in his own constituency of Serowe North, where he received 5,909 votes in contrast to 53 for the BIP and 39 for the BPP candidates. The BPP was successful only in the Francistown and Mochudi districts. Significantly, the BPP victory in Mochudi, the Bakgatla capital, was probably due more to the support received from the young, British-educated Chief Linchwe than to the propaganda activities of the party, and further demonstrated the strong role the chieftainship could play in the political development of the Territory. The BPP, however, insisted that its lopsided defeat was due primarily to corrupt practices which allegedly occurred before and during the election. It was estimated that some 75 per cent of Bechuanaland's eligible voters had participated in the country's first general election.

Immediately following the election, the Queen's Commissioner, Sir Peter Fawcus, who had led the Protectorate to this historic point, asked Seretse Khama to form Bechuanaland's first African government. The new Prime Minister reaffirmed his intention to welcome investment from all countries, including South Africa and Rhodesia, and emphasised his belief that economics and politics remained distinct. He indicated that, under his government, Bechuanaland would seek membership of the United Nations, the Organisation of African Unity and the Commonwealth, and would also be favourably disposed towards an economic grouping of Southern African states. Khama stressed that, while temporary asylum would be given to bona fide political refugees from South Africa, they would not be permitted to use Bechuanaland for subversion. Independence, he said, would be sought in September 1966.

For the whites of Bechuanaland and the Nationalists of South Africa, Seretse Khama's victory was the least of three evils and even a certain enthusiasm was expressed about him. As if in preparation for a Khama victory, the South African Nationalist press had ceased to treat his wife with scorn and hope was expressed for early independence so that the country might move into a new association of Southern African states. Verwoerd sent his personal congratulations to Khama while the Minister of Interior, Senator de Klerk, casually announced that the ban on Khama's entering the Republic had been lifted on October 21, 1964. This step was taken, said Verwoerd, 'after it had become clear, despite previous intentions, that Bechuanaland had been placed on the road to independence and after [he] had indicated, on behalf of the government, that since this was in accordance with the policy of separate development, the Republic would desire friendly relations with such a neighbour state'.[9] The actual details of these relations could be worked out only when Bechuanaland was fully independent. These remarks were made amid reports of a new South African tack, namely, that the projected Batswana Bantustan near Mafeking might be sacrificed to Bechuanaland in order to win the new government's genuine co-operation and ensure a sound buffer between South Africa and the north.

Bechuanaland's first Parliament was formally opened by the Queen's Commissioner on March 23, in the Lobatsi High Court, pending completion of government buildings in Gaberones. Sir Peter indicated the government's intention to promote gradual evolution of a fully unified state, without unduly forcing the pace at which tribal institutions would be integrated in the national polity. These assurances, however, were not sufficient for the members of the House of Chiefs, some members of which deplored government policy towards them. Although it was expected that one of the senior chiefs, such as Chief Bathoen II of the Bangwaketse—for twenty-seven years chairman of the African Council of Chiefs, and colleague of Tshekedi Khama—or Chief Linchwe of the Bakgatla would be selected Chairman, both declined the nomination. Chief Bathoen declared that he would not stoop to be Chairman of a House which he considered had no future, and one which allegedly was looked down upon by both the Queen's Commissioner and the cabinet.[10] The discontent of the senior chiefs set the stage for behind-the-scenes negotiations with various defeated political figures, a combination which might prove decisive in some future election.

Although Khama's victory stirred considerable hope in South Africa, and stimulated greater encouragement for the BNP in Basutoland, it was also evident that the new Prime Minister was not geared to Verwoerd's thinking. Whereas Verwoerd spoke of 'friendship', Khama spoke of 'neutrality'. Moreover, Khama gave no indication that he would seek to establish diplomatic relations with South Africa. Rather, he made an official visit to Zambia where, together with Kaunda's cabinet, he spent five days exploring the possibilities of closer economic ties between the two countries, so as not to be dependent 'on one nation'.[11] The Prime Minister thereby gave substance to his pre-election promise that South Africa and other nations would be used so long as necessary, in keeping with his declared policy 'of putting Bechuanaland's survival above all else'.

Post Election Difficulties: Drought and Opposition Regrouping

Unfortunately for the new government, the progressive worsening of drought conditions severely undercut efforts to prepare the country for independence and provided political capital for the opposition. By June, the most populous region of the country had been turned into a giant dustbowl, a tragic consequence of the fact that only 14,000 of 760,000 arable acres had been ploughed. The drought, with its resultant famine and disease, was the worst in a generation and, by April 1966, had caused the loss of some 400,000 head of cattle out of the total national herd of 1,300,000. In the last few months of 1965 the situation deteriorated dramatically. Instead of having to provide an emergency food rationing programme for an estimated 110,000, it appeared that provision would have to be made to feed 360,000 by the end of 1966, almost 65 per cent of the population. These efforts, which required a trebling of existing drought and famine programmes, strained government finances to the limit. Only the generous relief provided by the United Nations World Food Programme, the Oxford Committee for Famine Relief, the Colonial Development and Welfare Fund, and various church agencies prevented mass starvation. Significantly, however, while Bechuanaland's position was far more critical than that of Basutoland, no request for assistance was made to the South African government. The British government did agree to underwrite emergency food purchases in the Republic. The explosiveness of the situation was underscored in June by a march of some two hundred unemployed into Gaberones, the capital, demanding immediate assistance. Reports of a growing incidence of medicine murder indicated the total despair and demoralisation of many who sought remedies for the tragedy in ancient practices.

Acting against the backdrop of national economic disaster, the government faced growing opposition from three quarters—the parliamentary opposition led by Philip Matante, the chieftaincy, and a new, more nationalistic grouping which took shape under the guiding hand of Dr Kenneth Koma. Of the three, the government feared the likelihood of a combination of the latter two more than it feared the formal opposition.

Koma, who returned to Bechuanaland just before the election from an extended stay abroad, was educated at Cape Town University, Nottingham (United Kingdom) and Charles University in Prague, and he had completed his academic work at the University of Moscow. While he disclaimed any Communist affiliation, it was generally rumoured, with official concurrence, that he was a Communist. Certainly, the British CID chief at Mahalapye, Koma's home village, proceeded on that assumption, and most foreign visitors to the doctor (including the author) have been carefully interrogated. In the event, Koma worked quietly and effectively to bring together various disaffected elements and by June more formal meetings were in progress with Mpho (BIP) and Motsete (BPP), Chief Linchwe of the Bakgatla and the son of Chief Bathoen, Gaseitsiwe, chief-designate of the Bangwaketse and recent founder of the Botswana National Union. Also of special interest to Koma were organised workers and the civil service, most of whom strongly resented the government's heavy reliance upon expatriates and its cautious handling of obvious racism in the urban, South African dominated centres. Contrary to South

African circulated reports—which from the outset branded him as 'a channel for Moscow's influence'—that the new political grouping would seek to establish strong links with Peking and Havana, aimed at subverting the Republic, Koma insisted that he would never see Botswana used as a base for attacks against South Africa, Rhodesia or Portuguese-controlled Angola, however much he detested the policies of those states. However, banned from South Africa as a Communist, he stressed that independence would be an 'illusion' until the country became economically free of the Republic.

The new party, which Koma nursed into being as the Botswana National Front, was born in October at Mochudi, Chief Linchwe's village, with some 450 persons in attendance. Reedwell Molomo, a teacher in the Serowe Teachers' Training College, was elected President and Daniel Kwele Vice-President. Koma was named Secretary for External Affairs. In its statement of principles, the Front proclaimed that its aims were 'to unite the different communities in Bechuanaland on the basis of full equality, achieve national independence, arouse the political consciousness of the people in all fields, and mobilise the masses making them an integral part of the national liberatory movement in Africa'.

The formation of the Botswana National Union under Gaseitsiwe was probably more symptomatic of chiefly resentment at the erosion of their powers than an augury of a real political party. This resentment culminated in a vote of no confidence in the existence and functions of the House of Chiefs in November 1965. Instead, the eight principal chiefs demanded a bicameral legislature, in which a House of Chiefs would exercise real authority. Chief Bathoen, in particular, deplored government plans to leave the chiefs with little more than the mechanics of local government administration, and, in a stern warning, stated that 'a people who rely on their chiefs as heavily as the Bechuana can turn out a government that silences this traditionalism'. He was supported in this view by the young, popular, British-educated Chief Linchwe, a strong admirer of Koma. The BDP's reply to the chieftaincy's threat was voiced by Masire, who pointed out that 'while the chiefs may tell their people who to vote for, they can't go with them to the polling booths'. It was confidently expected that, during the BDP's remaining four year mandate, the people would be sufficiently weaned away from the chiefs to think independently. The chiefs were also warned by the BDP to be satisfied with the well-defined powers and functions of the traditional leaders, which it was asserted had again been restored to their proper exercise, lest they be guilty of 'digging their own graves' by associating with 'the Communist party'.

Although the formal legislative opposition received more publicity in its attacks upon the government, indications were that Matante's followers were decreasing in numbers. A motion of no confidence which he brought against the government was massively defeated along party lines but it did serve to circulate widely Matante's charges that the BDP had won the March elections because it was sponsored by the British administration and that the elections had really made no difference in the government since the BDP was the British administration. Reversing his party's position against the powers of chieftainship, Matante now saw in the new constitutional proposals a deliberate effort to undermine the chiefs who 'would not have much of a future' and whose powers 'would be liquidated'.

Independence Negotiations: A Republican Constitution

In December 1965, after a journey to the United States where he received an honorary doctorate from Fordham University, the Prime Minister tabled his government's proposals for the constitution of an independent Republic of Botswana. These proposals, which in many respects paralleled the American system, bore out the Prime Minister's contention that strong executive powers were required to initiate development projects and provide firm leadership. They were reportedly based on the conclusions reached in discussions with all groups that 'the time had come to move directly to a form of self-government, and that this should be achieved by constitutional arrangements which could lead naturally to independence'. There was no claim, however, that the proposals had actually received public approval but only that they 'were explained to the people, and the meeting of the House of Chiefs was postponed to permit those Chiefs who wished to do so to hold *kgotlas* to discuss the proposals'.[12] Apart from the change to a republican form of government under an executive President, they were in substance little more than the adjustments required to adapt the 1965 constitution to the circumstances of independence.

Having received legislative endorsement, the republican constitution was approved at an Independence Conference concluded in London on February 21, 1966. It provided for a President with full executive powers, whose election would be coupled with that of the National Assembly every five years. While himself not a member of the Assembly, the President with the Assembly constituted the Parliament. As he was to be elected by the Assembly, their majority support was necessary for him to retain office. He was given the power to address the Assembly, to summon, prorogue or dissolve it at any time, and ask non-local civil servants to resign (with compensation) to make way for locals. The Chief Justice would be appointed by the President while puisne judges and magistrates were to be appointed by a Judicial Service Commission. No provision was made for a House of Chiefs as a legislative body. Rather, its existing position as an advisory body on chieftaincy would be maintained. No dual citizenship was permitted, although provision was made for easy acquisition of citizenship by residents. The fundamental rights of all citizens were guaranteed, and derogations were made permissible only within very defined limits. Transitional provisions were made for the Prime Minister to become President on Independence Day, September 30, 1966, and likewise for the Deputy Prime Minister to become Vice-President. The first Parliament, automatically composed of the members of the existing Legislative Assembly, would dissolve on March 23, 1970, if not dissolved sooner.

Matante, representing the opposition at the London conference, walked out of the meeting and did not sign the document. He asserted that the government had no mandate to carry the country into independence, and denied that consultations with the people had been adequate. Instead, he called for the appointment of a special commission consisting of representatives of all political parties, the chiefs, the British government and the Bechuanaland government. Only then, said the BPP leader, could the people's will be accurately interpreted. Furthermore, he insisted that a general election was necessary before independence.

Foreign Affairs and the Future

While Khama adhered to his oft-repeated policy of co-existence with South Africa, the Rhodesian crisis in late 1965, touched off by the Smith government's unilateral declaration of independence, pulled Bechuanaland into the controversy. Britain's decision to counteract the banning in Rhodesia of BBC broadcasts by constructing a radio transmitter in Francistown, only fifteen miles from the Rhodesian border, and to embargo the shipment of oil, had serious implications for Bechuanaland. Although the Prime Minister firmly denied reports that he was unhappy with the construction of the radio station and had been pressured into acquiescence, he did voice fears that, if force were used to settle the question, it could not be confined to Rhodesia. In view of the vociferous white minority in the Francistown area, whose sympathy for South Africa and Rhodesia was undisguised, military activity in Bechuanaland could obviously strain the existing *modus vivendi*. So intense was this local feeling that Britain sent in a special military detachment to guard the station against sabotage. Still, Khama stressed that his government could not and would not recognise the 'illegal Smith regime' and he endorsed the banning of all shipments of arms, ammunition and oil through the Protectorate.

The invitation extended to the Prime Minister by President Nkrumah to attend the October OAU conference in Accra, as his 'special guest', enabled the BDP government to make other African states more aware of the Southern Africa situation. Substituting for the Prime Minister, Masire told the assembled heads of state that economic dependence on South Africa was a fact over which his government had no control, but emphasised that this did not reduce its abhorrence of apartheid. Although Masire was politely received, the OAU dealt him a stunning blow by going on record in support of the defeated opposition parties in each of the former High Commission Territories. The representatives of the Bechuanaland, Basutoland and Swaziland governments attending as observers decided to ignore this attack and instead expressed appreciation for a resolution ensuring and guaranteeing the independence of the Territories after each had become an independent state.

While the governing parties of the three Protectorates were all equally affronted by the Accra resolution, Seretse Khama did not respond to a subsequent proposal by the Basutoland National Party and the Swazi Imbokodo to form a joint committee to deal with this and other shared problems. On hearing reports that the Imbokodo might be willing to accept a less than normal diplomatic relationship with South Africa, Khama quietly reaffirmed his government's African character by commenting that it was difficult to see how South Africa and Botswana could exchange diplomatic representatives when the offer of the Zambian President, Kenneth Kaunda, had already been refused by Pretoria. Reference to Zambia was in line with frequent expressions of friendship toward that northern neighbour. While staying at the Zambian Embassy in Washington as the guest of Ambassador Soko, Khama said that Bechuanaland and Zambia 'understand each other more than a good many countries elsewhere because [they] are situated in a part of Africa which is turbulent, a part of Africa which has various racial conflicts'.

With independence assured and an expected four years in which to prove the wisdom of his government's middle course, Khama could only hope that as tribal ties weakened under the impact of democratic forms, they would not be replaced with internal support for a more vigorous Pan-Africanism than the charted course of his government could satisfy. Perhaps the greatest danger to his position might arise from the absence of a strong parliamentary opposition able to keep the government in tune with prevailing sentiment. In its absence, the government's essentially conservative character could be strengthened and it might fall too easily into the temptation to rely more heavily on even more conservative-minded expatriates at the expense of popular support.

10

THE ECONOMY OF BOTSWANA
by Dr H. George Henry

O F THE THREE former High Commission Territories, Botswana is the least well-endowed with agricultural resources. In the south and west, there are vast areas, amounting to more than half the entire country, of undulating scrubland: the Kalahari desert. In the south-west of the area, real desert conditions exist. Rainfall, highest in the northern regions, varies between twelve and twenty-seven inches a year. Because the Tropic of Capricorn passes through the centre of the country, the inhabitants are exposed to the common tropical disease of malaria, cattle are susceptible to foot and mouth disease and man and beast are constantly threatened by the dreaded trypanosomiasis, or 'sleeping sickness'.[1]

Water

The economic value of the Okavango river, which flows into the north-western corner of the country, is reduced by its absorption into a papyrus swamp teeming with the lethal tsetse fly. The critical shortage of water—far more acute than in Lesotho—is due to the poverty of the supply of surface water. The only sizeable source is the area of the Okavango swamps, which also nurture the richest wildlife in the country. Given this shortage and the frequent droughts with which the country is plagued, it is strange that the swamps have been left unexploited and undeveloped, particularly in the post-war period when more aid has been available to African communities than ever before. They are the largest swamps in Southern and Central Africa. It has been proposed that their waters be used to irrigate a cotton project that would dwarf even the Gezira scheme, the most important cotton-producing project in Africa and the backbone of the Sudan's economy.[2] Writing about this area of Bechuanaland as early as 1949, Professor John H. Wellington said: 'Two million to three million acres of swampland await drainage and development. . . . [What could be] a great food-producing area . . . [is] now only the playground of crocodiles, hippos and fish-hawk. There seems to be no other place in Africa where so much agricultural development is possible at so little cost.'[3]

However, the colonial government neglected to implement such development schemes as that proposed by Brind after his three-year study of the area about fifteen years ago. His proposal included controlling and conserving the water of the Okavango swamps, converting a part of them into a reservoir of 85,000 acre-feet and supplying water to the Gomare-Tube area, where good soils are said to exist. The only action taken by the government so far has been marginal: a limited number of boreholes equipped with pumping plants, quite inadequate as a stimulus to substantial growth.

Of the present 760,000 acres of arable land, only some 14,000 acres are under cultivation, chiefly in the eastern region. Apart from the lack of water, there is almost complete lack of knowledge of the various soil types and of their adaptability for efficient crop production. This absence of adequate data as a basis and guide for any kind of developmental programme is, of course, common to most underdeveloped countries.

Minerals

Gold was originally discovered, and gold mines developed, by ancient Africans in the Tati District of Bechuanaland. These mines are now controlled by the Tati Company, which has acquired the area and all mineral rights. Otherwise, little is known of the country's mineral resources, although Bechuanaland has been described as falling within that area of the earth which is richest in certain strategic minerals: 'It is a curious thing that the Kalahari, so spacious and so similar in geological history to its neighbours, should not share in these gifts of the gods to pioneer development. There is copper just over the border [of Bechuanaland] to the west, diamonds not so far to the south, gold on the east and Wankie coal on the north-east. The fact is that there probably *are* mineral deposits in the Kalahari, but how are we to find them when there is an almost universal covering of sand to hide all surface indications?'[4]

There is great need for comprehensive scientific surveys to ascertain the potential mineral capacity of the country. The British government undertook some geological surveys, but only of the most general type. These limited surveys have revealed the presence of deposits of limestone, asbestos, antimony, chromite, copper, iron, kyanite and lead,[5] though their commercial value remains to be proven. Recently, it was reported that rich and extensive coal deposits had been discovered in the Bamangwato tribal lands,[6] and the economic potential of the sodium carbonate-bearing brines of the Sua Pan region are also being investigated. Independent Botswana can now invite external capital and technology to survey and prospect for minerals. Their exploitation will, of course, depend on the provision of transportation, water supply and power; but convincing evidence of the presence of valuable minerals should make it easier to obtain the aid necessary for setting up the essential infrastructure. So far, the bulk of the mining has been on a small scale, concerned mainly with asbestos, manganese, gold and silver. The annual value of mineral exports since 1961 has been under £350,000. Among investors showing an interest in the mineral prospects of Botswana are the Rhodesian Selection Trust Exploration Company, the Standard Vacuum Oil Company of South Africa and De Beers Prospecting (Rhodesian Areas). It is possible that mining will become a factor of great economic significance for the country.

Population and Education

As in Lesotho, the major share of the burden of education rests on non-governmental shoulders. But whereas in Lesotho considerable encouragement was given to the churches to provide educational facilities, this has not been so in Botswana. As a result, there is greater political awareness among the Basuto and a proportionately larger and more articulate emerging middle class. The great majority of the primary schools in Botswana are administered by tribal school committees. This says much for involvement of tribal institutions but it also means leaving something which is vital for reducing human backwardness to an administration with very limited resources, horizons and objectives.

The entire educational system is weak in the provision of modern industrial skills and in supplying the leadership cadre of Batswana who are expected to assume positions of responsibility in this emerging African state. This weakness is only partially overcome by sending Batswana students to the university designated for the three Territories and situated in Basutoland. In 1963, this university was transferred to the British administration from the Roman Catholics, who had founded it as Pius XII College, but it has yet to attract a permanent faculty or provide a superior academic programme. Because of some noticeable retrenchments in faculty and courses, its attractiveness to 'foreign' students has decreased—an unhappy situation for, given the university's isolated position, it is essential that the student body reflects a healthy interaction of diverse national and ethnic backgrounds. In 1962, there were five Batswana students enrolled at the university; in the same year, the total number of Batswana in Bechuanaland holding BA degrees was thirty-five. A handful of students have received scholarships to study abroad, mainly in the United Kingdom and the United States.

Assuming an age-distribution roughly similar to that of Lesotho, about one-third of the total population comprises school-age children.[7] A recent estimate, based on a pilot census, put the population at between 500,000 and 600,000.[8] Thus there are roughly 160,000 to 200,000 children of school-going age, but, in spite of an increase in 1962, the total enrolled in primary and secondary schools was only 46,300[9]—less than a third of those eligible for education. Moreover, assuming the same level of educational opportunities for herdboys, the land-tenure system and the chieftainship together dictate that some sixty per cent of school-age boys, because of their duties herding cattle and acting as 'live fences', miss the chance of getting an education. Then, from the age of eighteen, they are forced into the market for cheap unskilled labour in South Africa, the only alternative for which they are eligible open to them. 'Some attempt is made to remedy this situation by having the herdboys leave the cattleposts for three or four years of school. But this is to a great extent a waste of funds, adding little to the numbers of the literate.' In many cases, the herdboy 'returns to the cattle and never reads a book again in his life'. Thus is established the invidious link between illiteracy and absence of industrial skills on the one hand, and a subsistence income on the other, and a high degree of human backwardness is perpetuated.

Medical services too are far from adequate for dealing with the large numbers of people suffering from preventable and other diseases. In 1962, there was in-patient accommodation for under 200 fee-paying and just over 1,000 non-paying patients.[10]

There is a clear need for the new Botswana government to give urgent attention not only to increasing the numbers of the literate but also to providing modern industrial and technical skills as one of the goals of economic development. Sources of aid hitherto ignored, such as the Peace Corps of the USA, can now be sought.

Agriculture

Crop production is a poor cousin to livestock-rearing in Botswana: only about five per cent of the arable land is cultivated, largely by Africans. The method of land allocation, the lack of adequate water supplies, the fact that the Batswana live in large villages at great distances from the farm lands—these are only some of the factors that adversely affect African agriculture and account for the very low outputs and subsistence methods of production of Batswana farmers. Substantial increases in the rate of output, without heavy capital investment, would be possible if changes were made in the distribution of lands and in the location of villages nearer the farms.

The concentration of the Batswana in relatively large villages is in contrast to the pattern of distribution of residences in the other former Territories. Equally different is the multi-tribal nature of the society and the consequent division of land-allocation authority among many chieftainship structures, as opposed to one in each of the other former Territories. Because of the distances between the fields and the villages, and the absence of modern means of transportation, a great deal of time is consumed in getting to work, although this is reduced somewhat by the desertion of entire villages at the planting and harvesting seasons, when there is the greatest demand for labour.[11]

Greater control over the production process is exercised by the chiefs in Botswana than in Lesotho or Swaziland. They tend to favour the planting of traditional crops and the use of traditional methods and, on many lands, ploughing and harvesting cannot begin until the chief gives the word. This is an 'irritant to the farmer who may not have the same crop as most of his neighbours, or simply has other ideas on when to plant and when to harvest. This custom no doubt had validity in older tribal days when the chief and his adviser had a monopoly on accumulated knowledge of the seasons. Although anachronistic, it persists as a deterrent to better individual farming'.[12] The system of land tenure prohibits individual exclusive rights and the fencing which is a symbol of such rights. It therefore represses and stifles all those innovations, enterprises and improvements which derive from the free expression of self-interest.

The common method of agriculture among the Batswana is that of shifting cultivation of subsistence crops, based on the tradition that, except for the essential minima of ploughing, planting and reaping nature need not be aided. 'No agricultural instruments are used other than the plough drawn by oxen or donkeys, for breaking the soil, and the hoe for weeding. Sowing is done by hand, the seed being broadcast and the harvest is done by plucking off the ears. Threashing is done in much the same manner as it was done in the days of the Old Testament, by beating the ears with long sticks on a specially prepared granary floor.'[13] There is a sharp contrast between the productivity of the Batswana and that of the non-African farmers, who more readily introduce rotation of crops and make use of selected quality seeds and fertilisers. Their output per acre is variously estimated as being between five and fifteen times greater than that of the Batswana.[14]

Sorghum, the most important crop grown by the Batswana, provides a surplus for export. Maize, although the staple food, is a marginal crop and domestic output is supplemented by relatively heavy imports from South Africa and Rhodesia. Between 1960 and 1962, maize imports averaged about £290,000 a year. As well as the sorghum surplus, other exports include beans and pulses, and wheat, maize and tobacco from non-African farms are sold in both local and external markets. Where some kind of irrigation is possible, production of citrus fruits has recently begun, and small quantities have been exported.

The problem of increasing agricultural output can be attacked at three different levels. At one level, without incurring over-heavy capital costs and without too much disturbance of the existing social order, very substantial increases in output can be achieved by massive extension programmes aimed at introducing such rudimentary agricultural practices as rotation of crops and the use of selected seeds and of fertilisers. There should also be investigation of the advantages of substituting crops for those at present imported. As a second level of change, increased productivity demands a reallocation of lands in compact blocks of economic size and the resiting of villages of smaller sizes nearer the farms. Such a change would shake long-standing values and traditions, threaten the power of the chiefs and involve huge outlays in capital expenditure—in fact it would constitute a revolution. At still another level, consideration must be given to increasing the water supply by irrigation, providing adequate means of transportation and communication, and devising and instituting marketing and credit facilities adapted to the conditions peculiar to

Botswana. This breakdown of the different orders of change should not be considered as sequences in a programme of development, nor as a listing of priorities, but as a conceptual breakdown of the problem into separate but inter-related phases. Different combinations of these phases may be adopted for the whole country or adapted to fit the needs of different areas.

Livestock rearing

The Batswana are primarily a pastoral people and livestock rearing is their most important form of domestic economic activity. During the period 1947 to 1955, it accounted for between 70 and 90 per cent of total commodity exports and constituted 80 per cent of the contribution of agriculture to geographical and national income.[15] Cattle rearing is the chief source of cash income for the African peasant and the farming community in general—about 90 per cent of the cattle population is owned by Africans.[16] Cattle are also used for ploughing and as a means of transportation.

The attitude of the Batswana to cattle is much more market-oriented than that of either the Basuto or the Swazi. They come much closer to accepting cattle as a marketable commodity to be exploited commercially as a means of providing a regular money income.[17] Unfortunately, there are still not enough Batswana who realise that improvement in quality should precede an increase in quantity. The problem of restricting the number of cattle to the available pasturage and water has become serious. Although an annual growth rate of 34,000 head a year was a cause of concern in 1958, the serious drought has substantially reduced the national herd, previously estimated at about 1,300,000. Cattle husbandry is generally primitive. Animals are normally herded on the bare unfenced veld and tended at cattle-posts by herdboys. There is no stall feeding, no silage production, no paddocks to ensure proper pasture management, no fencing to make scientific breeding possible. There are a few examples of the introduction of fencing, but where it is found it should not be construed as providing the high degree of exclusion or the individual ownership associated with fencing in European countries.

Whereas in Basutoland the British administration gave some attention to developing wool and mohair as products for the export market, in Bechuanaland heavier investments were made in the cattle industry, through the initiative and enterprise of the Colonial Development Corporation. In 1954, the Corporation built and started working the Lobatsi abattoir which now handles 80 to 90 per cent of the total export of carcases from Botswana.[18] On the base it provided, a tannery, a creamery, and bone-meal and soap factories have been established. The whole concern has been hailed as the greatest economic event in the history of the country. This has been followed up with great improvements in marketing. Overseas beef sales in 1964 were, for the first time, greater than those in the traditional markets such as South Africa.[19] Most of the increase went to the United Kingdom.[20]

A commendable feature of the Colonial Development Corporation, and one worthy of imitation, is its combination of external capital and know-how with the domestic resources of land, labour and cattle in such a way as to increase production and incomes and provide some profit. It also provides a means for teaching new skills to the Batswana. The Botswana government has now secured some shares in the enterprise, as has a group of trustees acting on behalf of the African and non-African producers—between them they hold exactly half the shares, with the Corporation holding the other half. The way is open for the next logical step, the conversion of the enterprise into a corporation owned and operated by the Batswana themselves. This, if successful, would constitute an excellent example of a scheme concerned with two main aspects of the state of underdevelopment—the exploitation of natural resources and the reduction of human backwardness by providing the Batswana with skills and economic opportunities at all levels.

Industrial and Commercial Sector

There are no industries in Bechuanaland apart from the agricultural industries centred on the Lobatsi abattoir. As in Basutoland, the bulk of the import and export trade is in the hands of non-Africans, chiefly South Africans. Under the British administration, law and custom tended to reinforce the monopoly rights and privileges granted in earlier days. According to a 1955 survey, 74 per cent of the general dealers' licences were held by Europeans, 15 per cent by Africans and 11 per cent by Asiatics. In 1955, of a total geographic income of £9,789,000, 43·3 per cent, some £4,240,000, came from trade and transport combined, but in a total net national income of £7,124,000, they provided only £1,048,000.[21] Thus a high percentage of the difference left the Territory in the form of interest, profits and dividends to the head offices of the trading stores, outside Bechuanaland. (On the other hand, migrant labour to South Africa provides a smaller but offsetting inflow of income.) In almost no instance have any of the non-African traders managed to establish partnerships or corporations in association with Africans, nor provided opportunities for them as business managers, auditors or accountants. The participation of Africans in the non-African trading stores has been limited to the role of shop assistants, maids and loaders and unloaders of merchandise. As a result of this limited experience and participation in commercial activity, among the Batswana there is a great lack of accounting skills, of knowledge of business management and of the techniques associated with successful entrepreneurship. At a very rough estimate, there are about 3,000 Africans employed in trade and industry. The average wage is about £5 10s. a month.

The Basuto are far in advance of the Batswana in the establishment of co-operative societies—chiefly because of the work done in Basutoland by the churches, especially the Roman Catholic Church. In Bechuanaland, the British administration, after initially opposing the attempts of the Roman Catholic Church to organise co-operatives, reversed its policy in 1948 and itself undertook responsibility for this. Such institutions, if successful, could help to increase the national income and both encourage necessary training and provide experience in business and commercial skills.

All the financial institutions are branches of concerns with head offices outside the Territory, and until recently these captured local savings were used almost entirely for financing developments beyond its borders. There were very limited opportunities for investment in Bechuanaland. The urgent need for economic development now makes it essential that new principles be introduced and new arrangements made to enable banking and other financial institutions to reverse the flow of funds on a basis other than what traditional banking practice would consider prudent. Such a departure from 'orthodox' financial practice is feasible as long as the necessary safeguards against default and insolvency on the part of debtors can be guaranteed, and it is the government that is best adapted to do so. To support any such guarantee, it will be necessary to provide the means and the incentives for increasing savings among the Batswana. Hence the development of an adequate system of financial institutions must go hand in hand with other forms of economic development, for these lie at the very nerve centre of any economy with an exchange sector. Until now no Batswana has been trained or given employment opportunities in the highly skilled jobs of banking and finance, but it is essential that they acquire these skills in order to help guide their country up the steep paths of economic development.

A small number of Batswana still supplement their incomes from agriculture with traditional handicraft, produced in the homes. Artifacts are manufactured from fibre, bone, wood, clay, leather and other home-grown materials, together with such imports as beads and paint.

The absence of any adequate degree of infrastructure is one of the main obstacles to industrialisation in Botswana, but is no reason for condemning the country eternally to an existence based solely on subsistence agriculture and livestock rearing. The country has vast resources of water and wildlife, 95 per cent of its arable land remains uncultivated and the potential of its mineral wealth is still largely unknown. Something can be done about the very poor state of the roads and communications. The water resources can be profitably exploited and better allocated, and power produced. The financial institutions can be broadened, deepened and tailored to the needs of a developing economy. These are by no means easy tasks, nor can they be accomplished overnight. What is required is a planned massive attack on all the problems but, if this is to be achieved, it will be necessary to obtain substantial aid in the form of both capital and skilled personnel from the developed countries and the international agencies.

As recent reports confirm, attempts to tackle some of the problems of preparing Botswana for economic development are under way. Several United Nations agencies have embarked on different projects which are essential preconditions for development. The International Development Association has granted a loan of about £1,285,000 for road development, which will, among other things, make the very rich wildlife of the Okavango swamps more accessible. The FAO will undertake a livestock and wildlife conservation project. The WHO will spend about £30,000 on tsetse fly control, UNESCO is to undertake a survey of secondary education, at present in a very poor state, and several other projects are to be sponsored by the ILO and the United Nations Children's Fund.[22] When the infrastructure has been provided, the stage will be set not only for the development of agriculture, including livestock rearing, but also for diversification of the economy, by exploitation of mineral resource potential and by the introduction of light industries.

The Government Sector

As in Lesotho, apart from agriculture and livestock rearing, the government is the largest employer of labour. Unlike Lesotho, however, where most of the non-Africans are employed by the government, in Botswana the main source of employment of non-Africans is the trade and commercial sector.[23] About 2,000 salaried and 1,500 wage-earning Africans are employed by the administration, and part of the reason for this number's being so small is that the government did not undertake responsibility for providing education of the quality necessary to produce an adequate leadership cadre of Africans.

Up until the 1950s, the efforts of the British administration to bring about social and economic development in Bechuanaland were negligible. This was especially so in the period preceding the Pim Report. How much concern the British administration had for the social and economic development of Bechuanaland may be inferred from an examination of its budget policy. According to the data available, revenue collected by the administration was 83 per cent of the total expenditure and grants for the twenty-three years from 1932–3 to 1954–5.[24] In keeping with the instructions to Resident Commissioners, expenditures were kept at a very low level—a policy out of touch with modern theory of fiscal policy as an instrument for development and for maximising social welfare. Modern theory emphasises the wisdom of spending rather than of parsimony.*

In trying to explain why the British administration gave so little attention to economic development in the period before the 1950s, consideration has been given to the historical and political conditions which caused Britain reluctantly to assume the responsibilities of protector: the uncertainty about the political future of the country; the prevailing ideology governing the relationship between a colonial

---

* 'It is a truth not confined to public finance that "our great need is economy". But there is a sharp distinction to be drawn between false and true economy, between spending as little as we can, regardless of the results attained, and spending whatever is necessary in order to produce the best results obtainable—in short, between spending little and spending wisely. If, therefore, public finance is to be treated as a branch of science, economic or political, and not merely as a string of catchpenny maxims, one fundamental principle must lie at the root of it. This we may call the Principle of Maximum Social Advantage. . . . As a result of these operations of public finance, changes take place in the amount and in the nature of the wealth which is produced, and in the distribution of that wealth among individuals and classes.' (Hugh Dalton, *Principles of Public Finance*, Routledge & Kegan Paul, London 1936, 9th ed., pp. 9–10.)

power and a dependent state; the 'disinclination to cause any sudden dislocation of native cultures through contact with the demands of white colonists'.[25] But this explanation is not entirely satisfactory: there is a further aspect. The attitude of a colonial power towards the economic development of its dependent states is necessarily regulated, to some extent, by the motive of self-interest. For this reason, the economic development of Bechuanaland by the British depended on: (*a*) the apparent coincidence of short-run or long-run interests and benefits from the projects to be undertaken; (*b*) the threat to British interests arising from the failure to develop the economy; (*c*) the effectiveness of the pressures of the Batswana for such development; and, more recently, (*d*) the pressures brought to bear on the British administration by the challenge of South Africa, which alleges that it will develop its Bantustans at a faster rate than Bechuanaland or the other two Territories.

Since the late 1950s, the improvement schemes introduced after the Pim Report have been expanded. The most important of these have been the projects connected with the livestock industry. The operations of the Colonial Development Corporation provide a useful model of the kind of co-operation—between government and private enterprise, and between external capital and technology on the one hand and domestic labour, land and other resources on the other—which could serve both domestic and external interests. Its greatest virtue lies in its potentiality for assisting with both phases of the developmental process—the exploitation of natural resources and the reduction of human backwardness.

The improvement schemes introduced by the British administration have so far produced only marginal benefits: it is structural changes, involving new methods of organisation, new and more efficient methods of production, new products and new and wider markets, that are required to push the economy over the hump. Such changes await the development of the infrastructure, the launching of massive research programmes and the introduction of a modern educational system designed to produce Batswana with technical and industrial skills. The African government recently installed can now negotiate for loans, grants and technology from many external sources, instead of relying on the United Kingdom alone. It can, more easily than the former British administration, modify or abolish those institutions which inhibit development, and create those likely to facilitate and induce growth.

PART III

SWAZILAND

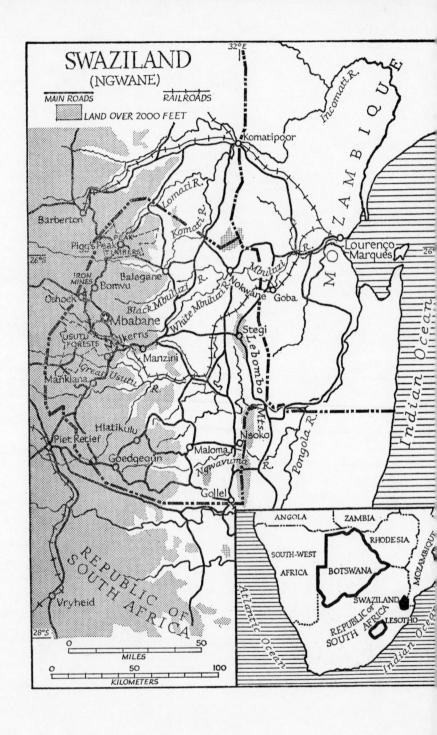

SWAZILAND
(NGWANE)

MAIN ROADS   RAILROADS

LAND OVER 2000 FEET

Barberton

Pigg's Peak
PEAK
(TIMBERS)

IRON
MINES

Bomvu

Balegane

Oshoek

Mbabane

Usutu
FORESTS

Malverns

Manzini

Mankiana

Great Usutu R.

Hlatikulu

Piet Retief

Goedgegun

Maloma

Nsoko

Gollel

Vryheid

REPUBLIC
OF
SOUTH AFRICA

Komatipoor

Lomati R.

Komati R.

Black Mbuluzi R.

White Mbuluzi R.

Nokwane

Mbuluzi

Goba

Stegi

Lebombo Mts.

Ngwavuma R.

Pongola R.

MOZAMBIQUE

Incomati R.

Lourenço
Marques

Indian Ocean

32°E

26°S

28°S

0   50
MILES

0   50   100
KILOMETERS

ANGOLA   ZAMBIA

SOUTH-WEST
AFRICA   RHODESIA

BOTSWANA

SWAZILAND

REPUBLIC or
SOUTH AFRICA   LESOTHO

Atlantic Ocean

MOZAMBIQUE

Indian Ocean

II

EARLY SWAZI HISTORY AND EUROPEAN
ASCENDANCY

TUCKED BETWEEN Mozambique and the north-eastern corner of the Republic of South Africa, Swaziland, with its 6,704 square miles, is one of the smallest countries on the African continent. The Swazi people, composed of various clan origins, have existed as a distinct tribe only since the beginning of the nineteenth century. The Nkosi-Dlamini, today the ruling clan of the Swazi, migrated from central Africa towards Delagoa Bay and then southwards into Tongaland in the fifteenth century. There the Dlamini remained for almost two hundred years until the reign of Ngwane III, the first ruler commemorated in present day ritual, who led his followers across the Lubombo mountains and built his capital, Lobamba, in what is now south-eastern Swaziland. Ngwane (died *circa* 1780), his son Ndunguanya (died 1815), and his grandson Sobhuza I, thereafter absorbed the small clans in the neighbouring district of Eshiselweni, a region since regarded as the birthplace of the Swazi nation.

Land disputes forced Sobhuza I and his people to move northward from Eshiselweni into central Swaziland, near the present site of Manzini (Bremersdorp). There the royal capital was established and, even to the present day, it remains the centre of royal villages. While consolidating his position through conquest and marriage alliances, Sobhuza was troubled with periodic raids from the Zulu who, after Shaka's succession to the chieftainship in 1815, controlled the area south of the Pongola river. Always a strategist, Sobhuza avoided conflict with his Zulu adversaries and at last, in 1836, forced them to retire from the country. While there is no evidence that Sobhuza had any personal contact with Europeans, in all likelihood some of his people met both British and Boers. When he died in 1839, Sobhuza left his infant son, Mswati, a strong kingdom which extended roughly as far as Barberton in the north, Carolina and Ermelo in the west, the Pongola river in the south, and the Lubombo mountains in the east.

After a troubled regency, Mswati ascended the throne in 1840. The new ruler continued the work of unification by developing the age-group system borrowed from the Zulu. This system not only provided the growing nation with a well disciplined fighting force, but introduced greater respect for the rule of the Dlamini, since it cut across clan and lineage affiliations. Through raids which carried his *impis* as far north as the present territory of Rhodesia, Mswati was able to construct a widely extended system of rule founded upon ties of loyalty, friendship and intermarriage. By this time it was also common for the members of the Dlamini and associated clans to use the name of Swazi, because of their allegiance to Mswati.

But as the Swazi reached the high-water mark of their expansion and influence, it was evident that the days of tribal warfare and expansion were being brought to a close. Everywhere African kingdoms were being crushed and subjected, either directly or indirectly, to the rule of the European. It was, in fact, only the British annexation of Natal which, by lessening the Zulu threat from the south, permitted Mswati's northern and western expansion. At the same time, however, Mswati appealed to Theophilus Shepstone, the newly appointed Diplomatic Agent to the Natives in Natal, and considered himself fortunate in securing British diplomatic protection inasmuch as Shepstone refused to permit even 'one small swoop' upon the Swazi by the Zulu.

The Arrival of Europeans: The First Concessions

Mswati's reign saw the arrival in Swaziland of growing numbers of Europeans, and contact with the foreigners brought a new era in Swazi history. Farmers from the Transvaal highlands seeking better pasture, traders from the coast eager to barter their various wares for ivory and skins, and hunters in pursuit of abundant game—all made their appearance in the country. In 1846, Mswati granted a cession of all land between the Olifants and Crocodile rivers to the Lydenburg Republic of the Boers. Another cession was granted to the Transvaal Republic and, though these cessions had no immediate effects, they proved to be the precursors of the confusion and final subjection of the Swazi.

Mswati's death in 1868 meant the passing of the last of the truly independent and fighting Swazi kings. Meanwhile, the traditional pattern of Swazi life was affected by the course of events in Southern Africa as Boers and Britons contended for supremacy. The Boers were especially interested in the Swazi country as it provided access to the eastern coast. Moreover, their relationships with the Swazi were fairly close during the lifetime of Mswati, and these were strengthened as a result of troubles arising over the succession to the chieftainship after his death. Having suppressed the conflicts between the factions supporting the rival claims of Mswati's sons, in 1875 the Transvaal Boers recognised the installation of Mbandzeni, a younger son of Mswati by a junior wife. A weak and depraved chief, much given to 'the white man's liquor', Mbandzeni and his council of chiefs formally confirmed the concessions made to the Boers by Mswati in return for their support.

Swazi Independence and Extension of Concessions

Unfortunately for the Boers, however, conditions of anarchy and financial embarrassment prevented the Transvaal Republic from capitalising upon its successful intrusion into Swaziland. The British, on the other hand, were able to act more forcefully in checking Boer aspirations towards the coast. But while checking the Boers, the British government hesitated to extend its own jurisdiction and thus increase its local commitments by annexing a country small in area, isolated from other territories and most likely to prove costly and troublesome to govern. Although restrained for vastly different reasons from assuming total hegemony, both British and Boers therefore settled for a mutual guarantee of Swazi independence in the two Conventions of 1881 and 1884.

Recognition of Swazi independence did not prevent, nor was it intended to prevent, the Transvaal Boers or other Europeans from acquiring land or other rights within this land of unknown promise. The arbitrarily-defined boundaries included in the Pretoria Convention of 1881, which guaranteed the Transvaal complete self-government subject to the suzerainty of Britain, encroached upon land to which the Swazi had already laid claim. Henceforth, thousands of Swazi found themselves domiciled in the Transvaal Republic (known after 1860 as the South African Republic) and removed from the jurisdiction of their king; and, while large areas were thus effectively severed from Swazi control, the granting of concessions served to reduce what was left of Swazi sovereignty to a legal fiction.

The granting of concessions, which extended as far back as 1860, had not been opposed by the Swazi chiefs. For, in addition to the prospect of profit, association with the Europeans meant protection against the Zulu. The discovery of gold in north-western Swaziland in 1879 brought many more concession-seekers to Mbandzeni's court. They requested not only land and mineral rights, but rights for all conceivable purposes. By the beginning of the twentieth century:

> Practically the whole area of the country was covered two, three or even four deep by concessions of all sizes for different purposes, and for greatly varying periods. In but very few cases were even the boundaries defined; many of the areas had been subdivided and sold several times, and seldom were the boundaries of the superimposed areas even coterminous. In addition to this, concessions were granted for all lands and minerals previously unallotted or which, having been allotted, might lapse or become forfeited. Finally it must be remembered, that over these three or four strata of conflicting interests, boundaries and periods, there had to be preserved the natural rights of the natives to live, move, cultivate, graze and hunt.[1]

Although Mbandzeni and his councillors were not entirely unaware of the consequences of their actions in granting concessions (during the peak of the concessions period they were apparently receiving more than £12,000 annually), it was manifestly impossible for these illiterate leaders to appreciate such concepts as leasehold, freehold, private ownership, trade monopoly, banking privilege, etc., all of which were embodied in the concessions. It may be accepted that, in granting concessions, Mbandzeni did not contemplate the permanent alienation of any of the Territory's natural resources but intended to grant only usufruct, for in Swazi law and custom there was no recognition of a right to alienate national assets.

However unaware of the consequences of their actions, the Swazi chiefs were soon made to realise the tragic implications of these grants. Immigrants proved to be without scruple in their treatment of the Swazi and frequently tended to disregard the authority of the chiefs. Relationships between the Swazi people and their traditional authority were thus set at naught. Moreover, the Boers made it clear that their guarantee of Swazi independence was purely nominal.

A Resident Adviser Appointed: Swazi Sovereignty Destroyed

Capitalising upon the breakdown of internal security as lawless elements among the whites strove for gain, the Boers advised Mbandzeni in 1866 to repudiate any obligations to the British. Such action, they argued, would permit the establishment of proper government. But Mbandzeni declined to follow this advice and instead sought British protection and asked for a British Resident. Both requests were refused. Mbandzeni thereupon turned to Theophilus Shepstone, who still enjoyed the confidence of the tribes in south-eastern Africa. Unable to accept this request, Shepstone recommended his son, Theophilus Shepstone, Jr, as Resident Adviser, and the appointment was made in 1886.

As a paid Adviser, Shepstone's task was to deal solely with the affairs of the whites in the Swazi territory. In this way, Mbandzeni hoped to reduce the possibility that anarchy might be used as an excuse by the Boers for taking over complete control of the country. Shepstone's appointment, however, had no official standing with the British government and he soon was as much out of favour with a faction of British concessionaires as he was with the Boers, most of whom were farmers.

It was Mbandzeni's intention to control the Europeans through their own institutions and at the same time to retain his sovereignty. With the King's sanction, Shepstone called a meeting of concessionaires, and a white committee of fifteen property owners was elected. Five additional members were appointed as the King's nominees. To this committee Mbandzeni, in 1888, reluctantly gave a 'Charter of Rights' which conferred the power of self-government. But he expressly reserved to himself the right to veto any decisions. Despite this safeguard, however, the introduction of a European system of government established a precedent thereafter utilised to supplant the indigenous Swazi administration and further impinge upon their sovereignty. Although Shepstone organised a concessions register and undertook the systematic collection of rentals, it was during his tenure as Resident Adviser that the majority of monopoly concessions were granted. Therefore, despite European 'assistance', Mbandzeni saw his heritage dwindle, his domain restricted by European boundary commissions, and his power questioned by European governments. When he was near to death, he mourned with good reason that 'Swazi kingship ends with me'.[2] In truth, when Mbandzeni died in 1889, his people were only nominally independent, since the entire country was owned by concessionaires.

The white committee established by Shepstone failed to exercise control, and discord between the two European groups made its work ineffective. It was dissolved by the Swazis themselves in 1889, shortly after the death of Mbandzeni. Meanwhile, a number of Europeans in Swaziland had joined in a request to Kruger's South African Republic (now enjoying restored autonomy after a brief British interlude, and with its treasury refurbished) to take over control of the country. President Kruger accordingly sought to take advantage of this opportunity to secure an eastern outlet through Swaziland. He proposed to respect British interests north of the Limpopo river if Britain would give its support to South African aspirations in Swaziland. The result of these endeavours was the creation of a joint commission of inquiry into the affairs of the Territory.

The Establishment of Dual Rule

The commission began its work a month after Mbandzeni's death. Despite the inclination of the British Commissioner to favour the incorporation of Swaziland within the South African Republic, commercial and philanthropic interests in Britian forced the Secretary of State to reject the proposal. Dual rule was the only acceptable alternative. This agreement took the form of the First Swaziland Convention, signed in 1890, and, with the approval of the acting Swazi Regents, a provisional government was established. It received full power to adjudicate in matters affecting the whites and to frame laws for them. It was composed of representatives of the two white powers, a representative of the Swazi (the Resident Adviser), various officials, and a Chief Court. The Court was further empowered to inquire into the validity of the concessions and discharged this function by confirming 352 out of a total of 364 concessions.

Although the Provisional Government Committee which the Convention provided proved to be short-lived, it laid down that no inroad should be allowed upon the independence of the Swazi, not even with the consent of the Swazi nation, unless approved by both the British and the South African Republic governments. It was also stipulated that no powers or jurisdiction were to be exercised by the Committee or any court over any matter in which Swazi alone were concerned. Subject to all existing rights, the sovereignty and ownership of the Swazi nation of all land within the boundaries of Swaziland was to be recognised. No new land grants or concessions were to have legal validity without the approval of the two contracting powers. But 'to responsible Europeans, settled in the country or having interests there, the necessity for a single administration became increasingly obvious.

... In the meantime black and white were becoming increasingly interdependent and the black man's institutions thwarted the white man's ambitions and autonomy. At the same time, a basis was required for dispossessing the Swazi of their sovereignty without violating too blatantly the pledges of the 1881 and 1884 Conventions.'[3]

Dual rule did not prove successful. South African concessions in various public services, revenue-raising and administrative procedures hampered British participation. Growing hostility between Boer and British officials reflected the attitudes prevailing throughout Southern Africa. While fewer in number than the British, the Boers were not deterred from seeking complete control of the country. 'The Republic believed itself entitled to acquire the country by virtue of the interests held there, not only by numerous of its citizens but by the government itself.'[4] In 1891, the Republic reminded the British government of its pledge to further consider Swaziland problems once dual rule was established. Moreover, the inherent weakness of dual rule was made more evident by the confusion which arose over the selection of a successor to Mbandzeni, a problem tardily solved by the selection of Bunu (sometimes known as Ngwane), the sixteen-year-old eldest son of the Queen Regent, Gwamile Mduli, a woman of exceptional intelligence and resolution, and widow of Mbandzeni.

South African Ascendancy Established

In view of the South African Republic's open hostility towards British interests, it is not easy to understand why the British government agreed to sanction Boer negotiations with the Swazi. But by the Covention of 1893 Britain consented to an agreement by which 'the rights and powers of jurisdiction, protection and administration over Swaziland, though without incorporation thereof into the South African Republic' could be made the matter of discussions between the Republic and the Swazi. Britain therefore intended to barter Swaziland for a free hand elsewhere, as the two European states pursued their larger aims. But there was a third party, without whose concurrence this pact was ineffectual. For the vital condition to the whole arrangement was the issuance of an Organic Proclamation by the Swazi Queen Regent, conferring on the Republic the necessary authority. Not only did the Queen Regent (who by Swazi custom enjoyed a position of unusual authority) and her Council refuse to agree to this proposed transfer, one so obviously contrary to the guarantee of Swazi independence contained in the

Convention of 1890, but they despatched a deputation to England to plead for British protection. However, the British government, believing it more important for the moment to curtail Boer ambitions in other directions, declined to accept Swazi allegiance. In addition, it was felt that some provision must be made for the effective governing of the country, lest serious disorders arise among the 750 European residents and the South African Republic be justified in outright occupation.[5] In December 1894, a Convention with the South African Republic was concluded, embodying most of the terms contained in the projected arrangement of 1893. It differed, however, inasmuch as it dispensed with the condition requiring the previous assent of the Swazi or the issuance by the Queen Regent of an Organic Proclamation. Faced with impossible odds and unwilling to suffer the fate of openly rebellious Bantu nations, the Swazi temporarily submitted.

It is from the date of the Convention in 1894 that the Swazi lost that formal guarantee of independence which was contained in the Conventions of 1881, 1884 and 1890. Although it is true that the Convention of 1894 stipulated that Swaziland should not be incorporated in the South African Republic, that King Ngwane should, after coming of age, be Paramount Chief of the Swazi, and that the internal affairs of the Swazi people should be administered by the chiefs, these conditions did not alter the fact that the South African Republic was given 'all rights and powers of protection, legislation, jurisdiction and administration over Swaziland and the inhabitants thereof'. Needless to say, the Swazi have consistently emphasised the fact that they were not a party to the Convention. This argument is ironically dismissed by Lord Hailey, who states: 'In the practice regulating these matters, the recognition accorded to a change of national status has more frequently depended on the decisions taken by exterior powers than on the wishes expressed by the inhabitants of the country concerned. There can be no doubt that from the legal standpoint the Transvaal acquired in 1894 a measure of authority in Swaziland which was qualified only by the obligation to observe the conditions laid down in the Convention. But the Swazi had no effective means of securing the observance of this obligation, except by appealing to the British to use their influence with the Transvaal government.'[6] Thus, by a stroke of the pen, Swazi sovereignty was not only destroyed but its destruction was justified in terms of legalistic casuistry.

In February 1895, a Resident Special Commissioner and other officials were appointed by the Republic by virtue of Article III of the

Convention of the Transvaal (1894). The British government was represented only through a Resident Consul. But the satisfaction of having obtained control of the Territory was short-lived. Only two months later, Britain annexed Tongaland to the east and thereby frustrated Boer aspirations towards the sea. The Jameson Raid of 1896 also augured ill for the future.

The Convention of 1894 provided, inter alia, for the introduction of a native hut tax three years after the signing. But, as the time approached, rumours spread that the Swazi intended to resist payment and that an army was being prepared to attack the whites. While inter-group feeling became increasingly hostile, a leading councillor, reportedly sympathetic to the whites, was executed in 1898 at the Swazi capital. Bunu, who by now had succeeded to the throne as 'Ngwenyama' (Paramount or King), was allegedly implicated in the murder. Summoned to appear in the court of the local Landdrost, Bunu refused and fled for refuge to a British magistrate in Natal. Milner, then High Commissioner, refused to surrender Bunu on the grounds that there was no court in existence competent to try the King. British refusal to surrender him was based on the admission of the South African President that he wished there to be no more Paramount Chiefs after Bunu. In Boer eyes, Bunu had already abandoned the throne by flight, despite the fact that by Swazi custom, 'if the king is dead, the queen is the king'.[7] A compromise was at last worked out whereby Bunu submitted himself to judgement, received a moderate fine, and was reinstated. But the incident also resulted in the promulgation of a protocol to the Convention of 1894 which severely limited the civil and criminal jurisdiction of the Swazi chiefs. It thus marked a further stage in diminishing the independence originally guaranteed by the Conventions of 1890 and 1891. European domination was now substantially accomplished.

12

SWAZILAND UNDER BRITISH
ADMINISTRATION, 1903–1959

WITH THE OUTBREAK of the Anglo-Boer war in 1899, it was agreed that neither side would engage non-whites lest the myth of white superiority be weakened. The Boer administration was therefore withdrawn from Swaziland and the Resident Special Commissioner handed over all authority to the Ngwenyama. The Swazi remained strictly neutral and the war had little effect upon the Territory. Bunu died during the early part of the war (December 1899) and the Swazi Council selected his son, Sobhuza II, born only five months earlier, as his successor. The Queen Regent took up the reins of government and continued to act, assisted by a younger son of Mbandzeni, until 1921 when Sobhuza, together with his mother, was formally installed.

Constitutional Implications of the Order-in-Council of 1903

After the Boer defeat in 1902, Britain assumed reluctant control over Swaziland. A special Commissioner was sent to take charge of the Territory and the Swaziland order-in-council of June 25, 1903, was issued to regulate relations between the two countries. This order, issued by virtue of the powers conferred in the Foreign Jurisdiction Act of 1880, provided the basic authority under which the administration of the country has since been conducted. It vested the control of the Territory in the Governor of the Transvaal Colony, now under British jurisdiction. The laws of the Transvaal were applied, and a small provisional administration was established. The jurisdiction of chiefs was further limited to 'civil disputes in which aboriginal natives only are concerned'. The jurisdiction of the Crown, affirmed the preamble to the order-in-council, was based on the fact that the South African Republic formerly exercised 'powers of protection, jurisdiction and administration in Swaziland', and that all the rights and powers of the

Republic over Swaziland had passed to the British Crown by virtue of the conquest and annexation of the Transvaal. When the Transvaal received self-government in 1906, the powers conferred on the Governor were transferred to the High Commissioner and a system of control by the imperial government was inaugurated. A Resident Commissioner was appointed as the head of local personnel. The Crown thus ignored a Swazi request for the establishment of a protectorate by treaty. No attention was given to the Swazi claim that, inasmuch as the country's nominal independence had not been taken away either by conquest or by treaty, the defeat of the Republic meant that, legally, Swaziland's protected status had fallen away and that full sovereignty was restored. Hopes for a restoration of internal sovereignty were thus dashed and Swazi chiefs were clearly subordinated in the system. The South Africa Act of 1910, which indicated conditions for future transfer of Swaziland to the newly formed Union of South Africa, completed the destruction of Swazi sovereignty.

Through these enactments the British government purported to have taken over complete legislative and administrative authority in the Territory, subject only to the conditions regarding respect for Swazi law and custom. However, the order-in-council did not provide any precise indication of the Territory's constitutional status. Swaziland continued to be regarded as a protectorate, although the juristic interpretation of that label changed with time and place. It has usually conveyed different meanings to officials, settlers and the Swazi. Whereas before the Berlin Act of 1885, the British government contended that complete internal sovereignty should remain with the protected people, after that date English politicians inclined towards a different interpretation. Realising that the economic interests of investors might be endangered by 'primitive' and unsettled conditions, they followed the system already practised by other imperial powers and steadily assumed control of both internal and external affairs.[1] From the English juristic point of view, the difference between a protectorate and a colony lies in the fact that a colony is in a full sense part of the possessions of the Crown, whereas a protectorate is a British possession only for international purposes. 'Where internal sovereignty gradually passes to the protecting power', notes Lord Hailey, 'it becomes extremely difficult to draw a line between a protectorate and a colony.'[2] The status of the 'protected' person appears, if anything, to be lower than that of the colonised, for 'the natives of British colonies are British subjects whereas the natives of a protectorate are not full subjects and have not the rights of British subjects in the King's dominions'.[3] While the Swazi have always insisted that they are a protected nation in possession of internal sovereignty, the British maintain the earlier guarantees of independence are meaningless. Thus, according to Lord Hailey, 'agreements made with native rulers and guaranteeing their independence cannot be allowed international force ... since they were made by people subsequently brought under protection'. Furthermore, he argues: 'Natives of protectorates are not subjects of the Crown and therefore in any suit against the Crown would seem to have only the status of foreign persons. Therefore such agreements cannot be held by the courts to have force where they conflict with subsequent legislation'.[4]

Although the irony of these statements requires no comment, to some degree they explain the tragedy of Swaziland and the other High Commission Territories. For while legalities stripped the Swazi nation of its sovereignty, thus depriving it of the means to deal with the modern world, the recognition of Swazi law and custom fettered the modern Swazi to traditional forms which could serve only to ensure that the people would be permanently exploited by whites bound by nothing save their own individualistic philosophy.

Defeat on the Land Claims Question

Before there could be either security or development under the new British administration, it was necessary to settle the question of land ownership. By 1904, the Governor of the Transvaal had appointed the necessary commission of investigation. As a result of its recommendations the Concessions Partitions Proclamation of 1907 provided that all land and grazing concessions in the Territory were subject to a deduction of one-third of their area for the sole and exclusive use and occupation 'of the natives of Swaziland'. The remaining two-thirds were declared free from such occupation, subject to the provision that, for five years from July 1909, no native actually resident on such land could be compelled to move, but that thereafter they could continue to occupy the land only on terms to be agreed upon between themselves and the concessionaires. Such agreements would in turn be subject to confirmation by the Resident Commissioner. The majority of all concessions granting exclusive rights, other than those to land and minerals, were expropriated at their value prior to the beginning of the Boer war.

This settlement came as a shock to the Swazi. A petition was drawn up and a deputation sent to London to protest against the terms of the Proclamation. Their anguish, says Dr Hilda Kuper, can be understood when it is remembered that the Swazi were almost entirely a peasantry. 'They won their subsistence from the soil; their major rituals were directed to increase its yield; the land was ritually identified with the king, with prosperity, health, and power; it was a focal point of national sentiment. To lose their land struck at the roots of their economic and political system.'[5] The Swazi petition was the first, but by no means the last, of the occasions on which the Swazi were to express a conviction that their history justified their claiming a status which, in constitutional terms, could be described as that of a 'Protected State'. Thus, while acknowledging the suzerainty of Britain, they claimed to be autonomous and in control of their domestic affairs. The deputation, which arrived in London late in 1907, made four points in particular: first, that they had had a right to expect the partition proceedings would give the Swazi not one-third, but a major share of the land; second, that the grant of land to the concessionaires in freehold was entirely contrary to the intentions of Mbandzeni, who had contemplated only a terminal leasehold; third, that the provision of an appeal from the Paramount Chief's court to that of the Resident Commissioner was an invasion of the right of the prerogative of the Paramount Chief; fourth, that some provision ought to be made (as for instance by the establishment of an Advisory Council of Chiefs) for formal consultation with the Swazi before legislation affecting them was enacted.

But the deputation was unsuccessful and the work of partition proceeded. Proclamation 24 of 1913 provided simple and effective machinery for the removal of Swazi from concessions after the five years had elapsed. Nevertheless, there was no large movement from the concessions. Those Swazi who moved did so voluntarily, while the remainder made terms with the concessionaires, subject to confirmation by the Resident Commissioner. The reaction among Swazi leaders was to encourage young men to go to the Transvaal in order to earn money with which the nation might buy back farms from their European holders, a procedure which has helped increase the Swazi holdings to about 52 per cent of the Territory.

The installation of Sobhuza II in 1921 as Paramount Chief again brought the land question to the fore in a dramatic manner. Following the lead previously taken by the Chief Regent, Sobhuza sought to question at law the legal validity of the whole of the land partition proceedings. Two issues were involved: the validity of the proclamations which gave effect to partition, and, second, the validity of the orders-in-council of 1907, 1908 and 1910, which had gone on to define as Crown lands all lands not held by concessionaires or demarcated during the partition proceedings as reserved for the exclusive use of natives.

Supported by the Council, Sobhuza brought suit in the Special Court of Swaziland in 1922 against the eviction of his subjects from the area covered by Unallotted Land Concessions. The main object of the suit was to challenge the whole range of proclamations and orders-in-council under which the partition had been carried out and certain areas declared Crown lands. But the court dismissed the petition in 1924, saying that, as the King of Great Britain was the only sovereign in Swaziland, not only was there the necessary jurisdiction for issuing the orders, but a court sitting in the King's name had authority over Sobhuza. Appeal was then made to the Privy Council in London, funds being provided by a levy which also financed the despatch to England of a delegation of Swazi chiefs headed by Sobhuza. The Privy Council advised rejection of the appeal in 1926. Although the judgement dealt only with the points raised in the suit, it had relevance also to some other issues arising in the administration of Swaziland. In the terms used by the Privy Council, the Territory had been a 'protected dependency' of the South African Republic, albeit unincorporated, over which the Republic had exercised extensive powers. All of these powers, said the Council, had passed to the British Crown. They were limited in exercise only by the pledge to respect native law and custom. However, this limitation could not be construed as constituting a bar to the issuance of the proclamations and orders-in-council in view of the nature of the powers exercisable in a Protectorate by a Sovereign Power. 'It may happen', said the Council, 'that the Protecting Power thinks itself called on to interfere to an extent which may render it difficult to draw the line between a Protectorate and a Possession.' 'This method of peacefully extending British dominion', said Viscount Haldane, 'may well be as little generally understood, as it is (when it can operate) in law, unquestionable.' Dismissal of the court challenge increased Swazi resentment and contributed to their distrust of the European settlers. It also militated against such attempts as there were to improve the living standards of the Swazi people. In 1941, Sobhuza sent still another petition to the British King in Parliament asking, as

well as other things, that old promises be honoured, and that proposed
legislation regulating the appointment and powers of the chiefs should
not be promulgated.

Difficulties in Establishing a Native Authority

The petition of 1941 had its origins in the administration's policy,
evident from 1929 onwards, to bring the Swazi into closer touch with
the government and to associate them with the Territory's development. Such a step, from the point of view of the administration, was
necessary to improve social and economic standards. Moreover, the
obvious inability or unwillingness of chiefs to effect necessary changes
seemed to require reform from above. In the absence of a consultative
body like the Native Advisory Council in Bechuanaland, the chiefs
remained extremely conservative and arbitrary in the conduct of tribal
affairs, while the general standard of education was far lower than in
Basutoland. The administration saw the solution to these problems in
applying to the Territory a system of native administration similar to
that which since about 1900 had been applied to most British dependencies in Africa. An attempt was simultaneously being made to constitute a regular native administration in the other High Commission
Territories.

However justified and enlightened the British position may have
been, it encountered suspicion and mistrust which, in the words of Sir
Alan Pim, was the permanent legacy of the partition period. 'One
heritage from the period', he said, 'will long remain a factor of importance in any endeavour to raise the standards of native life—the distrust
of the European, which has for its origin the character of the original
transactions confirmed by the partition.'[6] The Pim Report also criticised the administration of the Territory, which it described as too
intent on the negative tasks of collecting taxes and administering
justice. Officials were said to be too absorbed in the affairs of the
European population and lacked any initiative in devising policies for
the improvement of native interests. As noted by Kuper, Swazi fear
and distrust was also the result of British inconsistency in dealing with
chiefs: 'While accepting traditional leaders, the government [urged]
them to be docile and co-operative. Actually there [was] an inconsistency in the approach to the chiefs. In theory, British policy, under
the banner of democracy, gives responsibility to the people, offers
promotion to capable individuals and challenges leadership obtained

solely by birth or wealth. In fact, in British possessions, the administrators themselves form an aristocracy and, for political reasons, their alignment is with the aristocrats among the subject people. The hereditary chiefs are encouraged to be efficient and independent only within limits permitted, and along lines set, by the government. If they are not prepared to accept this subservience, the hereditary principle is attacked.'[7] Whereas the government had rejected any suggestion that the Swazi were sovereign people possessing an independent status, it had in effect recognised the existence of a native regime determined to maintain traditional ways.

Largely as a result of the Pim Report, proposals for administrative reform were put forward in 1940. But the Swazi chiefs vehemently opposed the draft Native Administration Proclamation of 1941 on the grounds that it would violate native law and custom and therefore contravene the 1894 Convention. It was still argued that, as representatives of the Swazi nation, they had inherent powers independent of the authority of the British Crown. But when these complaints were finally embodied in a Memorial to the King in 1941, emphasis was more realistically placed on the hardship suffered as a result of the land partition of 1907. A subordinate place was given to the argument that the draft would violate native law and custom, largely because the Swazi chiefs realised that a 1936 decision about a comparable situation in Bechuanaland placed them at a legal disadvantage. Perhaps feeling that the challenge to British authority had been sufficently reduced, steps were now taken by the government to add to native areas, partly by utilisation of Crown lands and partly by purchase of suitable properties with funds provided by the British government.

In the absence of a negotiator as skilled as the Resident Commissioners of the other Territories, and because the High Commissioner had no desire to push the matter through by force,[8] there was no alternative but to leave things as they were. In 1944, as the climax to protracted negotiations, a Native Administration Proclamation was promulgated. The Proclamation was stillborn, however, because it still failed to enlist the genuine support of the Paramount Chief and his people. Opposition to the Proclamation was maintained on point of principle. The purport of the Proclamation, said the Swazi chiefs, was to vest in the Resident Commissioner certain reserve powers which could be used in exceptional circumstances. But the Proclamation's failure was not solely due to the opposition of the chiefs. Its failure could also be attributed to the fact that it was not accompanied by any enactment prescribing the composition and powers of the native courts, and because no steps were taken to institute a native treasury system. These delays, however, were also due to prolonged Swazi objections sustained by considerable legal assistance from Johannesburg. At last, in 1950, the Native Courts Proclamation was enacted with Swazi concurrence, after revision of the Proclamation of 1944 had been agreed upon. The revised Proclamation was issued as the Swaziland Native Administration (Consolidation) Proclamation, No 79 of 1950, and was shortly followed by the National Treasury Proclamation, No 81 of 1950.

The Proclamation of 1950 had the same general form as the laws enacted in British colonies of East and Central Africa. It prescribed the powers and functions of the native authority recognised by the government. The dual purpose underlying the employment of these authorities as agencies of local rule was emphasised throughout the Proclamation. The statutory powers possessed by the authorities were expressly noted as being in addition to any powers vested in the authorities by native law and custom. However, in the case where the native authorities issued orders in pursuance of statutory power, their issue was made subject to the supervision and control of local administration officials.

The Swaziland Native Administration Proclamation was distinguished, however, by certain provisions which generally represent concessions made to the Paramount Chief and his Council. Whereas it was usual elsewhere for the law to express itself as imposing obligations or conferring powers on the native authorities recognised by the government of the Territory concerned (as was the case in the Proclamation of 1944), the Proclamation of 1950 referred expressly to the Paramount Chief in *Libandhla* (theoretically, all Swazi adult males sitting as a council) as the repository of the powers conferred. The term 'subordinate native authority' disappeared, the local authorities subordinate to the Paramount Chief in *Libandhla* being the chiefs appointed by him. The administration was not required to give its assent to these appointments unless unusual circumstances were involved. Generally speaking, the initiative in government remained with the chiefs who, unfortunately, in the light of modern conditions, were little prepared to exercise these powers. But in order to secure the co-operation of the Swazi aristocracy—deemed to be the more influential element among the Swazi—the Proclamation diminished the measure both of initiative and control possessed by local administrative officers elsewhere. They were envisaged less as an agency which could originate or regulate policy in local affairs, than as one which could on occasion exercise a veto in certain directions.

The Native Courts Proclamation of 1950 showed a similar departure from procedure inasmuch as the authority for establishing native courts, issuing warrants, prescribing the form of their records, or for making rules regarding procedure, etc., was vested in the Paramount Chief, subject to the prior approval of the Resident Commissioner. Further differences limited the power of review possessed by District Officers over criminal decisions and established a unique chain of appeal in civil cases.

The National Treasury Proclamation, No 81 of 1950, was in simple form and merely provided for the establishment of a native administration treasury, to be termed the Swazi National Treasury. It empowered the High Commissioner to allocate to the Treasury such proportion of the native tax as he might think fit and to make regulations for the form of accounts and for audit. The Paramount Chief in *Libandhla* was empowered to make regulations, with the prior approval of the Resident Commissioner, for the constitution and conduct of the National Treasury and for determining what monies should be paid into it and the purposes for which its funds should be used.

Swazi Traditional Rule and the Swazi National Council

The Swazi traditional system, which British 'protection' effectively preserved, has usually been described as aristocratic,[9] though it is never safe to apply to the condition of Africa a political phraseology essentially related to the circumstances of Europe. But in so far as control has been exercised under the Paramount Chief by hereditary chiefs, the system may rightly be called aristocratic. The Ngwenyama's position is enhanced by the emotional attitude of most Swazi towards their King; many would still say: 'Without a King we would no longer be a people.' This attitude reflects more than a simple awareness that the Swazi nation came into existence and maintained its identity under the leadership of a series of strong Kings. For, in addition to his being a symbol of national unity, in the minds of the majority of the Swazi the King has a direct physical association with the health of his subjects and the fertility of the soil. This mystical bond between King, subjects and soil requires an elaborate ritualisation in dance and song, and the present King, Sobhuza II, is most attentive to this duty.

Born in 1899 of the ruling Dlamini house, which traces its ancestry back some four hundred years, Sobhuza II attended Zombodze School and Lovedale in the eastern Cape. Since his installation as Paramount Chief in 1921, he has twice gone abroad, once in 1922 and again for the coronation of Queen Elizabeth II in 1953. Having lost his battle in the courts to withdraw the concessions made by his predecessors, Sobhuza has since believed that nothing should be done to alienate or disturb European inhabitants, whose presence and participation he feels are so vital to his country.

The Swazi traditional system also gives an important place to the King's mother, who enjoys the title of 'Ndlovukati' or Lady Elephant. The position of the Queen Mother is one of unusual authority and prestige, for the King is believed to derive 'the blood of kingship' from both parents. The Queen Mother's power is such that the Swazi system has even been described as having some of the elements of a 'dual monarchy'. To the present day, the Ndlovukati's village of Lobamba is the religious and ceremonial capital of the nation, whereas the Ngwenyama's village of Lozitehlezi is regarded as the administrative headquarters.

While it is necessary to emphasise the importance of the Ngwenyama, both in the operation of British indirect rule and in matters directly under Swazi jurisdiction, the inherent power of the Paramount Chief must not be over-exaggerated. 'Though it frequently happens in Africa that authority is vested in persons entrenched in hereditary office and fortified by ritual, yet power is seldom absolute, and its exercise is usually subject to a well recognised system of checks. To some extent this may be due to the strength of the equalitarian spirit born of the feeling that all those who are members of a tribe or clan or kindred group have copartnership rights which have to be respected.' [10] Swazi Kings, including Sobhuza, have occasionally been fined by the Council for infractions of tradition. Moreover, since the Ngwenyama has negotiated on occasion with the government, his people have sometimes blamed him for legislation for which he was in no way responsible and about which he possibly was not even consulted. Sobhuza has sometimes been criticised for being a passive partner in forcing changes on the country. 'The role of King-cum-Paramount Chief is particularly ambiguous', says Kuper. 'He is called upon to sponsor European projects and at the same time his people, to whom practically no education is available, demand that he defend their own conservative customs. No matter how careful he is, he occasionally co-operates without the sanction or knowledge of his councils. Then, when they learn of what has been done, he must either try to extricate himself by subterfuge—and be regarded as vacillating by the government—or abide by his initial reaction—and be condemned as a "Government servant" by his subjects.'[11] Over the years the Resident Commissioners have sought the suggestions of the Ngwenyama and his Council. Despite the constant erosion of the real power of the Paramount Chief over the past seventy years, the monarchy remains a vital institution.

The Ngwenyama is a constitutional ruler in the sense that he is advised by his kinsmen and chosen councillors and cannot initiate action without the approval of two formally-constituted councils. The smaller of the two councils, the *Liqoqo*, has sometimes been interpreted as an Inner or Privy Council. Strictly speaking, however, the word council as applied to this body is a misnomer, for it is not a council with defined functions and holding regular meetings. In origin, it was a development of a family council and has remained largely informal. The Paramount Chief discusses matters with such princes or family members as have his confidence, and other advisers are called upon as the occasion might demand. But the invitation to join the *Liqoqo* is not a matter of public announcement. It invariably includes the Queen Mother, whose influence has recently suffered some decline. This council obviously suffers from the same defects as the original Basutoland Council in its representation of the chiefs rather than the people.

The larger council is known as the *Libandhla*, and, in its widest extension, is a council of every adult male in the nation. It is recognised as the final body from which approval for any contemplated act or legislation should be obtained. The *Libandhla* meets only once a year, during the winter, when it sits for about a month in the cattle byre of the capital. The meeting is in the hands of a leading prince of the *Liqoqo*. Although the Paramount Chief attends the meeting, it is customary for him to refrain from speaking until the majority opinion has been expressed. The Resident Commissioner and administration officers meet the *Libandhla* on one day when matters affecting government are put before it.

Taken together, the two councils form the Swazi National Council, which in turn, through its Standing Committee, meets with representatives of the British administration. These meetings are held on a weekly basis and provide the channel along which all government business flows to and from the Swazi nation. The Standing Committee consists of a Chairman, the Treasurer of the Swazi National Treasury, the

Secretary to the Nation, and six members, one from each of the Territory's six administrative Districts. The latter have considerable influence in the areas they represent. There is also a Chief Liaison Officer between the government and the Paramount Chief. While nominated by the Ngwenyama, this officer is a government-salaried employee.

It is generally recognised that these two tribal councils are unable to comprehend and cope with the complexity of contemporary political and social matters. 'In the days when opinion was more uniform and knowledge coincided more closely with age, the inner council might well have included the wisest men of the nation. At present, young progressives, especially teachers and clerks, complain of their exclusion.'[12] Even the casual aspect of these institutions makes them suspect today as being opposed to modern thought and influences. The Swazi National Council has apparently achieved very little of a positive nature, and lack of confidence in the Council has become more widespread. Its aristocratic composition has, for all practical purposes, negated the theoretically democratic character of Swazi institutions. Without education, divorced and insulated from the common people, the Swazi aristocracy has become strongly self-conscious as a class and seeks to protect and entrench its position. Even at the *Libandhla*, it is not the custom for a commoner to criticise or advance new opinions. The Swaziland Student Union, speaking for the country's youth, has publicly called for the abandonment of 'these traditional institutions, good as they might have been in the past; [because] they cannot be of any real practical use in the modern complex society. While we have lost our respect for them, they have lost their prestige in modern society'.[13]

The White Community and the European Advisory Council

The power and privileges of the white community have increased spectacularly over the years, and the success of their enterprises has been reflected in the notable material development of the country. But this development of necessity brought the whites into closer contact with and greater dependence upon the indigenous people. Increased prosperity for the whites required that more and more Africans should receive additional training, not only in the essentials of reading and writing, but also in skilled and semi-skilled professions. Consequently, a growing number of Swazi detached themselves from tribal ways and sought to live in the European manner. Faced with this dilemma of their own making, the whites generally sought to perpetuate the advantages of their initial cultural superiority by means of racial oppression and exclusion. When, for example, the first Swazi succeeded in completing his BA (by correspondence) in the 1920s, considerable controversy arose over his further education. Of the Europeans who expressed themselves on the matter, the majority thought he should be discouraged on the grounds that 'he would get above himself', that 'Kaffirs must not be civilised', that 'raw natives are better workers', that he would put 'queer ideas' in the heads of the people, or 'create trouble'.[14] Such has been the general legacy of white feelings towards the Swazi. Although relations between the 280,000 Swazis and the 10,000 whites have been generally good, it is mainly because in the past Swazis have been content to stay within their traditional tribal ways and accept a lesser position in European society.

In 1921, a European Advisory Council was constituted as an administrative measure. In principle, its function was to deal with affairs affecting European residents. The Council had regular sessions until 1949 when it was reconstituted and established as a statutory body. According to the terms of the official Proclamation, its function was to advise the Resident Commissioner on matters directly affecting European residents of Swaziland and on any matters specifically referred to the Council by the Resident Commissioner. The Territory was divided into ten electoral divisions which in turn provided one member each on the Council. Every European British subject, aged twenty-one and over, domiciled and with Swaziland residence for five years, was eligible to vote. The Chairman of the Council was the Resident Commissioner and, in addition to the Deputy Resident Commissioner, there were six official members who attended in an advisory capacity but had no power to vote. The full Council usually met twice a year. While not enjoying official legislative power, the Council always exercised considerable influence on government policy because of the preponderant economic position of the white community. On the whole, the whites followed the leadership of Carl Todd, leader of the elected membership, and sometimes referred to as the 'Roy Welensky of Swaziland'. A director of more than thirty large companies in South Africa, Todd possesses the most extensive land holdings in Swaziland.[15]

The small white population at present owns 43 per cent of the agricultural land and virtually all the mines, industries, business and trading enterprises. The white population of Swaziland is unique for the former High Commission Territories, inasmuch as it contains numerous absentee landlords and 'weekenders'. Sir Alan Pim, for example, remarked in 1932 that of the 500 owners of land some 40 per cent were habitually absent from Swaziland. In the words of Dr Hugh Ashton, the majority of landlords 'make no contribution to the country's social, economic or political life; nevertheless they have a direct personal interest in the country's position and future and, in the past, have been treated with tenderness in deference to their supposed influence with the South African government'. Of the 'weekenders', 'wealthy business men from South Africa who spend short holidays [in Swaziland] and retire to their comfortable estates', Ashton asserts that 'their potential influence is disproportionate to their numbers. Like the absentee farmers, their interest in the country is likely to differ fundamentally from that of the local inhabitants'.[16]

But whatever their attitudes and prejudices have been, it is with white capital and skill that the country has been developed, and a large percentage of the settled white population at present feel they belong to the country. Fearful of any changes likely to endanger their privileged position, they have generally condemned trade unionism and have been prone to label most aspiring Swazi political leaders as 'Communist-inspired', 'demagogic', and 'power-grasping'. Even newspaper reporting of political speeches has frequently been condemned. In reply, the editor of the *Times of Swaziland* was forced to chide: 'To ignore the existence of politicians, or brush them aside as being little men with no influence among their people, as many in Swaziland tend to do, is stupid and dangerous.'[17] Whites in the Territory have essentially held the South African attitude towards 'the native', an attitude supported in law until the Race Relations Proclamation of March 1, 1962.

13

CONSTITUTIONAL DISCUSSIONS AND
POLITICAL DEVELOPMENT, 1959–1962

SWAZILAND'S isolation from the fast-moving currents of contemporary African development came to an abrupt end in 1959. The quickening of political life in the other High Commission Territories made clear that such change could not long be avoided in Swaziland. Not only would public opinion in Britain suspect the absence of a corresponding advance in Swaziland, but questions were already being asked at the United Nations about the constitutional status of the three Protectorates. True, there had been no Swazi petitioners in New York, but events in Nyasaland, only seven hundred miles to the north, were proof that the tide of African nationalism could not be held back or deflected from Southern Africa by the fragile barrier provided by the so-called 'racial-partnership' of the Federation.

Perhaps of more immediate consequence, however, for the acceleration of political change, was the impetus provided by the notable postwar expansion, especially in the mining industry, together with ever increasing pressure upon the land. While investments by the Colonial Development Corporation and private groups were showing magnificent results in the European sector of the economy, the disparity between whites and Swazi only increased. Road building and public works were vastly expanded but at the cost of a proportionate reduction in expenditures on agriculture, education and health. In overall terms, the ordinary Swazi was scarcely affected, except in a negative manner, by the economic boom, as 87 per cent of the population tried with increasing difficulty to eke out an existence on 52 per cent of the country's total area. Under such strained conditions, Sobhuza again petitioned the administration on the matter of land and mineral concessions.

Meanwhile, in July 1959, an Economic Survey Mission, led by Professor Chandler Morse, had been appointed to make a general survey of the requirements and natural resources of the Territories and to make recommendations on the utilisation of financial resources that might be made available. The Mission subsequently reported that, despite an abundance of natural resources, Swaziland's economic advancement would in great part depend upon changes being made in the existing political structure. It was imperative, said the Mission, that 'the present occasional opportunities for informal consultation between the groups (i.e. Black and White) . . . be developed into a regular and less informal association, and that a channel . . . be established along which joint advice will flow towards the Government'.[1] Some few years earlier, Lord Hailey, while believing that Swaziland was destined to follow a path 'leading only to a restricted measure of political advance', had also recommended the creation of a legislative organ in which both communities would be represented.[2]

Constitutional Discussions Initiated

While the improvement of the economic position of his people might require a certain amount of compromise with modern political forms, Sobhuza was also keenly aware that elsewhere in Africa all such innovations had been accompanied by a decline in tribal authority. As if to anticipate such a threat to his own position, Sobhuza outlined in May 1959 certain beliefs which became the foundation of Swazi National Council policy. The unrest prevailing in Central and North Africa, and specifically in Nyasaland, was, he said, 'due to people forgetting their own African customs and grasping at European customs with which they were not fully familiar'. He went on to accuse 'power-greedy' individuals of making use of alien western political forms so as to arrogate leadership to themselves. Such practices, tied as they were to the idea of political parties, were foreign to the Swazi and unwanted. The correct procedure, said Sobhuza, was 'for all matters to be brought to the *Libandhla* for discussion and for the proper position to be arrived at by all men putting their heads together'.[3]

The Ngwenyama's petition to the Secretary of State for Commonwealth Relations, together with the advice of the Economic Survey Mission, prodded the European Advisory Council into action. From the point of view both of the Swazi and of the European community, some form of political change was required. But the European Advisory Council was also fearful lest the 'winds of change' stir too forcefully in Swaziland. Rather than see the rise of a Swazi nationalist organisation dictating the terms of constitutional evolution, the

European Advisory Council took the initiative in calling for a constitution. By supporting the tribal authorities, who could hopefully con-
tain any nationalistic tendencies, the European Advisory Council
hoped to procure with the Swazi National Council a growing share in
the government of the Territory. It was therefore proposed that a joint
advisory council be created. In a memorandum presented to the Resident
Commissioner in January 1960, the European Advisory Council stated
that 'the time has been reached ... for the examination of a multi-
racial council in which both European and Swazi interests should be
represented. ... It is urged that the Swazi National Council should
nominate its Swazi representatives.'⁴

Before the Secretary of State could reply to this memorandum,
the Ngwenyama had seized the initiative and, in April 1960, rejected
the proposed joint advisory council. Such a council, claimed Sobhuza,
would mean a derogation of Swazi power, since the Swazi National
Council 'already had legislative and executive powers whereas the
European Advisory Council was still only advisory'.⁵ Sobhuza's real
concern, however, was somewhat different, since the distinction made
between the powers of the National Council and the Advisory Council
did not alter the fact that the British government was sovereign.
Sobhuza hoped to regain control over mineral rights, which the Crown
had arrogated to itself, while preserving intact the tribal system. To do
this it was assumed that the support of the European community
would be necessary. Therefore, rather than waste precious time with the
creation of an advisory council, which might then be subject to
demands for more unfettered Swazi representation, Sobhuza proposed
at once the establishment of a legislative council which would uphold
the tribal hierarchy in all its powers.

Concretely, the Ngwenyama called for the creation of a legislative
council in which whites and Swazi would 'come together on an equal
basis'. The council, however, would have no jurisdiction over Swazi
custom or land and mineral rights. The Europeans, he said, should
choose their representatives under their system of elections and the
Swazi should select their representatives 'in the way they are used to'.
This kind of association, he suggested, might be called a federation, in
which the number of representatives of each group would not matter.
'The Federal system', said Sobhuza, was 'suitable for the association of
groups which have not reached the same stage of development', and
would have the double advantage of avoiding the abuses resulting from
the idea of 'one man, one vote' while promoting economic integration.⁶

Sobhuza's fear of a 'one man, one vote' franchise was reinforced by the advice of his South African legal adviser, a strong Nationalist Party figure, who warned that such a system would mean the Swazis 'acting outside the framework of their Nation . . . the very foundation of the Nation . . . thereby . . . destroyed and the Nation . . . a stranger in its own land'.[7] It could be expected that the Ngwenyama's plan would receive white support so long as the real economic and political power of that group remained secure.

Sobhuza's 'race-federation' plan was evidently patterned on that advanced by Sir De Villiers Graaff, the leader of the United Party in South Africa, who called for the establishment of a 'race-federation' as opposed to apartheid. His proposal, which accepted racism as a pillar of South African life, would nevertheless make possible a certain amount of compromise. Those close to Sobhuza were long familiar with an outline of Sir De Villier's views, as printed in a *Rand Daily Mail* article, and which the Ngwenyama frequently produced as a model of his own thinking. Sobhuza's statement was given front page coverage in most South African newspapers and it seemed to strike a responsive chord among whites, both in Swaziland and South Africa. The plan was also welcomed by the Swazi National Council which endorsed the Ngwenyama's views as its own. But this very combination of traditionalists, white settlers and South African support served warning on the small number of 'detribalised' Swazi that their chances of leading Swaziland along the path of African nationalism might be permanently destroyed. This fear provided the impetus for the formation of the country's first political party.

Swaziland Progressive Party

The first political organisation supporting the general aspirations of contemporary African nationalism to make its appearance in Swaziland was the Progressive Party. Although it came into existence only in 1960, the roots of the Progressive Party went back some years, to the Progressive Association. Formed under the guidance of the Resident Commissioner in 1929, the Association included many educated men both in and outside government. It was not long, however, until senior administrative officers had serious misgivings about such an uncontrolled organisation. The group was accused of promoting its own interests, an action apparently considered inappropriate by government officials, and was severely criticised by some of the chiefs, who viewed with considerable suspicion any organisation of Swazi outside the tribal framework. Relying upon Sobhuza's support, the administration accordingly decreed the affiliation of the Progressive Association to the Swazi National Council. The Association was henceforth dominated by government-appointed members and government employees. Submerged in the tribal system, the Association had only a negligible influence on Swazi life. Yet its reduced scope did not prevent it from making constructive recommendations on such important issues as taxation and conditions of farm and child labour. As the first indigenous semi-political unit in the country independent of hereditary officials, the Association was of some historical significance, even though its membership in 1935 was still under a hundred. Four years later, the Association was further weakened by a split along tribal lines between its Swazi and South African born members.[8]

From 1945 until 1960, the Association was under the presidency of John J. Nquku. Born in 1899 at Pietermaritzburg, South Africa, of Pondo parents, Nquku qualified as a teacher and served from 1920 to 1930 in various supervisory positions in the Bantu schools of South Africa. In 1930, he was offered an appointment in Swaziland where he became the first African inspector of schools. After settling in the Territory, he founded in 1934 a vernacular newspaper, *Izwi Lam Swazi* (The Voice of the Swazi), and served as its editor until the paper was taken over by the Bantu Press. In 1940, he resigned as inspector and became an active member of the Swazi National Council. He was then given charge of co-ordinating missionary and tribal educational policy. His growing stature won him the presidency of the Progressive Association in 1945 and, ten years later, Nquku again achieved prominence by founding and becoming first editor of *The Swazilander*. But most important for leading him out of the purely academic and literary world and into the field of politics was Nquku's visit in 1957 to Britain, America and Western Europe. Finally, in July 1960, Nquku acted to transform the Progressive Association into the Swaziland Progressive Party.

By July 1960, events had clearly demonstrated to the Association's membership that if the white residents, in league with the traditionalists, continued to have a free hand in devising the country's first written constitution, all legal doors might henceforth be closed to future political development. Consequently, at a special meeting called on July 30, 1960, at Kwaluseni, the Progressive Association voted to change its name—and this without the approval of the Ngwenyama—

into the Swaziland Progressive Party, and issued a manifesto stressing four cardinal points:

1. A non-racial policy was required to bring about the democratic enfranchisement of all persons in Swaziland irrespective of race, colour or creed.
2. South Africa must be opposed in its efforts to incorporate Swaziland.
3. The country must adopt the United Nations Declaration of Human Rights.
4. Complete integration must be achieved in every walk of life and discrimination, in all its forms, must be ended.

By alluding to the United Nations, the Progressive Party served notice that Swaziland would no longer remain isolated from the African and international scene.

The Fragmentation of Nationalist Leadership

Unfortunately for the infant nationalist cause, before the end of 1961, a split occurred within the leadership ranks of the Progressive Party. The crisis ostensibly grew out of accusations made by Dr Ambrose Zwane, the Secretary-General, and Clement Dumisa Dhlamini, the party's Youth Leader, that Nquku seemed to regard the party as his personal property and had dictatorially closed meetings of the Executive whenever he found a majority ranged against him. They were also dissatisfied with the manner in which party funds were handled by Nquku in his capacity as Treasurer, and by his refusal to hold elections at the party's first general conference in 1961. Nquku reportedly had received over £60,000 from Ghana.

While the split within the Progressive ranks was primarily a difference of personalities and not of political ideology, various outside forces seemed to exert some influence on the party. Taken in the political context of Southern Africa, it is important to note that similar cleavages also appeared within each major nationalistic party in the other High Commission Territories. In each case the struggle for control, sometimes resulting in schism, reflected the same underlying tension which in South Africa had led to the formation of the Pan-African Congress as a breakaway from the African Nationalist Congress. As elements controlled by or friendly to either of the major African nationalist parties of South Africa jockeyed for position, their battle for power was reflected in the tensions which gripped the nationalist parties in the High Commission Territories. Notwithstanding the strong ties binding the nationalist parties of the Territories and the Pan-African Congress, each territorial party reflected a developing Botswana, Basuto or Swazi nationalism. These parties were scarcely more ready than nationalist parties in other African states to place Pan-African sympathies before concrete issues of national survival.

Whatever the causes of the Progressive split, a special conference of the party deposed Nquku as President at the end of February 1962 and elected Ambrose Zwane in his place, with Clement Dumisa Dhlamini as Secretary-General. Dhlamini, the nephew of King Sobhuza II, had vehemently rejected his traditionalist background while still a student at Pius XII University College in Basutoland. Although he did not complete his degree course, he was active in student politics and closely associated himself with the nationalist aspirations of South African and Rhodesian students. His militant and erratic role in Swaziland politics began as early as December 16, 1960, when he delivered a stirring speech in Msunduza Hall, Mbabane. His capacity for galvanising the crowds attracted the attention of the politicians and he was urged to join the Progressive Party. In January 1961, a Youth League Conference of the party elected him President, a position he held until his election as Secretary-General. As Youth League President, he attended the All-African Peoples' Conference in Accra and also represented Swaziland at the World Assembly of Youth Conference in Dar-es-Salaam in August 1961. His active participation in political agitation, labour organisation and protest movements earned him the keen antipathy of both the traditionalists and the white community.

The new President of the Progressive Party, Ambrose Zwane, was born in 1924 in Manzini, Swaziland. The first of his people to graduate as a doctor of medicine, he was the eldest son of Mdolomba Zwane, one of the councillors whom Sobhuza had sent to England in the 1920s on the matter of the land partition. A Catholic, Zwane was educated at various Catholic and Protestant mission schools. Having completed his matriculation in 1945, with a distinction in physical science, he was awarded a scholarship by the Swaziland government to Fort Hare, where he completed his first year of medicine. In 1947 he transferred to Witwatersrand University where he made the acquaintance of such African political leaders as Robert Sobukwe and Nelson Mandela. After qualifying as a doctor in 1951, he worked for a short time in

South Africa before he returned to Swaziland as a Government Medical Officer.

It was while working for the Swaziland government that Zwane especially felt the force of apartheid in his country. With his own protests against discrimination ignored and even those from the Swazi National Council of no avail, the Sharpeville massacre in South Africa on March 21, 1960, brought his immediate resignation from government service. Zwane thereupon resolved to give his attention to politics. Although originally intending to form his own political party, he instead accepted Nquku's request to join with him in transforming the Progressive Association. Elected Secretary-General of the Progressive Party at its organisational meeting on July 30, 1960, Zwane's step into politics proved to be a shot in the arm for political life in Swaziland. Party membership quickly increased, as his presence lent necessary respect to a movement hitherto viewed with considerable suspicion.

Following their split, both Nquku and Zwane travelled abroad soliciting support for their respective groups. Despite differences, they were equally adamant in their efforts to convince British colonial officials that the constitutional proposals then being advanced by the Swazi National Council-European Advisory Council coalition were unacceptable. Meanwhile, various incidents revealed growing hostility towards Nquku and seemed to confirm that he was no longer the recognised leader of the nationalist movement. In late February 1962, members of the Progressive Youth League attempted to prevent him from boarding his plane at Johannesburg. His new car was set on fire in early May and this was followed by the attempted burning of his house. Undaunted and still supported by a small section of the old party Executive, Nquku testified before the United Nations Committee on Non-Self-Governing Territories. After a brief return trip to Swaziland at the end of May 1962, both he and Zwane (who had only recently visited Ghana and Egypt) left for the All-African Peoples' Conference in Accra. Both leaders paid short visits to the Soviet Union, although Zwane vehemently denied that he was in any way subjecting himself to Communist influence. 'My experience', he said, 'has taught me that anybody who takes positive action for the liberation of his people is labelled "red". . . . These people forget that I am a Catholic, and if my politics clash with my religion, I would rather resign from politics.'[9] During the course of his travels, he was several times arrested in South Africa as a prohibited immigrant and the British Embassy in Pretoria was obliged to secure his release.

In August 1962, Nquku's own Executive announced his suspension as President, pending investigation of complaints. The Executive thereupon claimed to be the only legitimate Progressive Party and named B. M. Simelane as President with O. M. Mabusa as Secretary-General. Although Nquku termed the suspension 'nothing but fabrication', a large number of those who had remained loyal were now lined up against him. Deprived of all but a nominal following, Nquku henceforth sought merely to avoid revealing his own weakness. He therefore remained aloof from all attempts by the old Executive and Zwane to achieve party unity. By mid-September, efforts were under way to heal the breach but Nquku and his Secretary-General, Albert Nxumalo, chose to fly to New York to present an appeal for United Nations intervention. Again seeking to counteract his failing position at home by seeking international recognition, Nquku returned to the United Nations in January 1963. Claiming to be the only leader of Swazi nationalism, he protested against the composition of the Constitutional Committee and again called for United Nations intervention.

Swaziland Democratic Party

Organised in March 1962, the Swaziland Democratic Party (SDP) was something of an anomaly on the African political scene. Officially headed by Simon Nxumalo, but nurtured, advised and financed by a group of white liberals, in its first public statement the Democratic Party totally rejected the constitutional proposals advanced by the Swazi National Council-European Advisory Council alliance. Claiming to be the country's only non-racial party, the Democrats condemned the Progressive Party and its successor, the Ngwane National Liberatory Congress (NNLC), as racialist, citing as evidence its endorsement of Pan-Africanism and the financial support it enjoyed from Ghana. The SDP somewhat illogically contended that 'a policy of Pan-Africanism would mean the destruction of the economy of the country, because appointments would be made on political lines'. However, the tribal system was also condemned as being the acceptance in principle of apartheid. Any form of racial separation recognised in the political structure of the country was seen as 'leaving the door wide open for Communist infiltration and extreme nationalism, black or white', thereby endangering good race relations.

The SDP was able to enunciate its full programme in May 1962. Departing from the backward-looking approach of the white majority, the SDP advocated 'one Swazi nationality and citizenship for all under a unified system of government, law and taxation'. While the position of the Ngwenyama was to be respected, his future role was seen as that of a constitutional monarch in a nation remaining under the protection of Great Britain. Heavy stress was placed on the social responsibilities of the state in labour, education and general welfare. The party initially called for a limited franchise, 'until the people have had an opportunity to acquire more political experience'. This position, however, was abandoned in October. Nxumalo explained the reversal as due to the realisation that 'in the white community as a whole there was not the spirit of give and take which was essential if Swaziland was to be a non-racial nation'. More important was the realisation gained from the party's first public meeting that such a position would not permit genuine African support. Liberal parties advocating a limited franchise had been totally rejected everywhere on the continent and the SDP had no desire to be cast in a similar role.

In essence, the SDP accepted all the aspirations of contemporary African nationalism in so far as they implied an affirmation of human dignity and required rapid social and economic development. Private property, for instance, was to be respected, but not at the expense of the rights of labour. But the SDP separated itself from the mainstream of African nationalism by refusing to endorse Pan-Africanism, which it alleged to be subject to the dictates of Ghana, backed by Moscow and Peking. By rejecting Pan-Africanism, the SDP hoped to maintain friendly relations with South Africa and Portuguese Mozambique although unreservedly rejecting their respective apartheid and assimilado concepts. Indeed, because Swaziland was potentially a viable, self-supporting state, the SDP had a logical basis for its policy. More than the other Protectorates, Swaziland's economic prosperity was not so dependent upon a radical change in the 'white fortress' of South Africa so long as cordial formal relations could be maintained. Despite this desire for good relations, the SDP consistently opposed all efforts of the Advisory Council and the National Council to exclude and deport political refugees from South Africa.

Criticism of the SDP came from either side of the political spectrum. It was charged that the SDP, while attacking other political groups for soliciting outside assistance, itself enjoyed the support of the Liberal Party of South Africa and had its own 'back-seat drivers'. Moreover, allegations made by the SDP that other parties were racialist ignored the fact that they were open to members of any race, although no point was made of seeking such membership. The European Advisory Council, finding the SDP leaders particularly difficult to deal with or even to meet in intelligent debate, made various attempts, in conjunction with tribal authorities, to restrict its sphere of operations and to conduct a whispering campaign against its white supporters.

The SDP did indeed receive the backing of some members of the South African Liberal Party who emigrated to Swaziland. But the liberalism of the SDP was quite distinct from that known in former British possessions to the north. Thus, the demise of the Liberal Party in Northern Rhodesia was praised as a 'wise and realistic step' on the grounds that there was no room for a third force between Welenskyism on the one hand and the African nationalism of Kaunda and Nkumbula on the other. But South African liberalism, which the SDP claimed to follow, was not regarded as the rival of African nationalism. Rather, it was compared with Kaunda's UNIP, which also sought white support. It was claimed that 'the Democratic Party does for Swaziland what Kaunda's UNIP does for Northern Rhodesia',[10] but this comparison conveniently overlooked UNIP's Pan-African associations.

Behind the leadership of Nxumalo, the Liberal presence was especially felt in the persons of Vincent Rozwadowski, a prominent farmer of Polish origin and a member of the SDP Executive, and Jordon Ngubane. Formerly a national Vice-President of the South African Liberal Party, Ngubane was banned under South Africa's Suppression of Communism Act and fled the country to Swaziland. In 1963, he became an executive officer of the SDP. Rozwadowski had emigrated to South Africa after the war, but found the country's racialism too discomforting. His keen intellect and generous financial support largely made the SDP. By exposing and condemning white attempts to check political progress and even to subvert the Territory's independence, he earned himself considerable hostility from the white community. His firm allegiance to British principles of politics and his strong support for British ties apparently won him the respect, if not the encouragement, of the local British administration.

Mbandzeni National Convention

A peculiar twist to the Swaziland political scene was given by the formation of the Mbandzeni National Convention (MNC) in July 1962.

This was an amalgamation of the Mbandzeni National Party, founded by Clifford Nkosi in April 1962, and Dr George Msibi's Convention Movement. Basing its stand on the Convention of 1881, the MNC claimed that Swaziland had in fact never lost its independence. The party's goal was the restoration of sovereignty and the adoption of a one man, one vote system. Nkosi, first Secretary-General of the new organisation and then its President, maintained close ties with a firm of South African lawyers closely linked with the South African government. In some semi-intelligible public statements made before the amalgamation, Nkosi called for the return of Swazi land and recognition of the nation's sovereignty—both points being consistent with the demands of the tribalists.

Msibi, who apparently requested the merger and became the first President of the MNC, was trained for nine years in India and later went to Japan for further studies. According to SDP allegations, he was active in 'red-lined Indian youth organisations', and was tainted with suspicion of being a Communist supporter. When this charge could not be substantiated, he was said to have allowed himself to become a tool of Verwoerd by stirring up Swazis against Africans born in South Africa but residing in Swaziland.[11] Msibi categorically rejected these charges and made the following demands on behalf of his party:

1. The introduction of a territorial labour organisation under the Ngwenyama. Otherwise, trade unions, however legitimate, would continue to grow and thus provide the easiest route for Communism to enter the country.

2. A clear rejection of the 50-50 voting proposals of the European Advisory Council-Swazi National Council alliance and its replacement by universal adult franchise.

3. A national organisation devoid of any racialism or political factionalism to meet the challenge of political development.[12]

In early January 1963, the MNC at last set forth its aims in a Political Charter under the signature of Msibi. Emphasis was again placed on the idea of 'restoration' rather than 'independence' and on the supremacy of the Swazi nation which, it said, 'has always accepted into its fold other nationalities with the privilege of retaining their culture and identity but without prejudice to Swazi authority'. While thus ambiguously appearing to eschew racialism, it stated that 'the human resources of the Swazi Nation will be preferred as priority in all enterprises'—a statement generally interpreted as being directed against non-Swazi Africans and whites. Ominously, however, the party's call for universal franchise was negated by the provision that 'all laws shall be valid and legal when they bear the signature of the King, the Ngwenyama of Swaziland, as an expression of the counsel of the Council of Chiefs and the authority of the Swazi people as vested in Parliament'. Fundamentally, this was very much the same scheme put forward by the Constitutional Committee, except that the MNC took a step backwards by limiting the council to chiefs. Such an approach, however ambiguous, had considerable appeal for the tribalists, and indeed the group enjoyed a measure of support within the Swazi bureaucracy. In the words of the SDP, the Convention sought 'to enjoy the best of both worlds. It stands for restoration. It believes in Swazi supremacy (taking its cue from white supremacy) but adds that it wants to establish a non-racial state.'[13] The very adoption of the name 'convention' rather than 'party' was indicative of the organisation's basic object—the formation of a united front. By emphasising the restoration of sovereignty, it struck the lowest common denominator in terms of which tribalists and Swazi politicians could unite. To become more specific was to lessen the possibility of a united front. Perhaps this emphasis on the formation of a united front, a typical Communist tactic, explains why the Convention was at first incorrectly suspected of being a Communist tool.

However strong the common interests which prompted the alliance of Msibi with Nkosi, certain differences in their respective backgrounds and beliefs made the merger a most unrealistic one from the start. While both stressed the idea of Swazi sovereignty and unity, the motivation was different. Nkosi, a close relative of the King, seemed bent on preserving the traditional system along the lines adopted by Chief Kaiser Matanzima in the Transkei. Msibi, on the other hand, seeking modernisation of the traditional system, spoke scornfully of the reservations contained in the proposed Bill of Rights, a glance at which, he said, was sufficient 'to realise the dream-world in which the fathers of these proposals live . . . '.

The Constitutional Committee and Progressive Dissent

Meanwhile, the Secretary of State for the Colonies had replied to the European Advisory Council memorandum and welcomed the idea of a legislative council on which both European and Swazi interests would be represented. The Resident Commissioner, Brian Marwick, was instructed to pursue the matter.

In November 1960, the Secretary of State authorised the setting up of a constitutional committee in Swaziland. Its terms of reference were: (1) to examine the circumstances which militated against common purpose and coexistence; (2) to consider what form of constitution was desirable for Swaziland and to draft accordingly; (3) to consider the need for subordinate or local forms of government in Swaziland, e.g., at District level and for urban areas.

The Constitutional Committee, as it was duly appointed, consisted of representatives of the European Advisory Council, the Ngwenyama in *Libandhla*, the British administration, and the Swaziland Combined Executive Association, under the chairmanship of the Resident Commissioner. A small Working Committee was appointed and proceeded to invite evidence from interested parties. On the Constitutional Committee, though not on its Working Committee, were three members of the recently formed Progressive Party. Nquku, the President of the party, Dr Ambrose P. Zwane, the Secretary-General, and O. M. Mabuza, a member of the Executive, were given places on the Committee in their capacity as members of the *Libandhla* and not as members of the Swaziland Progressive Party. No representation was given to the Coloured community, notwithstanding the fact that they comprised a substantial minority and were accorded a separate status in law.

The first meeting of the whole Constitutional Committee took place on November 4, 1960. The sitting was then adjourned until February 17, 1961, ostensibly owing to the annual *Incwala* ceremony* and because the Swazi members wished to refer back to the Swazi National Council. During the recess, however, the Swazi National Council made good use of the time to send out messengers to all *tinkundlas* (local councils) to inveigh against the formation of political parties.

A procedural dispute which erupted on the first day of the resumed Committee sitting proved a portent of continued division. During the discussion, Todd, the leading spokesman for the European Advisory Committee, insisted, in opposition to the opinion of the Progressives, that members 'were expected to make their comments within the framework of the Ngwenyama's speech—not contrary to it'.[14] Addi-

* Although the meanings of the *Incwala*, the central ceremony of Swazi life, are disputed, it is certainly a first-fruits ceremony as well as a drama of kingship in which the collective strength of the nation is renewed.

tional controversy revolving around the freedom of independent expression, freedom of political organisation, and, more specifically, the right of the Progressive Party to exist, resulted in the suspension or expulsion of Nquku from the Swazi section of the Committee. The remaining Progressive members, having failed in their request that a constitutional adviser be appointed for the Committee, decided that their position was untenable. They then approached Professor Denis V. Cowen, Professor of Comparative Government at Cape Town University and author of the Basutoland constitution, to advise their party and the Eurafrican Welfare Association on constitutional reform. Finally, on June 11, 1961, Zwane and Mabuza resigned from the Committee. 'If we are to be discouraged from speaking out, as in Mr Nquku's case', said Zwane in his letter of resignation, 'we will be false to our convictions while giving the public the misleading impression that the Swaziland Progressive Party is having a hand in the shaping of the new constitution when, in fact, the position is quite different.' A formal request for representation on the committee was then made to the Resident Commissioner by the Progressive Party, but this was refused on the grounds that the Swazi National Council was the only body properly representative of the Swazi people.

Having been denied representation on the Constitutional Committee, the Progressive Party declined to submit Professor Cowen's report in the first instance to that body for comment and interpretation. Instead, the report was addressed to the people of Swaziland and to the British government. The report, submitted on September 20, 1961, contained the following major provisions:

1. The establishment of a Legislative Council with provision for a common voters' roll including Swazi, whites, and Coloureds, and allowing for universal adult suffrage.
2. The establishment of non-racialism, as against multi-racialism, in all aspects of Swaziland's political, economic, and social life, and the elimination of the very large number of racially discriminating laws in Swaziland, some of which had been kept in force since Swaziland was subject to the jurisdiction of the Transvaal Republic.
3. The entrenchment in the constitution of a court-enforced Bill of Human Rights, including full freedom of political organisation.
4. The peaceful integration of the traditional chieftainship into modern democratic structures of government.

5. The recognition of Swaziland as a Protected State and the establishment of the Paramount Chief's position as Head of State with a status similar to the Sultan of Zanzibar.
6. The establishment of responsible government.
7. The establishment of a democratic form of local government, especially in the main townships of Swaziland.[15]

Prior to the formal submission of this report, the recently-formed Swaziland Student Union, founded by Timothy Zwane, a student at Pius XII College in Basutoland, presented a memorandum to the Constitutional Committee. This memorandum, dated August 31, 1961, demanded that constitutional changes be based on the principles of non-racialism (as opposed to multi-racialism), universal adult suffrage, a common election roll, a legislature with a majority of elected members, and with the Ngwenyama as constitutional head of the whole non-racial nation. The Union also went on record as 'recognising the Swaziland Progressive Party as truly representative of the Swazi people's aspirations and interests' and therefore called upon the Committee and the government 'to invite the party to send full representation to the Committee and that their representatives constitute one half of the whole committee'.[16] Not only were the demands of the Progressive Party and the Student Union ignored, but the Committee continued its sittings behind a cloak of secrecy.

Meanwhile, the determination of the Ngwenyama and Todd to exclude the nationalists and to push through their own constitutional formula exasperated Marwick, the Resident Commissioner. His attempts to thwart these tactics soon led to an almost total estrangement and the Committee's work virtually ground to a halt. Finally, in an effort to inject a new element into the situation, Marwick persuaded the Secretary of State for Colonies, Reginald Maudling, to appoint Sir Charles Arden-Clarke as adviser to the Committee. But Arden-Clarke's experience in Nigeria, Bechuanaland, Basutoland and Ghana seemed to make little difference to the Committee and he submitted his own report to London.

When the final report of the Committee emerged, no comments or recommendations were given as those of the constitutional adviser and there was no word from London concerning his observations. Indeed, the likelihood that any of Arden-Clarke's advice had been accepted seemed minimal, and the report included such definitions, as 'a Bill of Rights is a list of things . . . '. The secretive pattern surrounding the Committee's activities was further revealed when, on December 13, the Secretary of State received a four-man delegation from the Committee which presented him with the final report. Since these proposals, dated November 20, 1961, had been drawn up and submitted to London without reference to the inhabitants of the Territory, Professor Cowen attempted to salvage the situation by requesting that a London conference be called prior to any constitutional decision. This proposal was vigorously opposed by the Swazi National Council and the European Advisory Council.

The Committee Report and British Reservations

On March 2, 1962, the Report of the Constitutional Committee was made public, although by that date its general contents had become known. While recommending an end to all existing discriminatory legislation and practices, it proceeded to urge the implementation of a constitution which would establish racialism as a basic principle of government, thereby entrenching the privileged position of both the white residents and the traditional hierarchy. 'A constitutional committee of local worthies, black and white', said *The Times* (London), 'has put forward proposals for a timid advance towards a communally-elected legislative council which would entrench all the most conservative characteristics of the Paramount Chief's regime. . . . The constitution makers have packed their proposals with elementary and proven errors.'[17]

The Committee Report recommended an Executive Council consisting of the Governor, three ex-officio members, one official and four nominated members, together with four unofficials (two Swazi and two European). The Legislative Council was to consist of equal numbers of Swazi (chosen by acclamation) and European members (elected by western methods) without regard to the numerical strength of each community. The 'special place' of the Ngwenyama in the Territory was to be recognised, giving him the right to withhold his consent to Bills, which would then be reserved for the Queen's pleasure. Finally, a Bill of Rights was to lay down personal liberties, such as freedom of expression and assembly, but it was also, in effect, to prevent any major change in the socio-political framework since it pledged to maintain the position of the Ngwenyama and the property rights of racial groups. It specifically excluded any constitutional reforms which might conflict with these principles.

The published report indicated that the four official members of the Constitutional Committee, including the Resident Commissioner, had certain reservations which had been communicated to the Colonial Secretary. 'It was understood', said Marwick, 'that the reservations, which were contained in a confidential document, would not be published.' Nevertheless, in early April, Marwick announced that copies of the reservations had found their way into the hands of members of the European community and that distorted versions were circulating in the Territory. Whether this leak was engineered by whites who hoped to embarrass the government or by someone in the employ of a political party was not known, but its effect was electric. Confessing that this action had been forced upon him, and with the permission of the Colonial Secretary, the Resident Commissioner released the reservations with the regret that they 'may give offence and cause embarrassment to the Ngwenyama, the Swazi National Council and the Swazi members of the Constitutional Committee'.[18]

The Note of Reservations indeed proved very embarrassing not only for the Swazi members of the Constitutional Committee but also for their white colleagues. Carl Todd informed a white gathering prior to its release that 'he had urged the government not to publish it as the government had a special relationship with the people and was not involved in politics'.[19] To the consternation of the Committee members, the official members had pointed out to the Colonial Secretary that the idea of 'racial federation' was 'inimical to the achievement of the ultimate objective of a non-racial state'. They considered it 'unrealistic and wrong to deny those educated Swazi who find the traditional system inadequate for their needs the right to take part by modern democratic process in the legislature'. Their exclusion from voting rights was cited as a clear example of racial discrimination. The official members declared that equal Swazi and European representation was difficult to justify, and went on to suggest that 'in the present friendly atmosphere between the races, now would be the time for the Europeans to give up their claim for 50 per cent representation rather than wait to have it wrested from them'. The illusory argument that potential investment depended on the 50-50 arrangement was said to be outweighed by the advantage of recognising the true position of the European minority. Aiming to be neither too conservative nor too bold, the official members proposed a scheme whereby eight Swazi members would be nominated by the Ngwenyama, eight Europeans elected on a European roll, and eight members (four Swazi and four

European) elected on a common roll with a qualified franchise in four double-member constituencies. Following the lead suggested by Lord Hailey, who had emphasised that future development required that 'the position of the Paramount Chief and his Council must become that of agencies recognised by the Legislature for the conduct of certain aspects of native affairs', the official reservations stated that 'the Legislative Council should not be restricted in an undefined manner' but rather should define the matters to be dealt with by the Ngwenyama-in-Council. The official members thus rejected the Committee's proposals which would deny the Legislature's competence to deal with 'matters affecting Swazi law and custom, Swazi institutions, and Swazi land and minerals'.[20]

The Colonial Secretary attached great importance to these official reservations. His preliminary comments, in the form of a letter to the High Commissioner dated February 14, 1962, were published as an annex to the Constitutional Report released in March. Maudling rejected the recommendation that official members of the proposed Legislative Council should not have a vote, and expressed his belief that the High Commissioner should be empowered to nominate additional members if necessary. Thus, any hope that the European Advisory Council-Swazi National Council alliance might have entertained of creating a situation analogous to that in Southern Rhodesia, wherein the British government disclaimed any internal responsibility, seemed completely dashed. While recognising that the Swazi might be anxious to preserve certain institutions, the Colonial Secretary did not want the Swazi 'to regard the proposed Legislative Council as a body in some way alien to and distinct from their own traditions. . . '. He therefore considered it undesirable 'to preclude the Legislature of the Territory from passing laws that might affect Swazi law and custom, [or] to prevent it from exercising a general power to legislate in respect of land and minerals in such a way as to affect Swazi land and minerals'.

He was not convinced by the Report's recommendations for electing Swazi representatives to the Legislative Council. He declared that a common roll, or something along those lines, would undoubtedly be required if the non-traditional elements among the Swazi were to be satisfied. He concluded his letter to the High Commissioner by stating that he would await the reactions both to the proposals and to his own comments before coming to a final decision. To further assist the High Commissioner in evaluating public reaction, he sent Denis S. Stephens to Swaziland in mid-July as constitutional adviser.

Reaction to the Constitutional Proposals: the Swazi Nation

Reactions in Swaziland to the constitutional proposals ranged from warm endorsement to bitter denunciation. The representatives of the Swazi National Council and the European Advisory Council tended to regard each major point as above negotiation, while the Resident Commissioner, supported by the local newspaper, the *Times of Swaziland*, endeavoured to accustom the conservatives to the idea of inevitable change. Swazi nationalists rejected the proposals in their entirety.

Still seeking to modify the attitude of the traditionalists, the Resident Commissioner met with the Ngwenyama and the principal officers of the Swazi nation in early June. While recognising the worth of traditional institutions, his words were clearly critical of the Swazi National Council. He reminded his hearers, to their embarrassment, that in 1960 he had cautioned against undue haste in advancing a constitution. His objections were based on the fact that the Swazi had never faced the basic problems arising from the clash of modern ideas with traditional approaches and positions. Yet, they had suddenly proposed a constitution embodying those very contradictions which they had not had the courage to face. Marwick also noted that his relationship with the Swazi National Council had deteriorated over the past two years. He pointed out that three years earlier he had proposed the reorganisation of the Council to meet modern needs but his suggestions had not found favour and the opportunity for reform had been missed. Even its Standing Committee had become incapable of dealing with the simplest matters. In brief, said the Resident Commissioner, the Council was disintegrating when it should have been at its strongest. He also found it necessary to speak out strongly against the racialism which had been all-prevailing and legally-supported in the country: only through a new attitude, by consciously building up a single nation of two races, could Swaziland advance as a modern nation.[21]

It was only after the release of the constitutional proposals that the Ngwenyama, for the first time, appeared to desire the opinion of his people. Rather than wait until the regularly-scheduled July meeting of the full Swazi National Council, Sobhuza summoned his people to a special meeting—the first such meeting in fifty years—at the Lobamba cattle kraal on February 27, 1962. Although the summons was addressed to 'all men', it was understood to mean the princes, chiefs and heads of kraals, and their councillors. While the Lobamba meeting thus constituted could hardly be considered fully representative of the people, even such a limited assembly was sufficient to reveal the split which sooner or later has overtaken most African societies as the educated youth confront the tribal elders. Thus the Swazi National Council proposals were rudely rejected and the meeting broke up in complete disorder. A few weeks later a Mbabane District Swazi Council meeting (*Inkundla*), attended by some 800 persons, again rejected the 50-50 proposal and demanded an elected majority.

The full meeting of the Swazi National Council, which officially convened on July 3, 1962, and lasted into early August, revealed, in its operational procedure, not only the inadequacy of the old tribal structure, but also the resolve of the traditionalists to carry through a predetermined plan. Conservative estimates put the total number of assembled delegates at over a thousand and these were drawn from all political, social and economic strata of Swazi life. For no clearly-defined reason, there were delays in placing before the delegates the real business of the conference. As days turned into weeks without the delegates knowing precisely what they were called to do, farmers and people in employment felt obliged to depart. Only the tribal chiefs could afford to stay on.

Prior to convoking the meeting which was to concern itself with the constitutional proposals, the *Liqoqo* decided to violate the basic assumptions of tribal democracy by denying political leaders the right to speak in full assembly. Only on July 29 were the politicians granted permission to present their views. But instead of addressing the full assembly, they were called to the offices of the National Council. Only *tinkundla* representatives—chiefs, indunas, and some Swazi members of the Constitutional Committee—were present for what turned out to be an interrogation of the assembled politicians. Each party leader appeared separately before the *Iqoqo* (small committee) and the Secretary of the Swazi National Council, Polycarp Dhlamini, informed the gathering that anyone who caused trouble would be arrested. The politicians were then interrogated on the membership of their parties and were reprimanded for speaking against the proposed constitution. To most of the questions, Nquku and other political spokesmen refused to give an answer and protested against their treatment.

A few days earlier, on July 21, the Resident Commissioner addressed the full meeting of the Council at Lobamba and administered a stern rebuke. He pointed out some of the problems arising from the constitutional proposals, specifically those dealing with the traditional powers of the Ngwenyama, the allocation of lands and tribal allegiance. Even more directly, he asked the assembly 'whether it was not possible to consider some of the proposals as being akin to the policy of apartheid in a neighbouring country'. Further, he said that the way in which the Swazi National Council had functioned in the last few years had caused him great misgivings. It was not performing the functions it should in the interests of the Swazi people and its reputation had suffered because of the way it had carried out its day-to-day affairs. 'You have a duty', he concluded, 'to see whether you have a council able to discharge [its] function. . . .'[22]

Despite the admonitions of the Resident Commissioner and the opposition of the politically conscious, the Swazi National Council officially announced on August 9 that the nation had unanimously accepted 'in principle' the draft constitution. This decision was reportedly based on the consent of the Ndlovukazi (Queen Mother), princes and 563 councillors and 'men'—about half the originally assembled number. Acceptance 'in principle' puzzled even the British constitutional expert, Denis Stephens, who was assessing public opinion. When he asked what such acceptance meant, National Council spokesmen began hedging behind nebulous talk of mineral rights. Obviously the National Council was not convinced that 'unanimous acceptance' truly reflected popular sentiment.

As interesting as it was typical was the fact that the Ngwenyama did not associate himself with the announcement. Although Sobhuza may indeed have been ill as announced, he had equivocated in early June in the face of strong opposition to the 50-50 proposal. According to published reports never denied, he had privately told a meeting of Swazi teachers: 'I never said that we should work on this 50-50 basis as I am alleged to have done. What I said was that we should be equals. . . . It seems that others are speaking for me.'[23]

Reaction to the Constitutional Proposals: the White Community

The release of the constitutional proposals in March was also the signal for a concerted effort on the part of the European Advisory Council to secure white and Swazi acceptance and to pressure Britain into dropping the reservations of the Swaziland government and the Colonial Secretary. The group's recognised leader, Carl Todd, and his white associates did not conceal their hostility towards the British government. 'I would prefer to rely on the agreement with the Swazi National Council and with equal representation in the Legislature', said Todd, 'than being solely in the hands of the British government and their officials to protect my interests against politicians who do not respect my rights and the true interests of Swaziland. . . . Under our proposals we can at least block any hasty action.' As for Swazi politicians and his relation to the Ngwenyama, he was also candidly clear: 'Swazi politicians can play their part in the affairs of the Swazi people by devoting their talents to the running of the Swazi National Council . . . [they] do not need to vote with Europeans and Coloureds, and they can improve the Swazi system, if this is necessary, without destroying it.' 'The Ngwenyama', he said, 'is such a wise friend of the Europeans that we should support and strengthen his position and not undermine it. . . .'[24] The proposed Bill of Rights was considered the best means for ensuring a favourable future, since it would preserve the traditional authority. 'The longer the traditional authority remained', he said, 'the better it would be for the country.' He was particularly angry that the British government had released the text of the official reservations, since they buttressed the fears of more far-sighted whites who considered the Committee report as 'wishful thinking', 'completely outdated by United Nations and British government policy', 'unimaginative, inelastic and dangerous', if not 'naked autocracy'.[25]

Even the announcement of a united front, formed by leaders of rival political parties, trade unions, academic bodies and the Anglican Church to protest against the racialism of the constitution, did not deter the leaders of the European Advisory Council from their course. Public meetings were called to mobilise support in favour of the proposals and, hopefully, to prevent British interference. On March 21, Sydney Gaiger, another prominent Advisory Council member, informed a white gathering that 'the futures of our political and property interests are at stake. and the public would be well advised to think, and to act, in a manner which will not jeopardise these two most important factors. . . . The purpose of this meeting, therefore. is to mobilise public opinion with a view to writing to the government in support of our proposals.'[26] In April, the European Advisory Council unanimously endorsed the proposals of the sub-committee.

A white voters' referendum held in May confirmed the position of the European Advisory Council by an overwhelming percentage: 697 in favour, 19 opposed. But also of significance was the fact that only

52·23 per cent of the white voters participated in the poll, thereby revealing indifference or reflecting an awareness of the futility of this course of action. Finally, on September 3, the European Advisory Council and the Swazi National Council joined forces in their effort to secure adoption of the constitutional proposals. At a joint meeting of these two bodies (Advisory Council official members were not included), the following resolutions were unanimously adopted:

1. The constitutional proposals be promulgated as a reflection of the will of the majority of the people in Swaziland.
2. A constitutional conference be held in Mbabane under the chairmanship of the Secretary of State.
3. The Ngwenyama be recognised as King of Swaziland. Europeans would continue their allegiance to other governments but would recognise and respect the position of the King therein.
4. A Treaty be signed clarifying the position of Swaziland as a protected state; this treaty to be concluded concurrently with the promulgation of a constitution.
5. The Secretary of State be requested to withdraw his conditions dealing with Swaziland mineral rights so that the Swazi Nation would be in control of the same.

With the announcement of the joint resolution, the strategy of the white-traditionalist alliance was made abundantly clear. First, constitutional arrangements entrenching the position of their respective rights and authority would be devised. Second, those proposals would be set forth as the will of the majority. Third, Britain would not only be pressured into granting a constitution on these terms, but at the same time would be asked to remove itself, through treaty, from any position whereby it might again be the arbiter of the country's political development. Such a course of action made a head-on clash with the British government inevitable. It came in early November, when Todd declared: 'The government is in fact a complete dictatorship. . . . Swaziland has no government by the people at all.'[27]

Reaction to the Constitutional Proposals: Political Elements

But while the Advisory Council and the National Council made frantic efforts to consolidate their apparent advantage and force the British government to accede to their demands as the voice of the majority, the very prospect of their success stimulated unprecedented political expression. A Swaziland Progressive Party manifesto, issued shortly before the July meeting of the Swazi National Council at Lobamba, denounced the Race Relations Proclamation of March 2, 1962, and the Liquor Licences Amendment Act as meaningless sops to confuse the people into believing that the constitutional discussions were already bearing fruit. It pointed to continued, if not worse, racial discrimination in education, and viewed the call for the formation of a police reserve as an indication of official intention to force a constitution upon the people. Zwane pointed out in a memorandum delivered in London to the Colonial Secretary that the proposed constitution enabled the white community to 'come up from a position in which their present Advisory Council has very little power—and then only in matters affecting Europeans—to a position in which they would exercise very substantial power over all persons in the Territory'. The memorandum called on the British government to refuse further mining concessions until Swaziland saw significant constitutional changes. Criticism of the absence of Swazi in high administrative posts, the differences in education expenditure for white and Swazi children amounting to £90 per annum in 1952, the dependence of Swaziland upon South Africa for news services, and a strong complaint against the banning of various British and Ghanaian publications was also set forward.[28]

In a letter to Members of Parliament, the Swaziland Student Union stated that the youth of the country 'are not prepared under any circumstances, to live under the proposed treacherous constitution which is an utter betrayal of our interests', and concluded by promising 'to use any means to see that the proposed constitution collapses, even if it means loss of life and collapse of the whole economy of the country'.[29]

The Swaziland Democratic Party (SDP) echoed the words of the Resident Commissioner and stated that certain pressing and controversial issues required full discussion before a constitution could be proposed. Otherwise, the basic contradictions of Swazi life would be incorporated into the constitution. The SDP also warned that adoption of the proposed constitution, 'vesting power in an alliance between white reaction and an anti-democratic and race-conscious tribal oligarchy . . . could very well [lead to] widespread disturbances in the Territory which would lead to conflict between black and white and paralyse economic development'.[30] In addition to these strong political statements and manifestos, a large number of public protest meetings were held during the last months of the year. Characteristic of Swaziland's situation, these meetings were invariably attended by South African security branch police.

A CONSTITUTION IMPOSED AND A
TRADITIONALIST VICTORY, 1963–1966

WITH NO AGREEMENT in sight on constitutional proposals for Swaziland, a London conference was convened in late January 1963. Although both the traditionalists and the nationalists expressed satisfaction that the conference was being held, the lines between the two were drawn as sharply as before. The Swaziland government was represented by two officials, including the Resident Commissioner, and Carl Todd led a four-man delegation from the European Advisory Council. The Eurafrican community selected A. Sellstroom as their representative while Dr David Hynd, a European medical missionary and long-time resident of Swaziland, sat as an independent spokesman. Six seats were reserved for the Swazi National Council (led, at the Conference, by Polycarp Dhlamini) and another three for the political parties—Progressive, Democratic and Convention. Simon Nxumalo and George Msibi were respectively invited to represent the Democratic and Convention parties, but the split in Progressive ranks gave the government the option of inviting either J. J. Nquku or Ambrose Zwane as the representative of that party, a decision made in favour of Nquku.

The London Conference: Nationalist-Traditionalist Confrontation

Whether the British decision to invite Nquku as Progressive Party spokesman was deliberately intended to ignore the bulk of Swazi nationalist sentiment, or to create a favourable reaction at the United Nations where he was then appearing, the effect was to encourage a growing movement towards unity among the nationalists. But protests from Nxumalo and Sellstroom on the exclusion of Zwane went unheeded, as did a Student Union declaration that the people of Swaziland 'felt insulted and betrayed by the decision of the Swaziland

Government to grant a ticket . . . to a supposed leader in this country and to turn down a leader who has genuine and popular support'.[1]

Although not admitted to the conference, Zwane, together with the Samketi faction of the Progressive Party, endorsed the Alliance of Political Organisations. This ad hoc alliance, formed on January 5 in response to Nxumalo's appeal for unity in the face of a 'united front formed by Black privilege and White privilege', was broadened in London by the adherence of Msibi, Sellstroom and Hynd. As a basis for common action, the nationalists or modernists called for the establishment of a non-racial democratic state, a sovereign and independent Swaziland, the recognition of the Ngwenyama as King and Head of State in a constitutional monarchy, and universal adult suffrage. While Nquku alone of the political leaders refused to join the Alliance, he too insisted on a one-man, one-vote franchise.

Nationalist ranks were further strengthened when Dr Allen Nxumalo, a top-ranking Swazi member of the Constitutional Committee, withdrew his support for the Committee's proposals. A well known and highly respected physician, Allen Nxumalo subsequently joined the Swaziland Democratic Party and succeeded his cousin, Simon Nxumalo, as party President. In explaining his decision to disassociate himself from the Swazi National Council, Dr Nxumalo stated that he was disillusioned with the Committee since 'it became clear that there was no intention to get a real mandate from the people [and] that all criticism was stifled'. Convinced that the National Council was likely to pursue these tactics, he denounced the idea of 'race federation' as 'apartheid in another disguise' and urged that there be no discussion of mineral rights until after a responsible government had been established.[2]

It was, in fact, around the question of mineral rights that the London conference revolved. Whereas the European Advisory Council and Swazi National Council representatives insisted that the conference was being held only to confirm the draft constitution drawn up a year before 'by the representatives of the majority of persons in the country', and that these proposals should accordingly be written into a formal treaty, the British government was determined that control of minerals and land should fall under the proposed Legislative Council which, open to modernising influences, would proceed with the development of a viable state. In implementing this policy, however, the government faced a dilemma somewhat unique in the annals of empire-shedding. Whereas in other colonial areas, the majority principle provided the immediate justification for each step of constitutional advancement, it could hardly be disputed that, on a strictly numerical basis, the Ngwenyama could claim to speak for the majority. On the other hand, it seemed certain that the future lay clearly with the political parties, which, it was further assumed, would soon politicise the masses.

As the conference floundered in deadlock, the British government endeavoured to persuade the Ngwenyama himself to come to London, a suggestion which Sobhuza resisted on the grounds that, as 'constitutional monarch' of Swaziland, he did not consider he should take an active part is discussing the future constitutional arrangement for the Territory, or that he should come under any pressure in that connection. If the Ngwenyama's refusal was not, as subsequent events seemed to indicate, a deliberate deception, it did give welcome comfort to the Political Alliance, which commended Sobhuza for his decision and pointed out that his participation would have been 'politically suicidal'.

Duncan Sandys, the Secretary of State for the Colonies, brought the conference to a close on February 12, with no sign of agreement yet in sight. Although the British government at one stage had almost given way to a substantially non-racial scheme providing for a majority of common-roll representation, strong lobbying and pressure had led to its abandonment. Thereafter, the British government moved ahead to effect a compromise formula of its own making. Further attempts at consultation in Swaziland were made through the Resident Commissioner, and on May 30 the official views of the British government were set forth in a White Paper.

British Views Announced

In form, if not in substance, the proposed constitution was a compromise between the views of the traditionalists, the white minority and the nationalists. The constitution provided for executive powers to be vested in Her Majesty's Commissioner (formerly the Resident Commissioner) assisted by an Executive Council of three ex-officio members and five members appointed by Her Majesty's Commissioner. The Legislature, it was announced, would consist of the Commissioner and a Legislative Council composed of a Speaker, twenty-four Elected Members, together with four Official Members and Nominated Members. Of the twenty-four Elected Members to sit in the Legislature, eight Swazi were to be elected through traditional methods, while of the eight Europeans, four were to be elected on a European roll and four on a National roll; eight persons of any race were to be elected on a National roll.

For the election of Europeans on the European roll, the entire country was to be treated as a single constituency, but, for the purposes of election on the National roll, Swaziland was to be divided into four constituencies, each returning three members to the Legislative Council. In each constituency, one seat was reserved for a European and candidates for these seats would require endorsement by twenty-five registered European voters. A European of twenty-one years or over would be qualified to vote on the European roll provided that he be a British subject or South African citizen and resident of Swaziland for at least three years. Any person of twenty-one years or over would qualify to vote on the National roll provided he be a British subject or British protected person, resident in Swaziland for at least three years and paying direct tax, or be the wife of a person paying direct tax. After one year the voting rights of South African citizens would be terminated. The constitution provided that the Ngwenyama would be entitled to see all papers to the Executive Council and receive a copy of every Bill passed by the Legislative Council. He was also empowered to bring matters before the Executive Council for consideration.

On the vital matter of minerals, their ownership, subject to existing rights, was formally vested in the Ngwenyama on behalf of the Swazi nation, but the Legislature was given power over them. Mineral rights, however, would be granted or refused by Her Majesty's Commissioner in the name of the Ngwenyama after consultation with him and with the Executive Council. Because of the Commissioner's very wide reserve and discretionary powers, both the Legislative and Executive Councils could in practice become merely advisory. Existing laws, including Swazi law and custom, were to continue in force until changed by a competent legislative authority.[3]

Swazi National Council Reaction to British Views

British refusal to compromise on the matter of mineral rights evidently came as a great surprise to the traditionalists, who had assumed that their European allies could win over the British government to Sobhuza's thinking. Since white support had not achieved the expected results, it was necessary for the traditionalists to revise their strategy. With minerals not excluded from the competence of the Legislative and Executive Councils, there remained little advantage in a numerical

50–50 legislative formula except for the whites. If the threat of the Swazi nationalists could be overcome, then the advantage of any racial formula might fall away.

Even before the Colonial Secretary had announced his preliminary views on May 30, the basic outlines of Whitehall's thinking were passed on to the Swazi National Council for discussion. At a meeting convoked on March 9 at Lobamba and attended by some 4,120 'councillors and men', the Council considered the Swazi delegation's report and the Colonial Secretary's views as presented in person by the Resident Commissioner, Marwick. Considering these views a complete departure from the idea of a 'racial federation', a resolution of March 14 referred the matter back to the people for a further mandate. Another meeting was set for April 15 and the views of the Swazi nation were promised to the government by April 23. This subsequent 'full' meeting of the National Council was attended by a smaller number, approximately 500, and political spokesmen were excluded. After repeating traditional positions on such matters as Swazi sovereignty, the Council rejected the proposal that Swazi land, minerals, law and custom should fall within the scope of the Legislative and Executive Councils inasmuch as both of these bodies were advisory to the High Commissioner, who exercised absolute control over them. Their transfer was thus seen as a surrender which could not be made until the reins of government were fully handed over to the Swazi. While again affirming the necessity of a 'racial federation', the Council suggested that the Secretary of State should 'give all the peoples of Swaziland the right to choose one or the other of the two systems, whether they wish to exercise their political rights through their traditional democracy or through the common roll modelled after the Westminster pattern', and that, on this basis, 'each group should be allocated seats in the Legislative Council in proportion to the number each element represents'.[4]

If the Council's proposal seemed to suggest that its white allies might now be expendable, the Ngwenyama lent even greater weight to the possibility when he stated that it was incorrect to hold that the Swazi nation stood principally for 50–50 representation. The mandate, said Sobhuza to the Swazi delegation, was to treat the whole issue on the principle or basis of a racial federal system 'which, by implication, amounts more or less to 50–50, or best understood to mean equality'. At the same time he could not accept the 'non-racial system or complete integration under the Westminster pattern'. Although the

Ngwenyama's and the Council's statements went beyond the very rigid interpretation of equal representation as understood or at least set forth by the National Council at the London conference, the racial principle was still intact. Since it would still permit white-traditional control for some time, it was endorsed by Todd as a 'democratic recognition of the rights of the minority who are entitled to seats in a Legislative Council in keeping with their numbers'. Nevertheless, the way would now be open, if not for a rapprochement with the nationalists, then at least for greater support from the illiterate masses who found any talk of 50-50 with the whites somewhat mystifying.

White Reaction to British Views

White reactions to the 'compromise' views of the British government were predictably bitter. Even before the British views had been officially revealed, Todd refused to be bound by the pledged secrecy surrounding the post-London conference consultations, and denounced the British government for attempting to impose an altogether new constitution 'that does not carry the support of the overwhelming proportion of Swazilanders, whether they be Swazis or Europeans'.[5] Such a move, he said, would be an act of imperialism by a colonial power, 'inconsistent with its pledge to the United Nations and intolerable during the twentieth century'.[6] If such accusations sounded somewhat incongruous in the mouth of the European Advisory Council leader, they were heartily endorsed by most whites in the Territory who rejected any proposals which would reduce them to a minority in the Legislature.

Still hoping to counter British policy, Todd also made an unexpected bid to the country's political parties. Imitating the tactics of the Convention, he sought to rally universal support by emphasising Swazi sovereignty. The Ngwenyama, he said, was the rightful King of Swaziland, not by reason of any constitution enacted by Britain but historically and factually: an imposed constitution would make Swaziland 'a conquered state without independent rights in the people'. He therefore called upon the politicians and the Ngwenyama to speak out forcefully on this matter. In particular, he appealed to Msibi, calling him 'a patriot with qualities of leadership', to see the logic of his plea. Although Todd could hardly separate this romantic excursion into history from the constitutional question, his approach obviously had its appeal for some, particularly for Msibi, as later events would show. Again utilising the slogan of Swazi sovereignty, Todd admonished the country's political leaders that it would be disloyal to exploit the nation's controversy with Britain to further their own political interests. With greater success, he urged upon the Ngwenyama his 'duty' to speak out and not stand aloof from an issue affecting the very foundation of his kingdom. 'An African king', he chided, 'is no figurehead on such an issue.' And finally, not satisfied with pressing his case in Swaziland, Todd published an appeal for a referendum in *The Times* (London) of March 23. In an obvious distortion of the facts, he linked existing labour discontent with the rejection of the Advisory Council-National Council proposals.[7]

But the very intensity of Todd's attacks upon the British government crystallised a certain amount of resentment in the European community. Unwilling to follow one whose leadership seemed to close the door to any further negotiation, some few whites endorsed the position of Frank Corbett, also a member of the Advisory Council, who questioned the wisdom of Todd's approach. According to Corbett, it was Todd's return from London and his violent outbursts against the British government which caused the breakdown of new Advisory Council-National Council compromise negotiations. He therefore requested Todd to justify his continued presence as leader of the European community on three points—his ability to represent European opinion, his acquaintance with the views of Swazilanders, black and white, and his personal relations with Swaziland and British government officials.[8] Sellstroom, of the Eurafrican community, who frequently associated himself with the European stand, supported Corbett's challenge. Desiring to give a political home to whites and Eurafricans discontented with Todd's leadership, Corbett eventually launched the Swaziland Independent Front in April 1964. The Front rejected apartheid and announced that it would resist 'any political pressure designed to insinuate Swaziland into any Bantustan scheme'.[9]

The King Enters Politics

But if the Front, with its 'progressive-business' outlook, hoped to gain at least the tacit support of the Ngwenyama, these hopes were quickly shattered. Preceded by Verwoerd's offer of September 3, 1963, to guide the Territories more quickly and efficiently to independence and prosperity than could be done by Britain, the King seemed intent upon an open clash with Britain. With South African endorsement, a resolution of the Swazi National Royal Club, supposedly representing some 15,000 Swazi living and working in the Republic, called for the severence of all ties with Britain. Supported by Todd, who continued to follow if not lead the Ngwenyama in his resistance to British plans. it was argued that both Britain and South Africa should recognise Swaziland's status as a Protected State under a constitution based on principles advocated by the Ngwenyama. These principles, presented to the House of Commons in the form of a petition from the Ngwenyama, were introduced in November on his behalf by the Conservative MP, Major Patrick Wall, a long-time champion of imperial interests in Central and Southern Africa. In this petition, Sobhuza specifically protested against the proposed system of elections and called for recognition of the country's status as a Protectorate, the rightful position of the Swazi King, the control by the Swazi nation of all land and mineral rights, and recognition of the rightful powers of the Swazi National Council.

The publication on January 3, 1964, of an order-in-council imposing a constitution along the lines of the May 30 White Paper induced Sobhuza to drop all pretence of co-operation. Ignoring government counsel, he called for an unofficial plebiscite on January 19 to register Swazi objections to the Constitution. Using a reindeer—a beast totally unknown to the Swazi—as the symbol of the Queen's Commissioner and the well-known lion to represent the Ngwenyama, the National Council confronted the country's illiterate population with a choice of accepting or rejecting their King. Although the issues were hardly so simple, 122,000 votes were announced for the Ngwenyama as opposed to a handful against him. All of the political parties, with the exception of Clifford Nkosi's MNC, from which Msibi had resigned in August 1963, asked their members to boycott the 'Reindeer Referendum'. The government also announced that it would ignore the exercise since it would merely prove what was already common knowledge: that Sobhuza enjoyed the loyalty of the majority of his people. The referendum was fully endorsed by Todd.

Whatever the hopes of the British government to effect an honest compromise between the nationalists, traditionalists and white community, the aims of the constitution were defeated in late April when it was announced that the King-in-Council would put up his own candidates for all National roll seats. Candidates would stand for continuance of the monarchy, Swazi customs, mineral and land rights, and the prerogative of the Ngwenyama. In making this decision,

Sobhuza completely frustrated the spirit of the new constitution, which had envisaged that as many as half the twenty-four seats would be chosen on a party basis. The decision also came as a severe blow to the main political parties, which now saw little hope of defeating candidates enjoying the support of the King and the National Council.

Sobhuza's decision to enter politics followed exactly the plan outlined by his legal adviser, van Wyk de Vries, a prominent South African Nationalist and member of the Broederbond. The eighteen page document, which fell into the hands of the *Rand Daily Mail* in October 1963, with its basic assertion that 'this constitution is a decisive step toward the extermination of the Ngwenyama, and of the Swazi Nation as an organic entity . . .', was calculated to fan the worst fears of Sobhuza. He was accordingly advised to press for explicit recognition of Swaziland as a Protectorate, for recognition of his own position as King of Swaziland, and for the vesting of all land and mineral rights in himself. It was recognised, however, that he alone could not reject the new constitution and so, after adopting a policy of procrastination, counter-proposals and petition, he was counselled to launch his own political party. It was predicted that Sobhuza's followers would easily win a majority in the Legislative Council. As the strongest political force in the country, it could then call for the removal of colonial rule.

Having decided on the formation of the Swazi National Council-sponsored Imbokodo ('Grinding Stone'), no attempt was made to apologise for the participation of the King and the National Council in politics. Charging that the political parties had already used bribery, intimidation, calumny and defamation, the National Council saw no need to permit politicians to put their case to Swazi living in Swazi areas. With that, perhaps some 80 per cent of the population was virtually delivered to the traditionalists.

Joining the protests of political leaders, the retiring Resident Commissioner, Sir Brian Marwick, speaking in his personal capacity, expressed his great disappointment with the National Council 'which for the most part was content to contemplate the imagined wrongs of the past'.[10] He also reminded the King that, while he might be in a safe and powerful position for some time if a particular political group gained control, at a later date he might well be cast aside by a rival group. In reply, the Committee of Imbokodo, led by Prince Makhosini Dhlamini, charged that Sir Brian and the government had done little or nothing towards the development and advancement of the Swazi during the past sixty years. The Commissioner was personally attacked

for granting mining rights in Swaziland without permission of the
Swazi and he was reminded that 'in Africa, Kings are leaders as well as
Kings', an approach amplified by George Msibi, who had accepted the
position of General Secretary of Imbokodo.

Reversal of British Policy

With the tax-payers' money now being diverted to the payment of the
expenses of a political party, the government had good reason, as Sir
Brian noted, for withholding the salaries of National Council officials.
But the government chose not to act. That Imbokodo would win the
elections seemed a foregone conclusion. Whether to placate South
Africa or to ensure the election of a 'moderate' government unlikely to
embarrass Britain in her relations with the Republic, all efforts to
stem the traditionalist tide were gradually ended. The very departure of
Sir Brian, after some thirty years in Swaziland, seemed to symbolise a
retreat in British policy. In his place, as the first Queen's Commissioner, came Francis A. Lloyd, CMG, OBE, formerly a Permanent
Secretary in Kenya and very much an old-style colonial administrator.
Henceforth, all efforts, direct and indirect, to prop up and even encourage nascent Swazi nationalism were abandoned.

If a change in British policy was as much due to government dis-
illusionment with the fissiparous character of the nationalist movement
as to the growing strength of the traditionalists, its own responsibilities
for this state of affairs could not be set aside. For while sympathetic
towards broad nationalist aims, the paternalistic administration headed
by Sir Brian had wished to dictate the pace of change and proved
intolerant of real dissent. With sweeping powers in its possession, the
administration had paid scant attention to the strenuous objections of
those who had long clamoured for improved living conditions and
government action against vested interests, white and black. In fact, it
was the high-handed policy of the administration during the great
strike of 1963, which, perhaps more than anything else, broke the back
of the nationalist movement and encouraged its fragmentation.

Labour Unrest and the Constitutional Questions

Even before the constitutional discussions had been brought to a conclusion in Swaziland and London, growing dissatisfaction with conditions of labour erupted in sporadic outbursts of protest and minor acts

of violence. In the past, instead of organising into industrial unions, the workers, as the employers well appreciated, turned to their leaders, who negotiated for them. But since the chiefs had no training in trade union organisation or any interest in political movements, they could not effectively put forward the demands of the workers.[11] However, from 1962 larger numbers of workers were awakening to the importance of trade unionism. A Swaziland Mining Workers' Union was formed in August 1962 at the Havelock Asbestos Mine, which had gone on strike as early as 1948. While disclaiming political affiliation, the Union declared that this did not mean 'it had closed its eyes to the present political struggle'.[12] Generally speaking, such union activities met with little appreciable success, for, while they could be recognised in law as workers' organisations, the employers were under no obligation to recognise them for purposes of negotiation. The usual response, therefore, of white employers to the labour awakening was to expel trade unionists or refuse to employ organisation-minded workers.

As the constitutional and political debates progressed, both labour and nationalist politicians grew conscious of their need for each other. Notwithstanding the arrival of an ICFTU organiser from the West Indies, the restrained, cautious and somewhat bourgeois approach of this organisation failed to evoke a profound response. Likewise, professions of interest on the part of the Swaziland Democratic Party also lacked emotional appeal. Seizing the opportunity, the Progressive Party of Zwane, soon to become the Ngwane National Liberatory Congress (NNLC), allied itself directly with the discontented workers who toiled for wages far lower than those prevailing for non-whites in South Africa.

General discontent prevailing at the large sugar estates of Ubombo Ranches gave the NNLC the appropriate opportunity to identify political issues with labour grievances. Zwane's Secretary-General, Clement Dumisa Dhlamini, together with Frank Groening, a Coloured collaborator, began mobilising the workers for a strike in late January 1963. Restrained by court order from entering the sugar properties, Dhlamini and his party workers urged the workers to demand a minimum monthly wage of R30.00 (£15, $42.00) in place of the existing wage of approximately R7.00 (£3 10s., $9.80). This agitation bore fruit on March 18 when 2,500 sugarcane workers in the Big Bend area went out on strike. Although the strike, lasting nine days, failed to gain the workers an appreciable wage increase, it served notice on their white employers, who had been stunned by the whole affair, that politics and labour would henceforth find common cause. The strike also troubled the Ngwenyama who felt compelled to address the country's employers, asking them to consider carefully the workers' legitimate causes of complaint. Otherwise, he said, trade unionism would be the only alternative. Frightened by the Ubombo strike, the government issued a labour decree forbidding strikes or lock-outs without three weeks' notice.

Shortly thereafter a government ban on the sale of sour milk, porridge and other cooked foods in the Mbabane market opened the door for renewed expressions of discontent and, at the same time, provided the politicians with another issue. A protest meeting on April 5 of about sixty market women was addressed by Dhlamini, who linked their grievances to the cause of Swazi nationalism. When the crowd refused to disperse as ordered by the District Commissioner, Dhlamini and a number of women were arrested. The next day, leaders of the SPP, the SDP and the MNC led an abortive march on the Residency in protest against these arrests and the constitutional proposals. Tear gas was used to disperse the crowds, which included many women.

On April 6 the country was alarmed by yet another sign of protest: this time at the Usutu Pulp Mill, where workers struck against low wages and the dismissal of two union organisers, one of whom was Clement Dhlamini. This strike, lasting three days, resulted in the reinstatement of the workers and a raise in the daily wage to R.50 (5s., $.70). It also led Gaiger, a close Advisory Council supporter of Todd, to link the strike with an attempt by subversive elements to take over the union, an interpretation of events contradicted by the Resident Commissioner.

The climax to several months of labour and political discontent came on May 20 when the workers at the Havelock Asbestos Mine, one of the world's five main producers, left their jobs in the largest demonstration the Territory had yet seen. Government attempts to intimidate the strikers by the arrest of twelve alleged ringleaders on June 9 precipitated a crisis. Tear gas was used to disperse the protesting crowd of more than 2000 and the arrested leaders were taken to Mbabane.

News of the Havelock disturbance and subsequent arrests had an electric effect upon the capital. A large meeting attended by more than 3,500 was held in Mbabane on June 9, and the following day the NNLC called for a general strike throughout the country. Dhlamini, free on bail, together with the NNLC Vice-President, Macdonald Maseko (a former ANC leader who escaped from house arrest in South Africa), led a procession numbering more than 3000 towards the British Residency. Although the police halted the march, the Resident Commissioner consented to meet the NNLC leaders, who demanded the release of the twelve strikers, a minimum daily wage of R2.00 (£1, $2.80), and the rejection of the constitution. They promised that the strike would continue until these demands were met. Thus, while the strike was ostensibly called to remedy labour grievances, its wider aims were to establish the NNLC as the major political party and to force rejection of the constitution.

As the strikes gradually spread throughout the Territory, and appeals from the Ngwenyama went unheeded by the workers, the High Commissioner ordered thirty-seven police from Bechuanaland to assist Swaziland's meagre security force of 370. This was immediately followed by the arrival of a battalion of troops from Kenya. By June 21, most Swazi workers in the capital had been forced to return to work and the troops were bringing their influence to bear in other parts of the country; an action which brought strong protest from the South African Congress of Trade Unions and various British Members of Parliament that the keeping of peace did not involve using troops to coerce strikers back to work.[13]

Again masters of the situation, the British authorities acted quickly against the NNLC. Dhlamini, fined R130.00 on June 13, was rearrested in court, together with Maseko. Dhlamini was charged with procuring or counselling an illegal strike at Havelock, and Maseko was arrested on a charge of taking part in an illegal procession. On June 26, Zwane was arrested in his consulting rooms. Recently returned from the Addis Ababa Conference, he had found the Havelock strike in process and had addressed the protest meeting of June 9. With all the NNLC Executive and known strike leaders apprehended, the total number of persons arrested in conjunction with the strikes was about 273.

On July 8 the chief accused were brought before Etienne Fourie, the same South African magistrate (later suspended from the bench for associating himself with a civil service protest) who had presided at Zwane's original hearing in June. Zwane reaffirmed his belief that the proper route to Swaziland's independence was 'by means of peaceful constitutional and democratic development'. He denied that he was guilty of any criminal offence, especially of the charge that he had attempted to incite a crowd of persons to burn down the Residency.

Although the Crown witness, who also testified that Zwane had ordered the killing of the Resident Commissioner, was dramatically exposed by the defence and subsequently imprisoned, it was not until early August that the preparatory examination ended and bail was arranged for the NNLC Executive. All the accused were committed for trial before the High Court. After several months of testimony, Zwane was acquitted on January 6, 1964, and mild sentences were handed down for his associates. In the meantime, however, the costs of the case—the longest in Swaziland's judicial history—reduced Zwane and the NNLC to near bankruptcy. Coming at such a crucial juncture in the constitutional evolution of the country, there was considerable suspicion that factors other than the strictly legal aspects of the strike were involved.

Swaziland's First Election: Traditionalist Victory

Although the political parties expressed their profound disappointment with the constitution for perpetuating a white-tribalist condominium, by late January 1964 all parties, including the NNLC, announced they would contest the National roll seats in the elections scheduled for June. The King, meanwhile, ordered that all Swazi should register for the elections. Eventually, over 88 per cent of the estimated potential electorate, or approximately 71,000 persons, registered for the National roll. On the European roll, some 2,209 registered out of an estimated potential electorate of 3,400. Most whites quickly identified themselves with the United Swaziland Association, a party created by Todd to work hand in hand with Imbokodo and pledged to lead Swaziland quickly to independence 'before Communistic influences were entrenched'.[14]

Polling for Swaziland's first legislature began on June 16, when Europeans and Eurafricans cast their votes for four seats. Of the twelve candidates, two ran as Independents, four were sponsored by the United Swaziland Association, and four were the nominees of the Swaziland Independent Front. But Todd's right-wing group easily captured all four reserved seats. The winners received from 983 votes to 1,129 votes while the highest Independent Front candidate received only 607 votes. Altogether, some 85 per cent of the 2,209 voters on the European roll cast their vote. The fact that the European roll included an estimated 1,000 South Africans, destined to lose their vote within one year, underscored the need, frequently expressed by Todd, for immediate independence. He promised that the first move of the new legislature, which was now assured of a traditionalist-white majority, would be to press Britain for a new constitution 'in keeping with the tradition and character of the people' and thus eliminate all elections.[15]

As the June 23–25 National roll elections drew near, the political parties moved in three directions in a belated effort to prevent a complete traditionalist victory. Efforts abroad to enlist financial support were stepped up; proceedings were initiated against certain Imbokodo candidates; renewed efforts were made to shore up the political alliance. Zwane, NNLC leader, and O. M. Mabuza, leader of one of the two Progressive parties, both visited various independent African states but had limited success in gaining support. The SDP, supported to some extent by the other political parties and the Independent Front, pressed unsuccessfully for the disqualification of Todd on grounds of insufficient residence.* Charges were also instituted against a United Swaziland Association candidate and two members of Imbokodo for printing election handbills in an unlawful manner, but the charges were dismissed. Indications of a political merger, first between the SDP, led by Allen Nxumalo, and Nquku's Progressive Party, failed to materialise and a last-minute four-party united front also collapsed. Consequently, with some forty-eight candidates representing six political parties contesting the twelve National roll seats, nationalist chances of gaining any representation were minimised. Government refusal to intervene in cases where chiefs forbade political campaigning made the parties' position hopeless. Not only was Clement Dhlamini refused permission to speak at the Royal Cattle Kraal at Lobamba, but the King himself refused to honour a promise to meet with all political leaders. For the nationalists, the elections now became a futile exercise.

The results of the three-day National roll elections gave a total victory to Imbokodo and its white supporters. Todd, running as an Imbokodo candidate, received 6,385 votes, while his nearest rival had 1,995 votes. Each of the four United Swaziland Association candidates elected for reserved National roll seats were wealthy businessmen and reputed supporters of South African Nationalist policies. All eight unreserved seats were won by Imbokodo candidates, who received 85·45 per cent of the valid votes (79,683); the eight official NNLC candidates gained 12·3 per cent (11,364); the eight SDP candidates only 1·4 per cent (1,271); Nquku's seven SPP candidates 0·6 per cent (589);

---

* Although Todd was twice disallowed registration as a voter by two Principal Registration Officers, he was enrolled on appeal to a magistrate, whose decision was final.

and Mabuza's SPP 0·25 per cent (247).While individual Imbokodo candidates polled from 8,799 to 13,561 votes, the highest nationalist contestor, Zwane, gained only 2,438 votes and his Deputy-President, Maseko, only 923 votes. Allen Nxumalo, who contested the same constituency as Zwane, received 237 votes and his Secretary-General, Simon Nxumalo, took only 147 votes. Nquku and Mabuza polled 56 votes and 34 votes respectively. A few days later, when the Ngwenyama certified the eight representatives of the Swazi nation chosen by traditional methods, the election was officially completed. Thus, of the new Legislative Council's twenty-four members, six were whites belonging to the United Swaziland Association, one white belonged to Imbokodo, one white was supposedly an Independent, and the sixteen Swazi were all Imbokodo or tribal representatives. Swaziland's first legislature was thus assured of a new-style one-party system without parliamentary opposition.

Decline of Political Parties

Post-election efforts on the part of the political parties to challenge electoral procedures and results came to nought. In replying to denunciations of the administration for refusing to penalise chiefs who threatened party members with ejection from their land holdings, the Queen's Commissioner, Lloyd, blandly stated that the Ngwenyama was responsible for prohibiting 'any act or conduct which might cause a riot, a disturbance or breach of the peace', and thereby implied that party meetings were equated with riots or disturbances.[16] Although aided in part by contributions from abroad, the NNLC could not meet the full costs of pursuing legal cases against some fourteen elected candidates, all of whom allegedly used intimidation or made illegal use of the lion symbol. The case dragged on from June 1964 to March 1965 and eventually the judge made an order allowing as an exception the use of the lion symbol. Charges of undue influence and corruption were dismissed.

Although the nationalist leaders continued to demand the convoking of a new constitutional conference which would then eliminate the Ngwenyama from politics and abolish the reserved seats, a joint effort by Zwane, Nquku and Allen Nxumalo to confer with the Colonial Secretary was unsuccessful. Straitened by financial difficulties and blocked in the courts, defeat served only to accentuate party differences. The failure of the two Progressive Parties to effect a much-announced union was symptomatic of the failure of the political parties. The Swaziland Democratic Party, for some time under a cloud because of its denunciation of the 1963 strike, was rent asunder by internal conflict as its two prominent white members, Vincent Roz-wadowski and Dr V. S. Leibrandt, were expelled at the party congress in October 1964. On the eve of the congress, Simon Nxumalo, Secretary-General of the SDP, had seen fit to resign from the party to work 'for wider national unity' and was thereupon given a senior SNC appointment. The following March, Allen Nxumalo, still President, announced that the SDP believed any opposition to Imbokodo was now meaningless and all members were urged to join with the Ngwenyama so as to gain early independence. The Imbokodo, said Nxumalo, 'is trying to be more progressive and the differences between them and us will narrow'. Even the NNLC, which alone of the nationalist parties had any sizeable following, was weakened by defections, internal strife and bankruptcy. The arrest of Zwane in April 1965 on three charges of debt default crippled the Executive and, as a culmination of fears that the Vice-President was attempting to subvert the party, Maseko was suspended from his position and then expelled from the party. Morals charges against Clement Dhlamini, NNLC Secretary-General, leading to his disappearance from the country in March 1965, took much of the steam out of party efforts. Even the appointment of Arthur Khoza, an able and intelligent university graduate, as acting Secretary-General, did not significantly revive nationalist chances.

The Opening of the Legislature

The Swaziland Legislative Council held its first meeting on September 9, 1964. The Council was opened by the Queen's Commissioner, Lloyd, who said the legislature was representative of peoples of all races and that it would not tolerate racial discrimination. He described Swaziland as a country richly endowed with minerals, good soil, and water, able to stand on its own feet by adopting progressive economic policies. In a speech read on his behalf, the Ngwenyama said that the march of progress made inexorable demands, whatever peoples' feelings might be, and these must be accepted. He also expressed regret that the constitution had been imposed, saying it would be hypocrisy to deny that confidence in the British had been shaken, but he hoped that the relationship with the government would change for the better.

Although the formalities of the opening session were carried through without incident, it was significant that additional British troops were flown in from Kenya to join the locally-based battalion in two days of military exercises and riot drill. While the authorities insisted that the move was quite coincidental, it was generally seen as an official show of strength should the political parties attempt a mass demonstration. In the event, some seven hundred party members, headed by Clement Dhlamini and Macdonald Maseko, chanted their grievances in a cordoned-off area. In anticipation of such a move, the SNC requested members of the King's regiments (*impis*) to demonstrate their support of the Ngwenyama. Accordingly, some one thousand Swazi, in traditional apparel, faced the party members across the barrier of the British First Battalion. For all its pageantry, the spectacle visibly demonstrated the confrontation between rival approaches to Swaziland's political development.

Imbokodo-White Split

While Europeans rejoiced in the defeat of the political parties and commended the Swazi people for their determination to retain traditional loyalties, a year of harmony in the Legislative Council ended with charges from the United Swaziland Association that the special position of the whites was in jeopardy. Shortly after the appointment in August 1965 of a Constitutional Committee, in response to a formal request for independence by the Ngwenyama, conflict developed within the Committee, composed exclusively of Council members, when the Imbokodo showed an unexpected determination to eliminate reserved voting. The split between Imbokodo and its erstwhile allies was further deepened in late October with the defeat of a motion introduced by the United Swaziland Association spokesman, Willie Meyer, seeking to extend the franchise rights of white South African nationals beyond the December 31 deadline. Although accepting defeat gracefully and urging South African residents to become British citizens (eventually an estimated 1000 South Africans changed their citizenship, comforted by the fact that the Republic announced its willingness to receive them 'back into the fold' in case of difficulty), the United Swaziland Association group remained adamant in its insistence on white representation.

The implications of the controversy over representation were also revealed in a letter dated January 26, 1965, addressed by Todd to the Ngwenyama. Todd's letter, which fell into the hands of the NNLC, was given widespread publicity as proof of European plans to subvert Swazi aspirations. Todd said he recognised that it was quite probable 'that pressure from the British government will result in the elimination of the European roll' and he therefore suggested 'some alternative protection for the European minority'. Such protection, he felt, could be provided if an understanding were reached with Imbokodo to reserve a fixed number of its seats, preferably eight, for Europeans. It would be understood, of course, that Imbokodo would use its numerical superiority 'to ensure that the right European candidates are voted into Parliament'. This understanding, said Todd, 'should be reached before any approach whatsoever is made to the government to encourage the government to start any new constitutional negotiations'. The white Imbokodo representative made no attempt to conceal his concern that European economic interests might be endangered without some arrangement for white representation.[17]

Unfortunately for Todd's plan, which would have secured white representation but outside the formal constitutional framework, the United Swaziland Association members could not trust even such an arrangement. In Meyer's words, 'verbal assurances were not enough because the Imbokodo might change—it had already changed a lot'. The fact that Imbokodo had been strengthened abroad through participation, as observers, at the OAU October Conference in Accra, and that Imbokodo had consolidated its strength at home through increased control over labour, commerce, industry and trade unionism, seemed cause for white concern. Thus, Meyer went so far as to insist that the original 50-50 plan of representation was necessary for the next five to ten years so that a Swazi middle class, having a stake in the economic future of the country, could be built up. The suggestion was even advanced that the British government provide money to buy land for the Swazis, a suggestion denounced by the Imbokodo as revealing a 'Kenya mentality'. Resentment was also expressed that the Imbokodo, which was born with white financial assistance, now wanted to become 'father of the man'. The breakdown of understanding between the two groups was attributed to the presence within Imbokodo of 'men belonging to a political party formerly supported by the British government transferring their ideas into the Imbokodo camp'.[18] Meyer publicly stated his belief that Imbokodo was being dictated to by Pan-Africanists and that the British government had 'infiltrated' into its ranks. Imbokodo was thus being 'brainwashed' by the British government. It was precisely, said Meyer, after members of the Democratic Party had joined Imbokodo that difficulties arose.[19]

If there was yet any doubt on Imbokodo's position, it was ended when the Ngwenyama announced in early February that whites would indeed have to become Swazis if they were to play their part in the development of the country. There could be no special representation, he said, and then pointed out that if one section started defending its 'rights' out of fear, it would drive the country into the very danger it feared.

After the failure of weeks of negotiation, it fell upon the British government to take the next step. Having received a number of recommendations directly from the unrepresented political parties, all of which called for a non-racial constitution and checks upon the traditional hierarchy, the British government released a White Paper at the end of March 1966. London indicated that Sobhuza would be recognised as King of Swaziland before the end of 1966, coinciding with the handing over of internal self-rule to the Swazis. Full independence was promised before the end of 1969. Recognition of the Ngwenyama as King of Swaziland even before independence was based on Britain's willingness to change Swaziland's official status to that of a Protected State. The White Paper also promised a code of fundamental rights and freedoms and a Parliament composed of a House of Assembly and a Senate, with universal adult suffrage. In the interim period, Britain would retain special responsibilities for external affairs, defence, internal security, finance and the public service.

As Swaziland thus entered what promised to be the immediate prelude to independence, it had yet to be determined whether the modernising influences within Imbokodo would indeed make of that group a nationalist force determined to preserve the integrity of the country and promote social and economic advancement. If it failed in this task, then the fear of the political parties that Imbokodo would become the tool of South African policy would be realised.

THE ECONOMY OF SWAZILAND
by Dr H. George Henry

SWAZILAND, with an area of 6,704 square miles, is divided into four distinct physiographic regions: the Highveld, the Middleveld, the Lowveld and the Lobombo plateau. The elevation falls from a range of 3,500-6,000 feet in the Highveld to an average of about 1,000 feet in the Lowveld. Agricultural production is affected by the quality of the soil, the slope of the land and the distribution of rainfall.[1] Rainfall ranges from 75 inches in parts of the Highveld in the west to 20-25 inches on the eastern margins of the Lowveld at the foot of the Lobombo plateau.[2] The best combination of these factors occurs in the Middleveld, and this area has always been favoured by the Swazi. The Lowveld is least favourable and is primarily ranching country. Roughly 8·8 per cent of the total area of Swaziland is used for agriculture.

The distribution of land between Swazi and non-Swazi has been markedly affected not only by the land tenure system but also by external influences. In contrast to Basutoland, where the shrewd Moshoeshoe I and his successors maintained a rigid policy of the non-alienation of land from the Basuto, the Swazi chiefs, as we have seen in Chapter 12, succumbed to a variety of pressures. The Paramount Chief, Mbandzeni, stands out as the principal agent in granting concessions of every conceivable kind to non-Swazi. The British administration tried to straighten out the confusion by the partition scheme of 1907, under which the Swazi received exclusive rights to about one-third of the entire Territory. Subsequently the Swazi bought back some of the land from the concessionaires through funds provided by tax payments. In addition, by means of a Colonial Development and Welfare Grant for a native land settlement scheme, land was purchased by the British administration, and certain Crown lands were added to this.[3] By 1961, roughly 52 per cent of the total area of the country was owned by the Swazi.[4] Because the Swazi have had long experience of non-Swazi forms of land ownership, it has been possible to launch, with the co-operation of the traditional administrative authority, a pilot project to provide a few hundred Swazi with freehold rights. Also, a smaller number is being given leasehold rights as participators in the Swaziland Irrigation Scheme sponsored by the Commonwealth (formerly Colonial) Development Corporation.

Minerals

In known and provable mineral resources, Swaziland is the wealthiest of the three former Territories. It possesses one of the world's five largest asbestos mines, developed at Havelock. In 1963, exports of this mineral were valued at about £2,500,000 and accounted for about 98 per cent of the total value of minerals. Large reserves of high-grade iron ore have been discovered at Bomvu Ridge, from which access to Lourenço Marques was obtained when Swaziland's first railway line, 140 miles long, was completed recently. Japan has contracted to purchase some 1,200,000 tons of ore per year for ten years. As the railway line passes close to the coal deposits of the Lowveld, it is expected that these coal mines will also be developed.[5] High-grade anthracite is already being mined near Maloma. The discovery of gold in the Barberton mountains, which was partly responsible for the great demand for concessions in the late nineteenth century, contributed little to the welfare of the Swazi. Production has remained at a low level over the last two decades. Other minerals mined in very small quantities are tin and barytes.

Water Resources

The Territory is amply supplied with rivers flowing through a terrain which makes them adaptable for producing hydro-electric power. At present they serve three important irrigation schemes. However, there exists the problem of distributing the water supply from the rivers in such a way as to reduce the effects of drought on crops, and to provide water for the drier regions where livestock are pastured. Irrigation schemes have been undertaken by several private enterprises and by the Commonwealth Development Corporation. By 1959, 52,750 acres of land had been brought under irrigation. The Morse Report cautioned that surveys to determine the suitability of the soils and careful training in irrigation methods should precede the extension of irrigation projects. The Commonwealth Development Corporation, relying perhaps on the success achieved so far, had, by late 1964, completed plans for the expansion of its irrigation scheme. This will involve construction of an earth dam and about one million cubic yards of earthwork.[6] The irrigation schemes facilitate the development of such important export crops as sugarcane, citrus fruits and rice. As either producers or entrepreneurs, a very small proportion of the Swazi benefits fully from these irrigation schemes, but a larger number profits to some degree by being employed as unskilled labourers for wages which supplement their agricultural incomes at subsistence levels.

Human Resources and Human Backwardness

In terms of the conditions set out when discussing human backwardness in Lesotho, it would be true to say that the Swazi are, on the whole, the most backward of all the Africans in the former Territories. This is not to lose sight of the fact that there are a very small number of Swazi farmers who, in terms of agricultural methods and techniques, are far in advance of either the Batswana or the Basuto. These few Swazi are also further advanced in their acceptance of the market mechanism as an institution governing the allocation of land and livestock and crop production.

Of the factors contributing to the very high degree of backwardness, three are among the most outstanding: (1) the autocratic rule of a conservative chief dedicated to traditionalism; (2) the illiteracy and ignorance of the vast majority of the Swazi, who find their security rooted in tradition and custom rather than in individual enterprise, initiative and change; (3) the very limited opportunities provided for acquiring skills and for employing them in the prevailing industrial and social environment.

The Paramount Chief, who has been ruling the Swazi for over forty years, has accumulated much power and influence. He is not completely unsusceptible to change and has in fact used his considerable influence to very good effect in several directions, two of which are of great economic significance. He greatly assisted the buying back of the land from the concessionaires with funds raised by a tax on cattle owners and migrant labourers. The success of the Rural Development Board, in its efforts to conserve land and water and to resettle villages as part of the programme for improving the allocation and use of land and agricultural practices generally, is due in great part to his support.

These are examples of enlightened paternalism. On the other hand, the Paramount Chief and the hierarchy of chiefs below him see in any universal widening of economic opportunity and growth of independence and individualism among the rank and file of the Swazi, a threat to the power and authority of the chieftainship.[7] Their attitude is shared by another power group—the non-Africans who dominate the economic life of Swaziland and who form a much larger percentage of the total population than in either of the other former Territories. They see in tribalism, in the very low living standards of the vast majority of the Swazi and in the maintenance of all the barriers against social and economic mobility for the Swazi, security from competition and from the democratisation of economic power. Hence they are strong advocates of the traditional way of life and firm supporters of the Paramount Chief.

The literacy rate is lower in Swaziland than in the other two countries: an estimated 75 per cent of all the Swazi are illiterate. However, some improvements have been made during the last few years. In 1958, it was estimated that 56 per cent of the primary school-age children were enrolled and 4·5 per cent of the secondary school-age group.[8] Literacy is much higher among the urbanised African (about 65 per cent) than among the rural African (about 28 per cent).[9] The churches, mainly the Church of the Nazarene, the Methodists, the Roman Catholics and a few others, were responsible for providing most of the educational facilities in the country. There were also three schools, one of which was secondary, managed by tribal authorities. But the segregation of the races and the offering of separate and unequal facilities for education was, until recently, much more marked, and followed the racialist pattern of South Africa more closely than in the other two Territories. In addition to the primary and secondary schools, there are two teacher-training centres, a housecraft-training centre for girls and a trade school from which about twenty students graduate annually with some knowledge of building, carpentry, motor mechanics and electrical installation. None of these graduates appears to meet the specific requirements of industry.[10]

Since education is basic and vital to a people lacking professional, technical and industrial skills, the legislation of 1963 (influenced, no doubt, by developments in the United States) which provides for the gradual integration of all schools, and which will subject the educational system more fully to one central authority, is of overwhelming importance. The implementation of this legislation will destroy one of those institutions which has worked effectively and insidiously to perpetuate cultural differences between Swazi and non-Swazi with nuances of superiority and inferiority, and will open up a much wider field of economic opportunity to the Swazi.

The Swazi are, on the whole, uneducated, inefficient and limited strictly to subsistence agriculture or else employed as unskilled labour in mining, trade and commerce and the light industries, or as poorly paid domestic servants in homes, offices and hotels. The recent evidences of acceleration of economic growth promise them very little, unless their educational opportunities are substantially increased and all traditional barriers to their social and economic mobility eliminated or severely reduced. The light industries now being established in Swaziland could play an important role in increasing Swazi participation by organising in-training programmes, providing instructors and offering other forms of assistance, so that the students from the Government Technical School would be more acceptable to industry. The fear of unequal distribution of the costs of such a programme could be greatly reduced if it were organised as a co-operative venture by private enterprise and government. At the same time, care should be taken not to restrict the freedom of workers who acquire skills and would like to move into jobs where the reward more closely matches productivity.

Agriculture

In the post-war period, industrial changes have been introduced which tend to reduce Swazi dependence on agriculture and to increase the opportunities for wage employment. But the impact of these changes has not caused any substantial improvement in agricultural practices, nor has it significantly reduced the numbers of those engaged in agriculture. Indeed, there is evidence of deterioration in the conditions of agriculture in some areas. For the vast majority of the Swazi, agricultural methods and practices are primitive and their production goals and values are subsistence-oriented. These are the uneducated Swazi, with very limited wants, who find great psychological security in the traditional institutions and customs which act as restraints on agricultural and other forms of economic development. But population pressure, soil erosion, the steady encroachment of the money economy and the slow introduction of new wants are exposing the inadequacies of the subsistence economy.[11] The development of transport and communication, the gradual urbanisation and industrialisation of the economy and the organisation of political parties are making the Swazi aware of alternatives to subsistence standards of living. Granted that material prosperity appeals to the Swazi, it follows that education, the provision of credit facilities for capital improvements in agriculture and the opening up of employment opportunities in skilled jobs are the most powerful tools for lifting the Swazi out of the subsistence economy.

There are a few Swazi farmers engaged in the production of cash crops, the most important of which are cotton and tobacco. According to the 1956 census, 25,928 Swazi were peasant farmers. In 1962, 3,411 of these peasant farmers were members of 116 Swazi Farmers' Associations and hence directly exposed to the effects of such organisations as the Agricultural Department, concerned with improving agricultural practices and increasing output. There is urgent need to expand organisations such as the Farmers' Associations in order to acquaint a much greater number of the Swazi with more advanced methods of agricultural and livestock husbandry. Many of these Swazi growers average an income from tobacco of roughly £15 per year, compared with about £110 to £220 per acre achieved by non-Swazi.[12] Even in maize, their basic foodstuff and the predominant crop grown by the Swazi, productivity is very low, and the total output insufficient to meet the needs of the Territory: in a season of good harvests, such as 1959-60, 55 per cent of all homesteads still had to buy maize. The most recent social survey suggests that extension of the irrigation system to serve more Swazi, coupled with sound practices of dry land-conservation farming, is essential for raising agricultural production to the level necessary for meeting domestic needs.[13]

By tradition, the Swazi have been a pastoral rather than an agricultural people. Their stock-raising industry has, however, been restricted by the lack of surface water in the Lowveld and the fact that quite a substantial area is owned by Transvaal sheep farmers and reserved for winter-grazing for their sheep.[14] In 1963, a total of 108,560 sheep were brought into the Territory from the Transvaal for winter grazing, the lowest number for seventeen years.[15] There has been some advance in upgrading the indigenous breed of cattle, and a few Swazi participate in this programme. Increasing numbers are also participating in the dairy industry being organised by the Agricultural Department. But on the whole the efficiency of the Swazi livestock industry is far below what could be achieved, due mainly to 'poor and uninformed animal husbandry; inbreeding, inevitable because of the lack of fencing and the necessary kraaling and herding of the animals; and insufficient nutriment'.[16] In general, the non-Swazi own better animals and enjoy greater knowledge and better facilities; thus 'their management of livestock is of a higher standard, and their losses from pests and disease are far lower'.[17] Livestock and livestock products are of less importance than in the other former Territories, accounting for between 10 and 15 per cent of total exports in recent years.

It is estimated that a quarter of the economically active non-Swazi are engaged in farming and forestry.[18] They are the main participants in the large-scale development of irrigation that has taken place during the post-war period. They are generally more familiar with modern agricultural practices, have easier access to capital and for them the environment of land rights and land distribution is more conducive to efficiency than among the Swazi. But there is evidence of poor farming practices and deterioration of soil fertility among some non-Swazi farmers.[19]

The large irrigation schemes have been financed by the Commonwealth Development Corporation and by several South African private enterprises. By 1962, 38,000 acres of the irrigated land were distributed among commercial crops as follows: 22,000 acres were planted in sugar cane, 6,000 in rice, 5,000 in citrus fruits and 5,000 in other crops.[20] There are three major forest areas; the largest, the Usutu Forests, covering 119,000 acres, was initiated by the Development Corporation in 1948. The other two are Peak Timbers Limited (75,000 acres) and Swaziland Plantations Limited (11,000 acres), the firm which pioneered afforestation. The growth rate of the conifers and eucalyptus in these man-made forests is among the highest in the world.[21]

The most important economic effect of all this agricultural development, so far as the Swazi are concerned, has been the creation of a domestic wage-earning agricultural labouring class and the consequent reduction of the numbers of those who would automatically turn towards South Africa for work. But because the Swazi are unskilled and the wages low, it has had negligible effect on the reduction of human backwardness. In fact this development seems to be having a 'polarising' effect on the dualistic nature of the economy as a whole and depressing the subsistence agricultural sector in particular. The availability of cash incomes renders subsistence farming less attractive and magnifies the opportunity cost of transforming subsistence farmers into commercial farmers. As noted already, the Swazi have not been able to produce adequate quantities of their basic foodstuff, maize, and there may be 'developing a trend to buy food from wage income, which is bound to affect rural production unless cash cropping can be made an attractive and realistic proposition'.[22] Unless the Swazi farmers can be assured of incomes from farming alone equal to the subsistence earned by sharing their labour between farm and wage-employment, and—more important—unless some arrangements can be made for paying the costs of 'waiting' between planting and harvest time, the Swazi may never be able to share in the agricultural development taking place, except at the subsistence level. It is the vicious circle of poverty which makes the Swazi farmer unable to exercise 'abstinence' or 'waiting'. He must abdicate his role of entrepreneur for that of labourer in order to earn mere necessities. This is perfectly rational behaviour. It is therefore a misrepresentation to suggest that the Swazi would not want to produce more from the land than his bare subsistence requirements.[23] For people living at this level, there is little flexibility for gambling with change. Their experience is tied to one certainty—subsistence and survival. Change offers too much uncertainty to be worth the risk.

Hence the expansion of non-Swazi agriculture and its employment of agricultural workers has tended, at best, to contribute to the maintenance of bare subsistence standards on Swazi farms, or, at worst, to depress them—a similar effect to that which migrant labour has had on subsistence agriculture in Lesotho. The employment provided is attractive enough to take labour from the land, and enough labour is withdrawn to make the opportunity cost greater than zero and to cause the increased employment of the less efficient labour of women and children on the African farms. But not enough income is earned by the Swazi agricultural labourer or Basuto migrant labourer to raise his standard of living above the subsistence level or to make it possible to increase agricultural capital.

The Commercial and Industrial Sector

Swaziland is well in advance of the other former Territories in power, irrigation, transportation and communication. Its first railway system was recently completed, providing an outlet to the sea through Mozambique. Such processing industries as sugar production and the manufacture of unbleached sulphate pulp have been set up on the basis of these developments. Other enterprises include a creamery, a malt factory, a fruit cannery, a mineral water factory, a printing works, two engineering concerns, a bonemeal factory and a clothing factory.[24] Plans were recently announced for the introduction of new industries, including an abattoir, a ginnery and oil storage installations.[25] Among the many factors responsible for the more rapid acceleration of economic growth in Swaziland as compared to the other countries, the following stand out: (*a*) the more generous endowment of natural resources; (*b*) the more attractive economic opportunities, including the right to buy and sell land, enjoyed by non-Swazi; (*c*) the more important role played by the British administration, directly and indirectly, in capital formation. During the period 1945 to 1963, loans and grants from the British government to Basutoland were £370,000 and £6,326,000 respectively, to Bechuanaland £3,197,000 and £12,457,000, and to Swaziland £12,928,000 and £7,252,000.[26] Swaziland received a higher measure of external aid from Britain than the other two put together.

Most of the production for export and the bulk of the wholesale and retail trade is in the hands of non-Swazi. All the financial institutions and all the cafes and hotels catering to the growing tourist industry are owned and managed by non-Swazi. There is not a Swazi enterprise on any of the main streets in any of the towns in Swaziland: a few Swazi tailors ply their trade on the footpaths in front of the non-Swazi concerns. Hand-made products for the tourist trade, including beadwork, brass and copperwork, pottery, carvings from wood and horn, grass mats, baskets and Swazi shields and spears are sold in the Swazi markets of the principal towns. Although the number of Swazi employed in commerce and industry has been increasing, it still represents a very small proportion of the potential labour force. In 1962, assuming a potential force of about 118,000, only 38,200 were in fact employed on a wage basis, and, of these, only some 4 per cent of the men and some 2 per cent of the women were engaged in manufacturing. It is estimated that, at any given time, some 40 per cent of rural Swazi males of working age are employed, and some 70 per cent of urban males.[27] Only 7 per cent of the Swazi live in towns.[28] The average earnings of Swazi employees in ten large firms, based on a sample survey conducted in 1963, were found to be around £120 per year. These facts, taken together, indicate that the Swazi share only to a very limited extent in the accelerating rate of economic growth.

The Government Sector

In the absence of other records, a time series of government revenue, expenditure and debt is a useful guide to the social and economic objectives of fiscal policy. From such records, supported by other information, inferences can be made regarding the impact of the British administration on the traditional society of Swaziland in terms of its contribution to the development of the Territory's resources. It should be borne in mind, however, that it is only since the 1930s and more especially during the post-war period that governments have been aware of the use of fiscal policy as an instrument for promoting economic development and social welfare.

The fiscal policy of the British administration in Swaziland seems to have followed the same general pattern as in the other two Territories until about the end of the second world war. Spending was kept at a minimal level and careful attention was paid to balancing the budget. Very little attention was paid to the economic and social welfare of the Swazi. Education, public health and agricultural improvement were left almost entirely in the hands of the chiefs or to voluntary agencies such as the churches. There were significant changes in this policy during the period following the second world war. The early financial history of the Territory shows that it was unable to meet the ordinary expenses of government between 1907 and 1932, except by using receipts from the sale of Crown lands.[29] The Territory received grants from Britain to help balance its budget three times during the period. It was the first of the three Territories to receive assistance under the Colonial Development and Welfare Act of 1929, and has been the greatest beneficiary since. This greater flow of capital to Swaziland has contributed to a higher rate of capital formation than the other two countries have experienced. Capital formation has centred on such projects as afforestation, highways, hydro-electric power stations and the more recent construction of a railway. But much more private, as opposed to government or semi-government, capital has been invested in Swaziland, especially in afforestation and irrigation,[30] and the decision to build the Swazi railway was essentially due to private enterprise. It is estimated that the contribution of private business to capital formation in Swaziland has been nearly double the £21 million spent by the Colonial (now Commonwealth) Development Corporation in all three Territories since 1949.[31]

A government's spending policy is naturally limited by the funds available. One source of such funds is taxation and, until the post-war period, the bulk of the Swaziland government revenues came from taxes paid by the Swazi. This was due largely to the regressive nature of the tax system, which burdened the Swazi more than the non-Swazi. For example, in 1938, of total government revenue of £116,000, the non-Swazi contributed £5,000 in income taxes and the Swazi paid £44,000 in direct taxes. The bulk of the remaining £67,000 was raised by indirect taxes, the major portion of which would be paid by the Swazi for they constitute roughly 97 per cent of the total population.[32] At the same time, the greater proportion of the expenditure provided social benefits for the non-Swazi. For example, from 1946 to 1950, in a population which had more than thirty Swazi to one non-Swazi, £76,774 was spent by the government on Swazi education and £34,383 on non-Swazi. By 1951, the tax structure had become more equitable. The income tax rates were kept very low until 1959 and, until recently, were paid only by non-Swazi. In 1959, a married person with a taxable income of £500 paid income tax of less than £2 2s. while, if that same person had a taxable income of £2,000, he paid £75 income tax. The marginal tax rates for incomes above £2,000 were much more steeply progressive, but purposelessly so. The income tax rate on the mining companies was 25 per cent on incomes not exceeding £10,000. The revenues from income tax of the Havelock Asbestos Company and other mines amounted to 56 per cent of the total revenue from income tax in 1963.[33] The personal income tax rates have been revised and increased since 1959. The tax rate has always been below that of South Africa and, in the interests of development, this differential should be maintained. However, it is recognised that income tax is being under-collected.[34] If the government is to increase its expenditures on social services (such as education) for the benefit of the Swazi, the efficiency of tax collection will have to be improved.

The inefficiency of tax collection, evasion by Swazi and non-Swazi, the less than proportionate expenditure on social services for the Swazi, the pattern of debts incurred for economic development purposes and the whole range and focus of fiscal policy help to explain the very high incidence of backwardness among the Swazi. Such an analysis makes it very clear that the British administration has paid far greater attention to the development of natural resources than to the development of African human resources. In Lesotho, human resources are rather more developed than natural resources, but there most of the credit belongs to the churches. Which of the two peoples, the Basuto or the Swazi, is economically better off is a highly controversial question. It is abundantly clear, however, that no significant improvement in the economic welfare of the Swazi can take place unless a massive effort is made to reduce human backwardness. This objective will have been attained when there is a major increase in the number of Swazi fully employed in the money economy, and when the proportion of the skilled vis-à-vis the unskilled labourers has been reversed.

The British administration has also contributed to the backwardness of the Swazi by its relatively firm support of traditional institutions and by its accommodation within Swaziland of certain South African economic and political principles which are not in the best interest of the Swazi. Support of the traditional institutions has meant, for example, encouraging the communal system of land tenure which, in its present form, is inconsistent with commercialised agriculture. It has also involved a concentration of power and authority for decision-making in the hands of hereditary chiefs, irrespective of their qualifications and ability. In the past few years, some attempts have been made by the administration to reduce human backwardness. Two fundamental institutional changes made in this respect are: (1) attempts to Africanise the high-level jobs in the public service; and (2) efforts to integrate the educational system. The first measure is rendered less effective by the great backlog of poor educational facilities and opportunities. For example, when the Swazi questioned the retention of a non-Swazi as head of the Public Works Department under the Africanisation programme, it was revealed that there was as yet no Swazi engineer, and that this was an essential qualification for the job.[35] The second measure can help to remedy the situation in the long run. According to an estimate made in 1962, the government sector employs just under 2,000 Swazi, more than three-quarters of whom were unskilled or semi-skilled workers earning between £5 5s. and £17 10s. per month. There are greater opportunities for the Swazi to be employed in skilled jobs in the government sector than elsewhere, but these opportunities are as yet available to less than 3 per cent of the potential labour force.

CONCLUSION

IN THE EARLY MONTHS of 1966, amid the heat of parliamentary elections in South Africa, Verwoerd and his Nationalist Party supporters expressed themselves with greater candour on the two closely related issues of Bantustan policy and future relations with Basutoland, Bechuanaland and Swaziland. Stung by repeated charges from the United Party opposition that the Nationalists were encouraging a real political fragmentation of the country, government candidates in many cases assured voters that the Bantustans would never attain a real independence—assurances which, while contrary to official policy, went uncontested by Pretoria. At the same time, however, the Deputy Minister of Bantu Administration and Development, M. C. Botha, confirmed in the Assembly that the government was contemplating land deals with the former High Commission Territories. While denying that there was any intention to include the 'conquered territory'—land taken in the Basuto war of 1865, ceded to the Orange Free State, and the cession confirmed, in modified form, by the Second Convention of Aliwal North in 1869—the Deputy Minister said the government was prepared to consider the exchange or sale of ethnically-compatible land adjoining Basutoland, especially such areas as Witzieshoek and the Herschel district. Even before this announcement, white traders in these areas had been unofficially advised, at ministerial level, to vacate and sell their businesses 'to Bantu buyers if the price was right'. Such moves, charged Marais Steyn, MP, Transvaal leader of the United Party, were only a preliminary for the turning over to Basutoland of all land in the Orange Free State west of the Caledon river.

If there was any contradiction between denial of ultimate independence for the Bantustans and a sale or exchange of lands with South Africa's independence-bound neighbours, the difficulty was resolved by Botha when he added, almost as an afterthought, that any such land deal 'was dependent on South Africa being able to play a part in guiding their [the High Commission Territories'] future economic and political development'.[1] This statement, a reaffirmation of the Prime Minister's speech of September 1963 in which he offered to 'guide' the Territories to independence, was further developed by Verwoerd on March 26, when he launched an attack on Britain and the United States for allegedly undermining South Africa in the Territories.

The provocation for his attack was a purported Anglo-American 'attempt to gain influence in the High Commission Territories, among others, through the officials they appointed there, to exclude and undermine friendship with South Africa rather than give those territories any further assistance'. Verwoerd said he wished to ask Britain and the United States 'whether for once they would not act wisely and instead of the chaos they left behind elsewhere in Africa, they would not allow Southern Africa to develop naturally'. South Africa, he said, 'neither wanted to incorporate nor to dominate those territories but was willing to grant them everything she wished for herself and to live with them as good neighbours'. Good economic relations were desired with them 'without outside interference'. These matters, he said, were referred to because of what was happening in the High Commission Territories, where it 'was also known that both Britain and the United States were creating spheres of influence' despite the fact that the prosperity of these countries depended upon their maintaining close relations with South Africa.[2]

Verwoerd's unexpected attack on Britain and the United States revealed the dilemma facing South Africa with the approaching independence of Britain's Southern African Territories. The allegation that the United States was seeking to create a 'sphere of influence' could scarcely be given credence, especially since the sum total of American involvement consisted of one American consul accredited to Basutoland and Swaziland, a USIS library in Maseru, and $100,000 annual assistance to the University in Basutoland. Announcement had also been made in March of the appointment of an American consul to Bechuanaland. If he meant to equate the appointment of diplomatic personnel with an attempt to exclude South African influence, it was obvious that only a total subservience of the Territories would ever satisfy South Africa. As one South African commentator observed, this was colonialism, and 'if it is to apply to countries which South Africa has never administered, it will apply even more to the future Bantustans, now part of South Africa but promised their independence. The danger lies in saying that countries are independent and acting as if they are not. .... If they are told one thing and see another, they will be in constant ferment. It is a strange role for a country which is pledged to non-interference in the affairs of other countries—but not apparently when they are emergent protectorates or Bantustans.'³

While Verwoerd's intent in this verbal assault was primarily to project an image of toughness to the electorate at a time when the United Party was capitalising upon the government's alleged 'betrayal' of Rhodesian whites through its failure to recognise or openly assist the break-away regime of Ian Smith, he might also have intended to deter any American action towards the Territories likely to increase the chances of their independent development. Indeed, the suggestion that the United States and Britain could most effectively demonstrate their repugnance of South African racialism through strong economic support for the Territories was being advanced by various groups seeking stronger measures against South Africa. In March 1966, hearings of the Sub-Committee on Africa of the US House of Representatives Foreign Affairs Committee received, from several sources, testimony to this effect, all of which was quoted in South African papers. Considering the large number of American officials, businessmen, military advisers and South African 'specialists' seeking to avoid an American-South African confrontation, Verwoerd's remarks, it could be assumed, might elicit a restraining hand on American actions should any meaningful policy be contemplated.

Despite formal renunciation of the policy of incorporation, the nature of South Africa's relationship to the Territories, as reflected in Verwoerd's speech of September 1963, revealed that the Territories, while destined for independence, were still of importance to the successful implementation of South Africa's policy. South African 'guidance', said Verwoerd, would not only benefit the countries economically, since they were already dependent on South Africa in that regard, but also aim at making them 'democratic states in which the masses would not be dominated by small groups of authoritarians' but instead would enjoy 'natural native democracy and its leaders, coupled with representative democracy—as in the Transkei'. Multi-racialism would be avoided by enabling whites to exercise political rights only in the Republic's white areas. And thirdly, 'wherever it might be necessary', South Africa would 'repurchase or exchange areas now wrongly occupied in order to include them in the white areas or the black'.⁴ By offering the Transkei and other reserve areas as a model for political and economic development—areas where recalcitrant chiefs had been deposed and all semblance of political organisation crushed—it could be expected that 'natural native democracy' under South African tutelage would produce similar results. In line with South African policy, industries would be set up in border areas, circumventing simultaneously minimum wage limitations, social insurance, joint ownership of industries, and all the other advantages which might normally accrue to a state in the process of industrialisation. The Territories would not only be privileged to share the economic stagnation promised the Bantustans, but, as the Prime Minister acknowledged, would assist South Africa 'to solve [its] own problems'. But as Basutoland's Minister of Economic Development, Charles Molapo, stated, border industries 'would strangle' that country's industrial growth 'and would prevent economic viability'.[5] The sale or transfer of lands, presumably areas already or likely to be designated as Bantustans, would offer South Africa the advantage of hastening its own project and bolstering up friendly governments in the Territories. These governments, it could be assumed, would enhance their own stature by claiming a 'victory' which would in turn render their own position more secure. Moreover, such land deals would relieve South Africa of an onerous burden should the government be obliged, for internal reasons, to push on with territorial apartheid. Through such steps, together with food or financial donations in times of hardship, South Africa could guarantee that its apartheid structure would not find a radical contrast in its independent neighbours.

Although Verwoerd's proffered helping hand was rejected, to a greater or lesser degree, by each of the Territories, the Prime Minister found cause to rejoice in the governments elected during the 1964-65 period. 'It is important', he said, 'that we give our friendship to such parties in these Territories when, as now, they are also the ruling parties. It is worth while for us to give friendship and support these governments when they ask for it and it would be foolish not to do so.' He said he would make no apology for the South African gift of grain to Basutoland, and would consider a similar offer in the future if necessary, just as 'Tshombe was helped in Katanga and then in the Congo'.[6] Not only would the Territories, albeit independent, complement South Africa's policies; they could also serve to shield that government from subversion, either real or imagined. Thus, professions of friendship were made contingent upon the willingness of the Territories to play such a role. It was especially important, he said, that no 'alien' influences be permitted to entrench themselves in the Territories, and he castigated Britain for 'allowing Communist Chinese money and influence to infiltrate into Basutoland'. This alleged Communist influence posed a threat 'not only to Basutoland and South Africa but also to the interests of the West ... and while Britain does not do anything about it, it is in our interest to see that the people in these three Territories have a sober outlook'.[7]

Despite Verwoerd's apparent mastery of the situation, a technicality of independence seemed to pose insuperable difficulties for South Africa's relations with the Territories. For, however well-disposed South Africa's neighbours might be, even the most conciliatory government would be hard-put to acquiesce in any diplomatic arrangement that failed to guarantee full and proper respect for accredited diplomatic representatives. If, for the sake of ideological conformity, no exception could be made to racialistic policies, South Africa would lose the potential benefit of contacts with countries likely to prove even more significant buffers against outside pressure, particularly Zambia, the Congo and Malawi. As government critics observed, 'relations established with even such a handful of countries, and based on self-interest rather than admiration, could make the critical difference in South Africa's international position'.[8]

Elections held between June 1964 and May 1965 in Basutoland, Bechuanaland and Swaziland, while marking important milestones in the constitutional evolution of the Territories, also served to focus the attention of the United Nations upon Britain's Southern African Territories. A working paper, prepared in May 1965 for the Special Committee on Colonialism, warned of South Africa's dominant position in the political and economic life of the Territories. As evidence of the Republic's growing interest in these areas, the report noted the high priority given by Verwoerd to his plan for positive co-operation between South Africa, the Territories, Mozambique, Angola and Rhodesia. South Africa's call for the early independence of the Territories, together with her pledge of economic assistance through the creation of a Southern African common market, were cited as major foreign policy objectives which certain elements in the Territories seemed determined to accept. Consequently, the report concluded, 'the chances of the Republic's increasing its hold over the three territories were considered enhanced'.

Whether the defeat of the Ngwane National Liberatory Congress, the Bechuanaland Peoples Party, the Basutoland Congress Party and the Marema Tlou Freedom Party, South Africa's most prominent opponents in the Territories, would correspondingly result in greater South African hegemony, remained open to question as the Territories approached independence. But, on first glance at least, South Africa appeared to have gained a significant victory. By an ironic twist of history, it was now South Africa that challenged Britain to grant the Territories their immediate independence, while defeated nationalist parties, alleging the danger of South African control, urged delay and revision of existing constitutions or constitutional proposals. If all the instincts of South Africa's Nationalist Party were in favour of supporting tribalism, the institution of chieftaincy and reactionary tendencies generally in African culture, it was apparent that these instincts could be held in check to permit an endorsement of an absolutist regime in Swaziland as 'truly democratic', to praise a formal Westminster pattern at the expense of the paramountcy in Basutoland as 'progressive', and to term the demands of the traditional chieftainship in Bechuanaland as 'obstructive'. In each case, a pragmatic decision as to whether South Africa's interests were advanced or hindered provided the criteria of judgement.

In Basutoland, the prospect of independence under the leadership of Chief Jonathan induced the Basutoland Congress Party and the Marema Tlou Freedom Party to abandon their bitter rivalry and make common cause with the Paramount Chief. Claiming that the basic interests of the people required his personal intervention, and supported by both opposition parties, Moshoeshoe demanded the right to exercise the reserved powers in order to ensure the integrity of the state. Then, in a swift-moving series of events, precipitated by the introduction in late April of independence motions in both the House of Assembly and the Senate, the Paramount Chief dismissed five senators of his own appointment, including the Minister of Economic Development, Senator Charles Molapo, who refused to endorse Moshoeshoe's demand for control of the public service, external affairs, defence and internal security. The Paramount Chief's action was thwarted, however, by an injunction of the High Court, which prevented the new senators from taking their seats. A decision on May 12, reinstating the dismissed senators, paved the way for the reintroduction of the independence motion, which, after the ousting of the Senate president, Dr Seth Makotoko, passed by a vote of 23 to 9—a vote which indicated that the MFP and the Paramount Chief had in the meantime lost the support of most of the principal chiefs. Even the announcement in early June that seventeen principal chiefs pledged their full support to

Chief Jonathan and at the same time deplored the activity of the Paramount Chief failed to deter Moshoeshoe. 'Prime Ministers', he said, 'come and go ... but a prime minister who wanted to maintain his position could well call in South Africa to help him'. Determined not to be 'a dummy any longer', he said that 'there is no room in Africa for constitutional fictions'. As proof that he himself must exercise the reserved powers, Moshoeshoe referred to the public order proclamation which he charged was a typical example of 'misuse of powers' since it 'virtually established a state of emergency in Basutoland'.[9]

Opposition to Chief Jonathan's independence move continued in London, where the Constitutional Conference belatedly convened on June 8. Armed with petitions claiming to represent some fifty thousand voters, and in the wake of a full split between the Prime Minister and the Paramount Chief—who was invited to the conference only as a 'distinguished observer'—the MFP and BCP representatives charged that the existing government had no mandate to lead the country to independence. Independence under Chief Jonathan, it was alleged, 'would in reality be handing over Basutoland to Dr Verwoerd [who] with his "gifts" and teeming men of the South African Intelligence Service, already has a stronger guiding hand on our present government than Mr Wilson has'. According to Mokhehle, it was only the bribes given to chiefs which secured the passage of the independence motion in the Senate. The general lack of confidence in the existing minority government, said the BCP leader, would most certainly result in that government 'exerting its authority in a panic stricken manner on the majority ... and in a manner which might result in an ugly situation which would impel the government to enlist the intervention of a foreign sovereign power—such as the South African Republic; which is the only hope they have ...'.[10] A joint statement, signed by the leaders of the two opposition parties, stated that 'they were not prepared for a conference whose conclusions were agreed in advance', and they challenged the British government to deny that there was no previous understanding about the outcome of the conference, where the opposition had been allocated the role 'of puppets in a carefully rehearsed pantomime'. Warning that there could be no certainty that the Basuto would quietly submit to a constitution which weakened traditional institutions and entrenched power in the hands of a minority, the opposition delegates withdrew from the conference and announced their intention to internationalise the issue through the Organisation of African Unity and the United Nations. Seth Makotoko, MFP leader, and G. M. Kolisang subsequently departed for New York, where an emergency meeting of the UN 'Committee of Twenty-Four' was convoked.

Having declined to sign the independence document, Moshoeshoe returned to Basutoland, amid rousing cheers from thousands who lined the three-mile route from the airfield to the royal palace in Maseru. He proceeded to castigate Britain for ignoring a mandate said to have been given him by 80,000 Basuto voters, demanding that he have a real voice at the independence talks and in support of his exercise of the reserve powers. Although ignored in London, Moshoeshoe made clear his intention to hold extensive meetings throughout the country to counteract the growing threat of South Africa's 'invisible government'. This move led the Prime Minister to re-emphasise his contention that the Paramount Chief must function strictly on the Westminster pattern as a constitutional monarch. In the event that the Paramount Chief did not see fit to confine himself to such a role, Chief Jonathan said that Moshoeshoe should abdicate. He thereupon urged the British government to prevent the Paramount Chief from 'abusing his position as representative of the Queen', while at the same time preparing for any emergency situation. Though quietly supplied with submachine guns and carefully purged of Congress Party supporters, the numerical weakness of the Basutoland Mounted Police made it unlikely that any mass disturbance could be quelled without additional help.

In Swaziland, the report of the Constitutional Committee, published on March 26, 1966, brought forth a storm of protest from the nationalist political parties and from student and labour organisations. According to its authors, the proposed constitution, which would grant Swaziland self-government as a Protected State in late 1966 and independence no later than 1969, combined 'the essentials of a modern democratic state with the traditional institutions of the Swazi nation and Swazi kingship'. This appraisal was not shared, however, by the bulk of the country's secondary and university students, represented by the Swaziland Student Union. The student group termed the constitution 'a political strategy calculated to entrench the interests of one group at the expense of the nation'.

Speaking for the Ngwane National Liberatory Congress, Arthur Khoza, acting Secretary-General, rejected the constitution and demanded that the British government immediately convoke a fully representative conference in London. This demand was supported by the Deputy Secretary-General of the Progressive Party, J. J. Gumede, who charged that the proposals had been formulated by 'reactionaries' and imposed 'a ruthless tribal dictatorship'. Claiming jointly to represent more than 26,000 Swazi, with the NNLC alone claiming a paid-up membership of 18,000, the two nationalist parties bitterly noted that they were deprived of representation both in the existing legislature and on the Constitutional Committee.

The Swaziland Mineworkers Union also denounced the proposed constitution as 'cold-blooded betrayal of workers and citizens in Swaziland' drafted by 'elements which have exploited and oppressed the workers' throughout Swazi history. The Union went on to warn 'that the labour force of the country is not prepared to live under the proposed treacherous constitution' and that 'if the voice of the workers is neglected, we will positively use all means to see the proposed constitution is rendered inoperative'.[11]

Although the attacks on the constitution were wide-ranging, certain provisions dealing with representation and royal powers came in for special criticism. The proposed creation of eight three-man constituencies, returning a total of twenty-four elected members to an Assembly augmented by six nominees of the Ngwenyama, was seen as a unique device to ensure that the opposition would never capture a parliamentary seat. Swamped by rural voters taking orders from the King, the urban centres would permanently be deprived of representation. Since the Senate was to be composed of six persons elected by the Assembly and six nominated by Sobhuza, his power over the legislature would be complete. Moreover, even such a rigidly-controlled body would have no power to legislate on Swazi law and custom, unless authorised by the Swazi National Council. The control of mineral rights remained exclusively in the hands of the Ngwenyama. Additional powers gave the King the right to refer back for reconsideration all except monetary bills, to appoint the Chief Justice, and even to block constitutional change in the face of a requisite 75 per cent vote in a national referendum. Although the elimination of a separate European role still rankled with some whites, it was obvious to Carl Todd, the principal white supporter of Imbokodo, that the King was thus well provided with the necessary powers to protect the interests of the white minority.

If the dissatisfaction of the Mineworkers Union and signs of reconciliation between Imbokodo's defeated opponents gave any reason for alarm, the intention of the Swazi government to counter this was revealed in two ways. On the one hand, Prince Makhosini Dhlamini, leader of Imbokodo, stated that an independent Swaziland would maintain and promote close relations with South Africa and Mozambique. And, on a more ominous note, George Msibi, Imbokodo Secretary-General, announced that the executive was preparing to meet a new challenge, allegedly posed by 'disturbing reports' of efforts being made to form an organisation 'controlled either directly or indirectly by the Communists' and believed to have the promise of 'a considerable amount of money from Peking'.[12]

Bechuanaland alone of the three Territories moved ahead, towards its September 30 independence goal, without serious danger that the government would be alienated from the electorate on the one hand or fall under the influence of a tradition-bound chiefly clique on the other. Strengthened by the knowledge that its choices in foreign affairs were somewhat broader than those of Basutoland or Swaziland, the Bechuanaland government embarked on a variety of contacts and programmes. These included the launching of the first Peace Corps project in the Territories, plans for a comprehensive hydrological survey, and the improvement of educational and civil service training programmes. Although South Africa was pointedly invited to attend the independence celebrations, Seretse Khama's government reiterated its abhorrence of apartheid and its intention to seek membership in the United Nations, and retain membership in the Commonwealth. The government also indicated that friendly relations with Basutoland and Swaziland would be maintained on an 'ad hoc basis' rather than through any permanent alliance. While deploring the OAU decision to offer assistance to opposition Pan-Africanist parties in the Territories, an action which was termed a 'flagrant violation of the organisation's charter and obviously not conducive to unity', the ruling BDP, at its April convention, reaffirmed its intention to seek membership of that body.

Even the fear felt in some quarters of the growing influence of Kenneth Koma's National Front was not borne out by local government elections held on June 13. Instead, Khama's government was enabled to consolidate its hold on the country, since the BDP took 136 out of 165 seats. The BPP and BIP won 21 and 5 seats respectively, and independents won 3. The overwhelming support given the Khama government seemed to indicate that it would not soon face a serious opponent. If the disgruntled chieftainship was tempted to link up with the government's opposition, the temptation was reduced by the prudent decision of the Khama government to make some concessions to their point of view. Consequently, the House of Chiefs was enlarged and given more extensive powers, while the eight principal chiefs were given the chairmanships of the new local councils. Although the problem of Rhodesia and the prolonged drought continued to vex the government, the road to independence seemed relatively free from serious obstacles.

The dramatic contrast between the constitutional formulas worked out for Basutoland and Swaziland served to point up one inescapable conclusion: that, having at last accepted independence as a legitimate goal for her Southern African dependencies, Britain was determined to withdraw as quickly as possible and on such terms as would obviate a painful choice between upholding British honour in the Territories on the one hand or British financial interests in the Republic on the other. Whereas the duplication of the Westminster pattern appeared as an absolute condition for Basuto independence—even if it meant a minority government in control and the reduction of the Paramount Chief to the position of a figurehead—in the Swaziland formula, the Paramount Chief emerged a virtual dictator under a constitution without parallel in the annals of British decolonisation. But, in both instances, the British government hoped to ensure that power would devolve upon governments intent upon shaping their destinies in full harmony with South Africa. As for the new governments, having carefully emphasised their determination to avoid all 'radical' contacts, and declining to focus any international attention upon their outstanding problems with South Africa, both governments indicated they would place their confidence in the good will of the Republic. Whether vague promises of continued British aid might yet offset the impact of political compromises with South Africa and enable the countries to realise their potential remained matters of conjecture. Even so, as a long-term observer of the Territories noted, a substantial injection of developmental aid would at least offer to Britain 'that chance, and that at a ludicrously low cost, to write a decent *finis* to her colonial history in Africa'.[13]

The belated decision of the British government to welcome an active United Nations involvement in the economic and institutional development of the Territories was a step in the right direction. Not only did it lend greater hope that they would yet benefit from international protection, but, given an active programme of assistance, their economic dependence upon South Africa might be considerably reduced.

The decision of the Swedish government to undertake a major assistance scheme to the Territories, totalling some £230,000 ($644,000), is of particular importance. Hitherto, Swedish action in Southern Africa essentially took the form of aid to anti-apartheid organisations and educational assistance for refugees. The extension of aid to the three countries was viewed as being within the framework of Sweden's policy of neutralising—via the United Nations—the effects of South Africa's apartheid policy. The Swedish decision, hopefully to be imitated by the United States and other governments which have officially condemned apartheid, will go far towards demonstrating the seriousness of their official statements.

Inasmuch as the political independence of the former Territories will be determined by the degree to which they can reduce their economic dependence on South Africa, there can be no more promising or positive way at this time to demonstrate support for non-racialism, encourage the defence of traditional liberties, and challenge South Africa's apartheid system than by a generous support of the former Territories. For it can be assumed that the example of even moderately prosperous and successful democratic societies in those areas will have far reaching consequences on the Republic of South Africa, where racialism is enshrined as the condition for the survival of the state.

NOTES AND REFERENCES

Introduction

1 Cmd 8707, *Basutoland, the Bechuanaland Protectorate and Swaziland: History of discussions with the Union of South Africa,* p. 7
2 *Ibid.,* pp. 46–9
3 *Ibid.,* p. 54
4 Lord Hailey, *The Republic of South Africa and the High Commission Territories,* p. 76
5 *Cf.* J. E. Spence, "British Policy Towards the High Commission Territories", *Journal of Modern African Studies,* vol. II, no. 2, 1964, p. 240ff
6 Hailey, *op. cit.,* p. 85
7 L. S. Amery in *The Times,* Dec. 23, 1937
8 Cited in R. C. Fitzgerald, "South Africa and the High Commission Territories", *World Affairs,* vol. IV, no. 3, July 1950, p. 317
9 N. Mansergh, ed., *Documents and Speeches on British Commonwealth Affairs, 1931–1952,* vol. II, p. 922
10 Fitzgerald, *op. cit.,* p. 319
11 L. E. Neame, *The History of Apartheid,* p. 181
12 *The Economist,* Oct. 15, 1955
13 Tshekedi Khama, *Bechuanaland and South Africa,* p. 9
14 *Cape Argus,* March 2, 1965
15 Spence, *op. cit.,* p. 243
16 Dr H. F. Verwoerd, *Crisis in World Conscience,* p. 17

PART I: FROM BASUTOLAND TO LESOTHO

1: The Basuto Nation, from Birth to Colonial Status, 1823–1884

1 Donald L. Weidner, *A History of Africa South of the Sahara,* p. 115
2 G. Tylden, *The Rise of the Basuto,* p. 2
3 Wiedner, *op. cit.,* p. 124
4 Tylden, *op. cit.,* p. 11
5 E. Walker, ed., *The Cambridge History of the British Empire,* vol. VIII, p. 400
6 Cited in Tylden, *op. cit.,* p. 65
7 *Cambridge History, op. cit.,* p. 423
8 Sir Godfrey Lagden, *The Basutos,* vol. I, p. 315
9 *Cambridge History, op. cit.,* p. 429
10 E. A. T. Dutton, *The Basuto of Basutoland,* p. 44

11 *Cambridge History, op. cit.*, p. 430
12 *Ibid.*, pp. 432–3; *cf.* Tylden, *op. cit.*, p. 89
13 *Cambridge History, op. cit.*, p. 434
14 Lagden, *op. cit.*, p. 474

2: Indirect Rule and the Development of Advisory Institutions, 1884–1910

1 Cmd 8209, *Basutoland Medicine Murder*, p. 9
2 Cmd 4907, *Report on the Financial and Economic Position of Basutoland*, p. 49
3 Lagden, *op. cit.*, p. 560
4 Spence, *op. cit.*, p. 222
5 High Commissioner's Despatch, no. 4, March 8, 1909, cited in *Report on Constitutional Reform and Chieftainship Affairs*, p. 22
6 Lagden, *op. cit.*, pp. 483–4
7 Council Papers, vol. I, Archives, Maseru, cited in *Report on Constitutional Reform and Chieftainship Affairs*, p. 27
8 *Ibid.*, p. 28
9 *Ibid.*, p. 31
10 Text in *Orders in Council, High Commissioner's Proclamations, etc.*, p. 121
11 *Native Administration in the British African Territories*, Lord Hailey, Pt. V, p. 62
12 Tylden, *op. cit.*, p. 209

3: The Failure of Indirect Rule and Administrative Reform, 1910–1959

1 Cmd 4907, *op. cit.*, pp. 48–9
2 Margaret L. Hodgson, *Indirect Rule in Southern Africa*, p. 25
3 E. H. Ashton, "Democracy and Indirect Rule", *Africa*, Oct. 1947, p. 241
4 *Report on Constitutional Reform and Chieftainship Affairs*, p. 34
5 Hodgson, *op. cit.*, p. 29
6 Sir Charles Dundas and Dr Hugh Ashton, *Problem Territories of Southern Africa*, pp. 52–3
7 Tylden, *op. cit.*, p. 219
8 Cmd 4907, *op. cit.*, p. 49
9 Cited in Spence, *op. cit.*, p. 222
10 Dundas and Ashton, *op. cit.*, p. 52
11 Cmd 8209, *op. cit.*
12 *Basutoland: Report for the Year 1963*, p. 125
13 Leo Marquand, *The Peoples and Policies of South Africa*, p. 268
14 Lord Harlech to the Basutoland Council, Jan. 1, 1944, cited in *Basutoland: Report for the Year 1962*, p. 119
15 Basil Davidson, *Report on Southern Africa*, p. 218
16 Hailey, *Native Administration . . .*, Pt. V, p. 93
17 *Report on Constitutional Reform . . . , op. cit.*, p. 51
18 Cmd 637, *Basutoland, Report on Constitutional Discussions*, p. 4

4: The Politicising of Basuto National Life

1 Herbert J. Spiro, *Politics in Africa*, p. 73
2 Colin and Margaret Legum, *South Africa: Crisis for the West*, p. 175*ff*
3 Spiro, *op. cit.*, p. 73
4 Tylden, *op. cit.*, p. 222
5 E. H. Ashton, *The Basuto*, p. 313
6 Ronald Segal, *African Profiles*, p. 42
7 BCP, *Mohlabani*, vol. V, no. 1
8 *Makatolle* (Maseru), vol. I, no. 4, Dec. 15, 1960
9 Comité d'Information Sociale, "Pour les Prochaines Elections", (Mazenod) no. 8, Aug. 10, 1958
10 Basutoland National Party Constitution (n.d.)
11 Edward Roux, *Time Longer than Rope*, p. 217
12 *Contact*, Sept. 7, 1961
13 *Ibid.*, June 14, 1962
14 William E. Griffith, "Africa", *Survey*, Jan. 1965, pp. 182–3

5: The Road to Independence, 1960–1966

1 J. P. I. Hennessy, "The First Basutoland General Election", *Journal of Local Administration Overseas*, July 1964, pp. 145–55
2 Spiro, *op. cit.*, p. 74
3 P. Hughes, "The Introduction of Local Government to Basutoland", *Journal of Local Administration Overseas*, July 1963, p. 156
4 Basutoland National Council, *Legislative Council Debates*, Third Meeting-First Session, Sept. 18–22, 1961, vol. B, p. 141*ff*
5 *Ibid.*
6 *Ibid.*, Second Meeting-Second Session, Mar. 14–16, 1962, vol. II, pp. 4–19
7 *Ibid.*, p. 19
8 *Ibid.*
9 *Ibid.*, p. 38
10 *Makatolle*, vol. II, nos. 7-8-9, Oct.-Dec. 1962, p. 9
11 Resolution repeated in July 1963; cited in *United Nations Review*, vol. X, nos. 8–9, Aug.-Sept. 1963, pp. 38–9
12 *Makatolle*, vol. II, nos. 3–4, Mar.-Apr. 1962
13 *Rand Daily Mail*, June 28, 1963
14 *Star*, Dec. 4, 1963
15 *Rand Daily Mail*, Apr. 7, 1965
16 *Friend*, Oct. 21, 1964
17 *Rand Daily Mail*, Aug. 18, 1964
18 *Rand Daily Mail*, Dec. 30, 1964
19 *Friend*, Apr. 28, 1965
20 *Star*, Apr. 4, 1965
21 E. 'Mabathoana, OMI, "An Attack on the Church", June 1965.

6: *The Economy of Lesotho*

1 W. W. Rostow, *The Stages of Economic Growth*, pp. 4–5
2 H. Myint, "An Interpretation of Economic Backwardness" in *The Economics of Underdevelopment*, p. 106
3 *Basutoland, Bechuanaland Protectorate and Swaziland: Report of an Economic Survey Mission* (hereafter referred to as the *Morse Report*), p. 225
4 *Ibid.*, p. 308
5 *Ibid.*, p. 314
6 *Ibid.*, p. 327
7 Lord Hailey, *African Survey*, pp. 176–81
8 Stockley, *op. cit.*, pp. 70, 81, 90
9 *Confidential Report of the Director of the Geological Survey and Mines Department of Swaziland*, based on his visit to Basutoland, Feb. 5–8, 1962
10 Colonial Office, *An Economic Survey of the Colonial Territories*, vol. I, p. 65
11 *Morse Report*, p. 254
12 *Ibid.*, p. 256
13 *Ibid.*, p. 398
14 *Southern Africa Financial Mail*, Oct. 11, 1963
15 *Friend*, Feb. 19, 1963
16 H. T. Andrews, ed., *South Africa in the Sixties: A Socio-Economic Survey*, pp. 209-10
17 Colonial Office Survey, *op. cit.*, p. 13
18 WHO Summary Report of Nutrition Survey conducted in Basutoland, Dec. 1959
19 A. O. Hirschman, *The Strategy of Economic Development*, p. 183
20 Hailey, *Native Administration . . .*, Pt. V, p. 117
21 *Ibid.*, p. 117
22 *Morse Report*, p. 202
23 See Ashton, *The Basuto*, p. 124; and Vernon Sheddick, *Land Tenure in Basutoland*, pp. 31–2, 150–1
24 E. L. Ashton, *Political Organization of the Southern Sotho*, pp. 204–6
25 Lagden, *The Basutos*, p. 302

PART II: FROM BECHUANALAND TO BOTSWANA

7: *The Establishment of the Bechuanaland Protectorate*

1 A. Sillery, *The Bechuanaland Protectorate*, p. 19
2 Text cited in Sillery, *op. cit.*, p. 41
3 C. W. de Kiewit, *British Colonial Policy and the South African Republics*, pp. 260–1
4 J. Mockford, *Khama: King of the Bamangwato*, p. 80
5 J. Mackenzie, *Austral Africa*, vol. I, p. 118
6 Sillery, *op. cit.*, p. 50
7 *Blue Book* C.4588, p. 52
8 Mackenzie, *op. cit.*, vol. II, p. 209
9 Mockford, *op. cit.*, p. 100

10 Cited in Hailey, *Native Administration* . . . , Pt. V, p. 193
11 *Ibid.*, pp. 193-4

8: *The Protectorate Administration, 1885-1961; Native Authorities and Reform*

1 *Blue Book* C.4588, p. 106
2 Cited in Hailey, *Native Administration* . . . , Pt. V, p. 202
3 M. Hodson and W. Ballinger, *The Bechuanaland Protectorate*, p. 31
4 Tshekedi Khama, *Bechuanaland and South Africa*, p. 19
5 Cmd 8707, *History of Discussions with the Union of South Africa, 1909-1939*, p. 6
6 Cited in Hailey, *Native Administration* . . . , Pt. V, p. 207
7 Dundas, *op. cit.*, pp. 52-3
8 *Ibid.*, p. 48
9 Sir Alan Pim, *Financial and Economic Position of the Bechuanaland Protectorate*, p. 38
10 *Cambridge History*, vol. VIII, p. 700
11 Hailey, *Native Administration* . . . , Pt. V, p. 219
12 Dundas, *op. cit.*, pp. 52-3
13 *Bechuanaland Protectorate Report, 1959*, p. 83
14 Dundas, *op. cit.*, p. 52-3
15 Mary Benson, *Tshekedi Khama*, pp. 153-61. This authoritative biography has been drawn upon freely for details of Tshekedi Khama's role in the development of modern Bechuanaland.
16 Colin Legum, ed., *Africa: A Handbook to the Continent*, p. 355
17 Khama, *op. cit.*, p. 9
18 *Ibid.*

9: *Political Parties and Constitutional Advancement, 1961-1966*

1 Ronald Segal, *African Profiles*, p. 48
2 *Contact*, July 26, 1962
3 *Ibid.*, Sept. 6, 1962
4 *The Economist*, June 10, 1961
5 Edwin S. Munger, *Bechuanaland: Pan-African Outpost or Bantu Homeland?*, p. 16
6 *Contact*, May 3, 1963
7 *Rand Daily Mail*, Jan. 4, 1964
8 *E.P. Herald*, Feb. 27, 1964
9 *Star*, Mar. 4, 1965
10 *Sunday Express*, May 2, 1965
11 *Natal Mercury*, Feb. 20, 1965
12 *Bechuanaland Independence Conference, 1966: Report*

10: *The Economy of Botswana*

1 Harm J. de Blij, *A Geography of Southern Africa*, pp. 117-18
2 Darrell Randall, *Factors of Economic Development and the Okavango Delta*, pp. 1-2

3 Cited in Randall, *op. cit.*
4 Frank Debenham, *Kalahari Sand*, p. 184
5 Randall, *op. cit.*, p. 83
6 *Mafeking Mail*, Apr. 12, 1964
7 E. Batson, *Social Survey of Basutoland, 1959*
8 Munger, *op. cit.*, p. 5
9 *Bechuanaland Annual Colonial Report, 1961 and 1962*, pp. 54–9
10 *Ibid.*, pp. 50–1
11 Sillery, *op. cit.*, pp. 200–1
12 Munger, *op. cit.*, p. 55
13 Sillery, *op. cit.*, p. 205
14 See *Morse Report*, p. 125; *cf.* Munger, *op. cit.*, p. 54
15 D. P. Erasmus, "The National Income of Bechuanaland Protectorate, 1955" in L. H. Samuels, ed., *African Studies in Income and Wealth*, p. 274
16 *Morse Report*, p. 53
17 Sillery, *op. cit.*, p. 203
18 Reference Division, Central Office of Information, *The High Commission Territories*, Jan. 1963, British Information Service, p. 20
19 Alan Gray, "Three Islands in South Africa", *New Commonwealth*, July 1961, p. 433
20 Munger, *op. cit.*, chart at end of book
21 Erasmus, *op. cit.*, pp. 277, 282
22 *Star*, Sept. 22, 1964
23 Erasmus, *op. cit.*, p. 281
24 Randall, *op. cit.*, p. 254
25 J. E. Spence, "British Policy Towards the High Commission Territories", *Journal of Modern African Studies*, vol. II, no. 2

PART III: SWAZILAND

11: Early Swazi History and European Ascendancy

1 *Swaziland: Annual Report for 1907–8*, pp. 11–13
2 Cited in H. Kuper, *African Aristocracy*, p. 24
3 *Ibid.*, p. 27
4 Dundas and Ashton, *op. cit.*, p. 24
5 *Ibid.*, p. 26
6 Hailey, *Native Administration* . . . , Pt. V, p. 367
7 Kuper, *op. cit.*, p. 28

12: Swaziland under British Administration, 1903–1959

1 H. Kuper, *The Uniform of Colour*, p. 49
2 Hailey, *An African Survey*, p. 270
3 *Ibid.*, p. 271
4 *Ibid.*, pp. 272–3
5 Kuper, *African Aristocracy*, p. 30
6 Cmd 4114, *Financial and Economic Position of Swaziland (Pim Report)*, p. 18

7 Kuper, *Uniform of Colour*, p. 98
8 Dundas and Ashton, *op. cit.*, p. 53
9 Hailey, *Native Administration* . . . , Pt. V, p. 356
10 *Ibid.*
11 Kuper, *Uniform of Colour*, p. 103
12 *Ibid.*, p. 104
13 *Swaziland Student* (Mbabane), vol. II, no. 1
14 Kuper, *Uniform of Colour*, p. 32
15 *Who's Who of Southern Africa*, p. 620
16 Dundas and Ashton, *op. cit.*, p. 40
17 *Times of Swaziland*, Apr. 6, 1962

13: Constitutional Discussions and Political Development, 1959–1962

1 *Report of the Economic Survey Mission, 1959*, p. 422
2 Hailey, *Native Administration* . . . , Pt. V, p. 428
3 ST 176/1959, SNC, Lobamba, Swaziland (mimeographed, pages not numbered).
4 Cited in Government of Swaziland Report, *Proposals for a Swaziland Constitution*, p. 12
5 *Ibid.*
6 ST 280/1960, SNC, Lobamba, Swaziland, pp. 1–10
7 "Opinion—Constitutional Development of Swaziland", p. 12
8 Kuper, *Uniform of Colour*, pp. 105–6
9 *Contact*, Nov. 29, 1962
10 *Sibani*, vol. I, no. 15, Dec. 1962
11 *Ibid.*, vol. I, no. 9, Nov. 2, 1962
12 *Times of Swaziland*, Nov. 30, 1962
13 *Sibani*, vol. I, no. 9, Nov. 2, 1962
14 "Working Paper on Swazi Institutions", para. 40. (Working Papers were prepared by officers of the administration.)
15 Swaziland Student Union, *Memorandum to the Swaziland Constitutional Reforms Committee*, Aug. 1961
16 *Student*, vol. I, no. 3, 1961
17 *The Times*, Apr. 6, 1962
18 *Times of Swaziland*, Apr. 13, 1962
19 *Ibid.*, Mar. 30, 1962
20 *Report of the Swaziland Constitutional Committee: Note of Reservations by the Chairman and Official Members* (mimeographed, pages not numbered).
21 *Times of Swaziland*, June 22, 1962
22 *Ibid.*, July 27, 1962
23 *Ibid.*, June 22, 1962
24 *Ibid.*, Mar. 23, 1962
25 *Ibid.*, Mar. 30, 1962
26 *Ibid.*, Mar. 23, 1962
27 *Ibid.*, Nov. 9, 1962
28 *Contact*, Sept. 6, 1962

29 Swaziland Student Union, *Open Letter to Members of Parliament*, Dec. 30, 1962
30 *Sibani*, vol. I, no. 2, Sept. 14, 1962

14: *A Constitution Imposed and a Traditionalist Victory, 1963–1966*

1 Swaziland Student Union, *A Brief Review of the Political Situation in Swaziland, 1960–63*, (mimeographed, pages not numbered).
2 *Times of Swaziland*, Jan. 18, 1963
3 Cmd 2052, *Swaziland Constitution*
4 *Times of Swaziland*, May 3, 1963
5 *Ibid.*, Mar. 1, 1963
6 *Ibid.*, Mar. 8, 1963
7 *The Times*, Mar. 23, 1963
8 *Times of Swaziland*, May 10, 1963
9 *Ibid.*, Apr. 10, 1964
10 *Ibid.*, Apr. 24, 1964
11 *Contact*, May 17, 1962
12 *Ibid.*, Sept. 6, 1962
13 *New Statesman*, June 21, 1963
14 *Times of Swaziland*, Apr. 10, 1964
15 *Star*, June 19, 1964
16 *Letter of Joint Meeting of Political Parties to H.M. Commissioner*, July 7, 1964
17 *Letter from Mr Carl Todd to the Ngwenyama*, Jan. 6, 1965
18 *Rand Daily Mail*, Feb. 9, 1966
19 *Times of Swaziland*, Feb. 18, 1966

15: *The Economy of Swaziland*

1 *Morse Report*, p. 429
2 J. F. Holleman, ed., *Experiments in Swaziland: Report of the Swaziland Sample Survey, 1960*, p. 206
3 *Morse Report*, p. 420
4 *Southern African Financial Mail*, Swaziland Supplement, Nov. 2, 1962, p. 57
5 *Star*, Sept. 8, 1964
6 *Friend*, Sept. 25, 1964
7 E. S. Munger, "Swaziland: The Tribe and the Country", *Central & Southern African Series*, vol. X, no. 2, p. 4
8 M. J. Herskovits and M. Harwitz, ed., *Economic Transition in Africa*, p. 273
9 *Swaziland Annual Colonial Report, 1963*, p. 15
10 *Morse Report*, p. 449
11 Holleman, *op. cit.*, p. 251
12 *Morse Report*, p. 481
13 Holleman, *op. cit.*, pp. 224–5
14 Hailey, *Native Administration . . .*, Pt. V, p. 341
15 *Swaziland Annual Colonial Report, 1963*, p. 49
16 *Morse Report*, p. 485
17 *Ibid.*, p. 485

18 *Swaziland Annual Colonial Report, 1963*, p. 20
19 *Morse Report*, pp. 451, 457
20 *Swaziland Annual Colonial Report, 1962*, p. 41
21 *Morse Report*, p. 438
22 Holleman, *op. cit.*, p. 335
23 *Ibid.*, p. 333
24 *Swaziland Annual Colonial Report, 1962*, pp. 55-6
25 *Rand Daily Mail*, Nov. 5, 1964
26 Cmd 2147, *Aid to Developing Countries*, Sept. 1963, p. 42
27 *Swaziland Annual Colonial Report, 1963*, pp. 20-1
28 Holleman, *op. cit.*, p. 251
29 Hailey, *Native Administration . . .*, Pt. V, p. 346
30 *Ibid.*, pp. 340, 344
31 J. E. Spence, "The High Commission Territories", *The Journal of Modern African Studies*, vol. II, no. 2, Aug. 1964, p. 234
32 Hailey, *African Survey*, p. 683
33 *Swaziland Annual Colonial Report, 1963*, p. 29
34 *Morse Report*, p. 29
35 *Times of Swaziland*, Feb. 12, 1965

Conclusion

1 *Star*, Jan. 28, 1966
2 Press Release, Information Service of South Africa, Mar. 1966, Washington DC
3 *Cape Argus*, Mar. 29, 1966
4 South African Dept. of Information, *The Road to Freedom for Basutoland, Bechuanaland and Swaziland*, Fact Paper, 107, 1963
5 *Rand Daily Mail*, May 10, 1966
6 *Friend*, Sept. 22, 1965
7 *Star*, Oct. 1, 1965
8 *Star*, Sept. 27, 1965
9 *Rand Daily Mail*, June 13, 1966
10 Colonial Office, Information Dept., Basutoland Independence Conference: Official Opening Speech by Ntsu Mokhehle
11 *Star*, May 27, 1966
12 *Star*, June 21, 1966
13 Halpern, Jack, *South Africa's Hostages*, p. 472

SELECT BIBLIOGRAPHY

LESOTHO (BASUTOLAND)

Ashton, Edmund H., *The Basuto*, Oxford University Press, London and New York 1962.
Basutoland Constitutional Conference, Cmd.2371, HMSO, London 1964.
Basutoland: Annual Reports, HMSO, London.
Basutoland Medicine Murder, Cmd.8209, G. I. Jones, HMSO, London 1951.
Batson, E., *Social Survey of Basutoland*, University of Cape Town Press, Cape Town 1959.
Council Papers, BNC, Vol. I, Archives, Maseru.
Dutton, Eric A. T., *The Basuto of Basutoland*, Juta, Cape Town 1923.
Edwards, Isobel, *Basutoland Enquiry*, Africa Bureau, London 1955.
Ellenberger, D., *History of the Basuto, Ancient and Modern*, Caxton, London 1912.
Lagden, Sir Godfrey, *The Basutos*, Hutchinson, London 1909.
Laws of Lerotholi, Morija Sesuto Book Depot, Basutoland 1955.
Legislative Council Debates, Maseru.
Report of the Basutoland Constitutional Commission, Basutoland Government, Maseru 1963.
Report on Constitutional Discussions, Cmd.637, HMSO, London 1959.
Report on Constitutional Reform and Chieftainship Affairs, Basutoland Government, Maseru, 1958.
Report on the Financial and Economic Position of Basutoland, Cmd.4907, HMSO, London 1935.
Rosenthal, Eric, *African Switzerland: Basutoland of Today*, Hutchinson, London and New York 1948.
Sheddick, Vernon, *Land Tenure in Basutoland*, HMSO, London 1954.
Tylden, G., *The Rise of the Basuto*, Juta, Cape Town 1950.
Williams, John G., *Moshesh, the Man on the Mountain*, Oxford University Press, London 1950.

Articles, Pamphlets, Miscellaneous

Basutoland National Party Constitution, n.d.
Basutoland Newsletter, BCP, Cairo.
Basutoland Petitions the United Nations, BCP, Cairo 1962.
Colonial Office, Information Department, *Basutoland Independence Conference: Official Opening Speech by Ntsu Mokhehle*.
Comité d'Information Sociale, "Pour les Prochaines Elections", Mazenod, Basutoland, No. 8, August 1958.

Hennessy, J. P. I., "The First Basutoland General Election", *Journal of Local Administration Overseas*, July 1964, pp. 145–55.

Houlton, Sir John, "Basutoland", *Geographical Magazine*, Vol. 26, July 1953, pp. 132–8.

Hughes, Peter, "The Introduction of Local Government to Basutoland", *Journal of Local Administration Overseas*, July 1963, pp. 154–9.

"Labor Problems in Basutoland", *International Labour Review*, Vol. 32, November 1935, pp. 682–8.

Maue, D. R., "Basutos' Rise from African Savagery", *Current History*, Vol. XXVI, August 1927, pp. 778–84.

Makotolle, BCP, Maseru.

Mohlabani, BCP, Maseru.

"Political Development in Basutoland", *International Bulletin*, African Institute, Pretoria, Vol. II, March 1964, pp. 69–83.

Spence, J. E., "British Policy Towards the High Commission Territories", *Journal of Modern African Studies*, Vol. II, No. 2, July 1964, pp. 221–46.

BOTSWANA (BECHUANALAND)

African Advisory Council, Minutes, Mafeking.

Bechuanaland Independence Conference, 1966: Report, Colonial Office, London, February 21, 1966 (mimeographed).

Bechuanaland Protectorate Annual Reports, HMSO, London.

Bechuanaland Protectorate: Constitutional Proposals, Cmd.1159, HMSO, London 1960.

Bechuanaland Protectorate (Constitution) Orders 1960 and 1963; Basutoland, Bechuanaland and Swaziland (High Commissioner) Order 1963; Bechuanaland Royal Instructions, HMSO, London.

Benson, Mary, *Tshekedi Khama*, Faber, London 1960.

Debenham, Frank, *Kalahari Sand*, Bell, London 1953.

European Advisory Council, Minutes, Mafeking.

Hodgson, M. L., and Ballinger, W. G., *Bechuanaland Protectorate*, Lovedale Press, Alice, South Africa, 1933.

Joint Advisory Council, Minutes, Mafeking.

Khama, Tshekedi, *Bechuanaland and South Africa*, Africa Bureau, London 1955; *Bechuanaland, a General Survey*, Institute of Race Relations, Johannesburg 1957.

Mockford, J., *Khama, King of the Bamangwato*, Cape, London 1931; *Seretse Khama and the Bamangwato*, Staples, London and New York 1950.

Munger, E. S., *Bechuanaland, Pan-African Outpost or Bantu Homeland*, Oxford University Press, London 1965.

Pim, Sir Alan, *Financial and Economic Position of the Bechuanaland Protectorate*, HMSO, London 1933.

Randall, Darrell, *Factors of Economic Development and the Okavango Delta*, University of Chicago Press, Chicago 1957.

Redfern, John, *Ruth and Seretse: 'A Very Disreputable Transaction'*, Gollancz, London 1955.

Report of a Mission to the Bechuanaland Protectorate to Investigate the Possibilities of Economic Development in the Western Kalahari, HMSO, London 1954.

Report of the Commission Appointed by the Secretary of State for Dominion Affairs, Commission on Financial and Economic Position of Bechuanaland Protectorate, HMSO, London 1933.

Report on the Establishment of a Legislative Council and Executive Council for the Bechuanaland Protectorate, Joint Advisory Council, Bechuanaland Government, Mafeking 1959.

Schapera, Isaac, *A Handbook of Tswana Law and Custom*, Oxford University Press, London and New York 1938; *Native Land Tenure in the Bechuanaland Protectorate*, Lovedale Press, Alice, South Africa, 1943; *Tribal Legislation Among the Tswana of the Bechuanaland Protectorate*, Lund, Humphries, London 1943; *Migrant Labour and Tribal Life*, Oxford University Press, London and New York 1947; *The Ethnic Composition of the Tswana Tribes*, London School of Economics, London 1952.

Sillery, A., *The Bechuanaland Protectorate*, Oxford University Press, London and New York 1952; *Sechele: the Story of an African Chief*, George Ronald, Oxford 1954.

Thomas, Elizabeth M., *The Harmless People*, Knopf, New York 1959; Secker and Warburg, London 1959.

Van der Post, Laurens, *The Lost World of the Kalahari*, Hogarth, London 1961.

Articles, Pamphlets, Miscellaneous

Barnes, L., "Tshekedi and After", *Nineteenth Century*, Vol. 114, November 1933, pp. 573–82.

Bechuanaland Newsletter, BPP, Cairo.

"Black and White in South Africa; the Bechuanaland Flogging", *Review of Reviews*, Vol. 84, October 1933, pp. 13–16.

Brown, J., "New Hope for Africa's Thirstland", *Fortnightly*, Vol. 179, No. 173, June 1953, pp. 394–8.

Chirgwin, A. M., "Bechuanaland: Its Poverty and Prospects", *Empire Review and Magazine*, Vol. 59, March 1934, pp. 158–63; "Future of Bechuanaland", *London Quarterly Review*, Vol. 159, October 1934, pp. 441–8; "Tshekedi, Chief of the Bamangwato", *Mississippi Review*, Vol. 58, March 1935, pp. 109–12.

"Crown and the Protectorate", *Round Table*, Vol. xxvii, March 1937, pp. 448–51.

Day, J. W., "Tshekedi; the Price of Shame; the Treachery of the Premier and Mr. J. H. Thomas", *Saturday Review*, Vol. 156, October 7, 1933, p. 362.

Erasmus, D. P., "The National Income of Bechuanaland Protectorate: 1955", *Finance and Trade Review*, Vol. iv, March 1961, pp. 261–75.

"Events in Bechuanaland", *African Labour Monthly*, Vol. xv, December 1933, pp. 753–60.

Flavin, M., "African Chief in an Oldsmobile", *Harper*, Vol. 198, May 1949, pp. 74–87.

Harris, J., "Slaves Under the British Flag", *Spectator*, Vol. 161, July 15, 1938, p. 99.

Houlton, Sir John, "The High Commission Territories in South Africa: Bechuanaland", *Geographical Magazine*, Vol. xxvi, August 1953, pp. 175–81.

"Labour Recruiting in Bechuanaland", *International Labour Review*, Vol. 45, February 1942, p. 199.

Legassick, Martin, "Bechuanaland: Road to the North", *Africa Today*, Vol. xi, April 1964, pp. 7–9.

Macmillan, W. M., "Real Moral of the Tshekedi Case", *New Statesman and Nation*, Vol. vi, September 23, 1933, pp. 345–6.

Masa, BPP, Cairo.

"Political Developments in the Bechuanaland Protectorate", *International Bulletin*, Africa Institute, Pretoria, Vol. ii, February 1964, pp. 42–53.

Schapera, Isaac, "Herding Rites of the Bechuanaland Bakgatla", *American Anthropology*, Vol. xxxvi, October 1934, pp. 561–84.

Sillery, A., "Founding the Bechuanaland Protectorate", *Fortnightly*, Vol. 173, April 1950, pp. 209–14.

Therisanyo/Consultation, BDP, Kanye.

"Tshekedi Affair", *Round Table*, Vol. xxiv, March 1934, pp. 438–42.

Wade, W. W., "Khama Case Becomes Focus for African Tensions", *Foreign Policy Bulletin*, Vol. xxix, April 7, 1950, pp. 3–4.

SWAZILAND

Barker, Dudley, *Swaziland*, HMSO, London 1965.

European Advisory Council, Minutes, Mbabane.

Holleman, J. F. (ed.), *Experiment in Swaziland: Report of the Swaziland Sample Survey 1960*, Oxford University Press, Cape Town and New York 1964.

Kuper, Hilda, *An African Aristocracy*, Oxford University Press, London 1947; *The Uniform of Colour*, Witwatersrand University Press, Johannesburg, 1947; *The Swazi*, International African Institute, London 1952; *The Swazi: A South African Kingdom*, Holt, Rinehart and Winston, New York and London 1963.

Marwick, Brian A., *The Swazi*, Cambridge University Press, Cambridge 1940.

Munger, Edwin S., *Swaziland, The Tribe and the Country*, American Universities Field Service, August 1962.

Pim, Sir Alan, *Financial and Economic Situation of Swaziland: Report of the Commission Appointed by the Secretary of State for Dominion Affairs*, Cmd.4114, HMSO, London 1932.

Pott, Douglas, *Swaziland: A General Survey*, Institute of Race Relations, Johannesburg 1955.

Swaziland: Annual Reports, HMSO, London.

Swaziland Constitution, Cmd.2052, HMSO, London 1963.

Swaziland: A General Survey, Institute of Race Relations, Johannesburg 1955.

Articles, Pamphlets, Miscellaneous

Akeley, M. L. J., "Swazi Queen at Home", *Natural History*, Vol. 42, June 1938, pp. 21–32.

Brief Review of the Political Situation in Swaziland, 1960–63, Swaziland Student Union, Mbabane.

Davidson, Basil, "Country of King Sobhuza", *New Statesman*, Vol. 46, September 19, 1953, p. 308; October 3, 1953, pp. 367–8.

Doveton, D. M., "Economic Geography of Swaziland", *Geographical Journal*, Vol. 88, October 1936, pp. 322–31.

Gordon, W. R., "Swaziland", *Contemporary*, Vol. 177, February 1950, pp. 91–4.

Harrington, L., "Afforestation Brings Wealth to Swaziland", *Canadian Geographical Journal*, June 1959, pp. 180–1.

Houlton, Sir John, "The High Commission Territories in South Africa: Swaziland", *Geographical Magazine*, Vol. XXVI, June 1953, pp. 95–105.

Letter from Mr Carl Todd to the Ngwenyama, January 26, 1965, mimeographed and distributed by NNLC.

Letter of Joint Meeting of Political Parties to H.M. Commissioner, NNLC, Mbabane, July 7, 1964.

Memorandum to the Swaziland Constitutional Reforms Committee, Swaziland Student Union, Mbabane, August 1961.

Open Letter to Members of Parliament, Swaziland Student Union, Mbabane, December 30, 1962.

Opinion—Constitutional Development of Swaziland, Swaziland National Council, Lobamba 1960 (typewritten).

"Political Development in Swaziland", *International Bulletin*, African Institute, Pretoria, Vol. 2, April 1964, pp. 119–33.

Proposals for a Swaziland Constitution (with Reservations by Official Members), Government of Swaziland, Mbabane 1962.

Scott, P., "Mineral Development in Swaziland", *Economic Geography*, Vol. XXVI, July 1950, pp. 196–213; "Land Policy and the Native Population of Swaziland", *Geographical Journal*, Vol. 117, December 1951, pp. 435–47.

Sherwood, Edward T., *Swazi Personality and the Assimilation of Western Culture*, University of Chicago Library, 1961 (microfilm).

Sibani, SDP, Mbabane.

Swaziland National Council, ST 176/1959, ST 280/60, Lobamba.

Southern African Financial Mail, Swaziland Supplement, November 2, 1962.

Stevens, Richard P., "Swaziland Political Development", *Journal of Modern African Studies*, Vol. I, No. 3, September 1963, pp. 327–50.

Swaziland: Report on Constitutional Reform, Denis V. Cowen on behalf of Swaziland Progressive Party and the Eur-African Welfare Association, Mbabane 1961.

Swaziland Student, Swaziland Student Union, Mbabane.

Welch, Claude E., "Constitutional Confusion in Swaziland", *African Report*, Vol. VIII, April 1963, pp. 7–9.

Zwane, Timothy, "The Struggle for Power in Swaziland", *Africa Today*, Vol. XI, May 1964, pp. 4–6.

HIGH COMMISSION TERRITORIES—GENERAL

Aid to Developing Countries, Cmd.2147, HMSO, London 1963.

Basutoland, Bechuanaland and Swaziland; an Economic Survey, Barclay's Bank, DCO, London 1962.

Basutoland, the Bechuanaland Protectorate and Swaziland: History of Discussions with the Union of South Africa 1909–1939, Cmd.8707, HMSO, London 1952.

Basutoland, Bechuanaland Protectorate and Swaziland: Report of an Economic Survey Mission, HMSO, London 1960.

Blue Book, Cmd.4588, HMSO, London.

British Information Service, *The High Commission Territories*, January 1963.

Cambridge History of the British Empire, Vol. VIII (*South Africa, Rhodesia and the High Commission Territories*), Cambridge University Press, Cambridge 1963.

Dalton, Hugh, *Principles of Public Finance*, Routledge and Kegan Paul, London 1936.

Davidson, Basil, *Report on Southern Africa*, Cape, London 1952.

de Blij, Harm I., *A Geography of Southern Africa*, Rand McNally, Chicago 1964.

de Kiewit, C. W., *A History of South Africa, Social and Economic*, Oxford University Press, London 1941.

Doxey, G. V., *The High Commission Territories and the Republic of South Africa*, Royal Institute of International Affairs, London 1963.

Dundas, Sir Charles, and Ashton, Dr Hugh, *Problem Territories of Southern Africa*, South African Institute of International Affairs, Cape Town 1952.

Economic Survey of the Colonial Territories, 1951, Vol. I (*Central Africa and the High Commission Territories*), HMSO, London 1952.

Edwards, Isobel E., *Protectorates or Native Reserves?*, Africa Bureau, London 1956.

Greaves, Lionel B., *The High Commission Territories: Basutoland, Bechuanaland Protectorate, and Swaziland*, Edinburgh House Press, London 1954.

Green, L. P., and Fair, T. J. D., *Development in Africa: A Study in Regional Analysis with Special Reference to Southern Africa*, Witwatersrand University Press, Johannesburg 1962.

Gunther, John, *Inside Africa*, Hamish Hamilton, London 1955; Harper, New York 1955.

Hailey, Lord, *An African Survey*, HMSO, London 1938; *Native Administration in the British African Territories*, Pt. V (*The High Commission Territories: Basutoland, The Bechuanaland Protectorate and Swaziland*), HMSO, London 1953; *The Republic of South Africa and the High Commission Territories*, Oxford University Press, London and New York 1963.

Halpern, Jack, *South Africa's Hostages—Basutoland, Bechuanaland and Swaziland*, Penguin Books, Harmondsworth and Baltimore, Md., 1965.

Hatch, John, *Africa Today and Tomorrow*, 2nd rev. ed., Praeger, New York 1965; Dobson, London 1965; *A History of Post-War Africa*, Praeger, New York 1965; Deutsch, London 1965.

Herskovits, M. J., and Harwitz, M. (eds.), *Economic Transition in Africa*, Northwestern University Press, Evanston, Ill. 1964.

High Commission Territories and the Union of South Africa, Royal Institute of International Affairs, London 1956.

Hodgson, Margaret L., *Indirect Rule in Southern Africa*, Lovedale Press, Alice, South Africa, 1931.

Legum, Colin (ed.), *Africa: A Handbook to the Continent*, rev. ed., Anthony Blond, London 1966; Praeger, New York 1966.

Legum, Colin and Margaret, *South Africa: Crisis for the West*, Pall Mall Press, London 1964; Praeger, New York 1964.

Mackenzie, J., *Austral Africa*, Vol. I, Sampson Low, London 1887.

Mansergh, N. (ed.), *Documents and Speeches on British Commonwealth Affairs, 1931–1952*, Oxford University Press, London 1953.

Marais, J. S., *The Fall of Kruger's Republic*, Oxford University Press, London and New York 1961.

Marquand, Leo, *The Peoples and Policies of South Africa*, Oxford University Press, London and New York 1962.

Neame, L. E., *The History of Apartheid*, Pall Mall Press, London 1962; British Book Centre, New York 1963.

Orchard, R. K., *The High Commission Territories of South Africa*, World Dominion Press, New York and London 1951.

Orders in Council, High Commissioner's Office, Proclamations, etc., Cape Times, Cape Town 1913.

Perham, Margery, and Curtis, Lionel, *The Protectorates of South Africa; the Question of their Transfer to the Union*, Oxford University Press, London and New York 1935.

Problems of the High Commission Territories in Southern Africa, US Office of Strategic Services Research and Analysis Branch, Washington DC 1945.

Report on the Structure of the Public Services in Basutoland, Bechuanaland and Swaziland, 1961, Sir Richard Ramage, High Commissioner's Office, Cape Town 1962.

Roux, Edward, *Time Longer Than Rope*, University of Wisconsin Press, Madison, Wis., 1964.

Segal, Ronald, *African Profiles*, Penguin Books, Harmondsworth and Baltimore, Md., 1962; (ed.), *Sanctions Against South Africa*, R. M. Bostock, "Sanctions and the High Commission Territories", Penguin Books, Harmondsworth 1964.

Sheddick, Vernon G., *The Southern Sotho*, International African Institute, London 1953.

Spiro, Herbert J., *Politics in Africa*, Prentice Hall, Englewood Cliffs, NJ, 1962.

Walker, Eric, *A History of Southern Africa*, Longmans, London and New York 1957.

Who's Who of Southern Africa, Donaldson, Johannesburg 1960.

Wiedner, Donald L., *A History of Africa South of the Sahara*, Random House, London and New York 1962.

Articles, Pamphlets, Newspapers, Miscellaneous

Africa Digest, Africa Bureau, London.

Ashton, E. H., "Democracy and Indirect Rule", *Africa*, October 1947, pp. 235–51.

"Atlantic Report: Basutoland, Bechuanaland and Swaziland", *Atlantic Monthly*, Vol. 213, April 1964, p. 234ff.

Baring, E., "Problems of the High Commission Territories", *International Affairs*, Vol. XXVIII, April 1952, pp. 184–9.

Caminada, J., "Malan and the Protectorates", *Spectator*, Vol. 192, May 14, 1954, p. 576.

Clark, W., "Problems of the Protectorates", *Spectator*, Vol. 183, November 25, 1949, p. 731.

Contact, Cape Town.

Eastern Province Herald, Port Elizabeth.

Financial Mail, Lusaka.

Fitzgerald, R. C., "South Africa and the High Commission Territories", *World Affairs*, Vol. IV, No. 3, July 1950, pp. 306–20.

Friend, Bloemfontein.

Gray, Alan, "Three 'Islands' in South Africa", *New Commonwealth*, July 1961, pp. 431–5.

Gross, S. I., "Basutoland, Bechuanaland Protectorate, Swaziland", *Board of Trade Journal*, Vol. CLXXXIII, September 28, 1962, pp. 641–6.

Halpern, J., "South Africa: Enclaves of Trouble", *Nation*, Vol. 197, July 27, 1963, pp. 49–52.

High Commission Territories in Southern Africa: Aide-Memoire handed to the Prime Minister of the Union of South Africa by the Secretary of State for Dominion Affairs on 15th May, 1935, HMSO, London 1935.

High Commission Territories of Basutoland, Swaziland and Bechuanaland Protectorate: Summary of Current Economic Information, US Office of International Trade, Washington DC, July 1947.

"High Commission Territories: Politics and Administration", *Round Table*, Vol. 42, March 1952, pp. 141–51.

Hodgson, M. L., "Britain as Trustee in Southern Africa", *Political Quarterly*, Vol. III, July 1932, pp. 398–408.

Houlton, John, "The High Commission Territories in South Africa", *Geographical Magazine*, Vol. XXVI, August 1953, pp. 175–81.

"Labour Problems of Basutoland, Bechuanaland and Swaziland", *Labour Review*, Vol. XXIX, March 1934, pp. 397–406.

Mafeteng Mail, Mafeteng.

Maud, Sir John, "The Challenge of the High Commission Territories", *African Affairs*, Vol. 63, April 1964, pp. 94–103.

Natal Mercury, Durban.

New Statesman, London.

Pim, A., "Question of the South African Protectorates", *International Affairs*, Vol. XIII, September 1934, pp. 668–88.

"Protectorates and the Union", *Round Table*, Vol. XXIV, September 1934, pp. 785–802.

Rand Daily Mail, Johannesburg.

"Reform in the Protectorates", *Round Table*, Vol. XXV, September 1935, pp. 746–53.

Sillery, A., "British Protectorates in Africa", *Fortnightly*, Vol. 176, December 1951, pp. 801–8; Vol. 177, January 1952, pp. 26–30.

"South Africa and the High Commission Territories", *International Bulletin*, Africa Institute, Pretoria, Vol. II, January 1964, pp. 9–24.

"South Africa: The High Commission Territories", *Round Table*, No. 165, December 1951, pp. 90–4.

South African Department of Information, *The Road to Freedom for Basutoland, Bechuanaland and Swaziland*, Fact Paper 107, 1963.

"South African Protectorates", *Round Table*, Vol. XXV, March 1935, pp. 318–23.

Star, Johannesburg.

Stevens, Richard P., "Basutoland: Vigorous Nationalism in a Stagnant Economy; Swaziland: A Constitution Imposed; Bechuanaland: the Reconciliation of Traditional and Modern Forces", *Africa Report*, Vol. IX, April 1964, pp. 9–17.

Sunday Express, Johannesburg.

The Economist, London.

The Times, London.

Times of Swaziland, Mbabane.

"Trust in Africa; the Problem of the Protectorates", *Round Table*, Vol. 40, March 1950, pp. 121–6.

United Nations General Assembly, *Information from Non-Self-Governing Territories:* March 4, 1959, A14083 Add. 3: Bechuanaland; March 5, 1959, A14083 Add. 2: Basutoland.

United Nations, *Report of the Special Committee on the Situation with Regard to the Implementation of the Declaration on the Granting of Independence to Colonial Countries and Peoples*, Reports of the General Assembly; *Progress of Non-Self-Governing Territories Under the Charter* (April 1963), Vols. 1–5, etc. September 3, 1963, A/AC, 109/L.81.

United Nations Review, August-September 1963.

Uys, S., "Protectorates Under the Gun", *New Republic*, Vol. 149, September 28, 1963, pp. 9–10.

Verwoerd, Dr H. F., *Crisis in World Conscience*, Fact Paper 107, Pretoria 1964.

Young, B. S., "High Commission Territories of Southern Africa", *Focus*, Vol. XIV, December 1963, pp. 1–6.

INDEX

Act of Union (S. Africa), 4–5, 7, 126
Adams College, 56
Addis Ababa Conference (1963), 64, 83, 235
Aden, 86
African Auxiliary Pioneer Corps, 58
African National Congress (ANC), 56–7, 64–5, 141–2, 203; Youth League, 59
Afro-Asian Peoples' Solidarity Conference (1963), 74
Age-group system, 176
Agriculture: Basuto, 27, 99–101; Bechuana, 132, 165–8, 170; Swazi, 243, 247–50
Aliwal North, 21–4, 255
All-African Peoples' Conferences (Accra), 60, 204–5
Alliance of Political Organisations (Swaziland), 224–5
Anglican Church, 17–18, 107, 220
Anglo-American Corporation, 102
Angola, 156, 259
Anti-Communist League, 61–2
Anti-slavery movement, 18
Apartheid policy, 9–10, 12, 57, 258; condemnation of, 67, 81, 84, 159, 205, 258, 266
Arden-Clarke, Sir Charles, 48, 58, 132–3, 213
Asbestos mines, 2, 163, 233–4, 244
Ashton, Dr Hugh, 197

Bakgatla tribe, 113, 125, 152, 155
Bakoena clan, 54
Bakwena tribe, 113, 116, 120–1, 125, 135–6
Ballinger, W. G., 42–3
Bamalete tribe, 113, 125n.
Bamangwato tribe, 113, 115–17, 120–1, 125, 127, 129–30, 134–8, 142, 144–5, 163; Tribal Council, 142, 144
Bangwaketse tribe, 113, 120–1, 125, 131, 144, 155
Bantu Authorities Act, 137
Bantu Press, 202

Bantustan system, 9–10, 255–8
Barberton, 175, 244
Barkly, Sir Henry, 26
Barolong tribe, 113, 116–17
Basutoland, Lesotho: administration and history, 2–12; annexed to Cape Colony, 26–8; associations and groups, 58; Basutoland Council, 36–8, 41, 44–50, 54, 57–8, 60; British loans and grants, 251; British Protectorate, 2–4, 19, 24, 28, 31; climate, 100–1; conflict with Boers, 2, 19–23; constitution (1959), 49–52, 67, 79–81; Constitutional Commission, 70–9; Crown Colony, 28; diplomatic representation, 77; economy of, 30, 39, 42, 98–109; Executive Council, 50–1, 69–70; first general election, 67; independence, 70, 76–7, 81, 93, 97; indirect rule by Britain, 29–52; laws, 32, 36, 41, 44, 49–51; monarchy, 76; National Council (1903), 33–6; National Council (Legislative, 1960), 50–1, 54, 68–71, 73, 78–9, 88, 127, 139; National Treasury, 44, 48–9, 51; new name (Lesotho), 76; new title of chief, 80; physical features, 1; political parties, 59–66 (see also separate entries); Regent's Advisory Council, 45; resources, 1, 98–107; South African relations, 4–12, 46, 52–7, 64–7, 74–96, 101, 103, 150; tribes and clans, 15–28; university, 256
Basutoland African Congress (BAC), 59–61
Basutoland Congress Party (BCP), 61, 66–71, 73–4, 78–84, 86, 88–92, 259–60
Basutoland Disannexation Act, 28
Basutoland Freedom Party (BFP), 63–4, 83
Basutoland Labour Party (BLP), 66
Basutoland National Party (BNP), 62, 64, 66–8, 82, 84–97, 159
Basuto War (1865), 23, 255